The Manipulation of Cultural Imagery in Canada's Prairie West

The late 1800s was a critical era in the social history of the Canadian Prairies: racial tensions increased between white settlers and the Native population and colonial authority was perceived to be increasingly threatened. As a result, white settlers began to erect social and spatial barriers to segregate themselves from the indigenous population. In *Capturing Women* Sarah Carter examines popular representations of women that emerged at the time, arguing that stereotypical images of Native and European women were created and manipulated to establish boundaries between Native peoples and white settlers and to justify repressive measures against the Native population.

One of Carter's themes is that women were not always in a position to invent or project their own images, identities, or ideas of themselves, nor were they free to author their own texts entirely. Focusing on captivity narratives, Carter looks at depictions of white women as victims of Aboriginal aggressors and explores the veracity of a number of accounts. She also examines depictions of Aboriginal women as sinister and dangerous. These representations of women, and the race and gender hierarchies they created, endured in the Canadian West long after the last decades of the nineteenth century.

Capturing Women is part of a growing body of literature on the question of women, race, and imperialism. Carter adopts a colonial framework, arguing that fundamental features of colonialism were clearly present in the extension of the power of the Canadian state and the maintenance of sharp social, economic, and spatial distinctions between the dominant and subordinate populations. She highlights similarities between images of women on the Prairies and symbols of women in other colonial cultures, such as the memsahib in British India and the Indian captive in the United States.

SARAH CARTER is associate professor of history, University of Calgary. Her previous books include *Lost Harvests: Prairie Indian Reserve Farmers and Government Policy* (McGill-Queen's).

McGill-Queen's Native and Northern Series
Bruce G. Trigger, Editor

Capturing Women
The Manipulation of Cultural Imagery in Canada's Prairie West

SARAH CARTER

McGill-Queen's University Press
Montreal & Kingston · London · Buffalo

© McGill-Queen's University Press 1997
ISBN 0-7735-1655-7 (cloth)
ISBN 0-7735-1656-5 (paper)

Legal deposit fourth quarter 1997
Bibliothèque nationale du Québec

Printed in Canada on acid-free paper

This book has been published with the help
of a grant from the Humanities and Social
Sciences Federation of Canada, using funds
provided by the Social Sciences and Humanities Research Council of Canada.

McGill-Queen's University Press acknowledges the support received for its publishing
program from the Canada Council's Block
Grants program.

Canadian Cataloguing in Publication Data

Carter, Sarah, 1954–
Capturing women: the manipulation
of cultural imagery in Canada's Prairie West
(McGill-Queen's native and northern series,
ISSN 1181-7453; 17)
Includes index.
ISBN 0-7735-1655-7 (bound)
ISBN 0-7735-1656-5 (pbk.)
1. Prairie Provinces – Ethnic relations –
History – 19th century. 2. White women –
Prairie Provinces – History.
3. Native women – Prairie Provinces –
History. 4. Indian captivities –
Prairie Provinces. 5. Prairie Provinces –
Social conditions.
I. Title. II. Series.
HQ1459.P6C37 1997   971.2'02
C97-900891-3

This book was typeset by Typo Litho
Composition Inc. in 10.5/13 Baskerville.

For Walter and Mary

Contents

Illustrations

Preface

This study focuses on a critical era in the history of the Prairie West, the region to the west of Manitoba. In the last three decades of the nineteenth century the Aboriginal majority became a small minority, and any coexistence or mixture of Euro-Canadian and Aboriginal societies came to an end. The new arrivals erected spatial and social boundaries that defined them as members of a particular community. This community became increasingly segregated from the indigenous people as boundaries were clarified and racial categories sharpened. White women, projected as "civilizing" agents, were central to the creation and reproduction of the new community; also central to the new notions of spatial and social segregation were representations of Aboriginal women as dangerous and sinister. Women in the West were polarized at this time into those who were regarded as the virtuous and pure agents of the salvation of (white) men and civilizers of the new region of the new nation, and those regarded as the promiscuous agents of ruin of the same.

Historians of the post-1870 Canadian West have tended to view the region in isolation, as unique and exceptional. In an effort to show that there were no similarities to the American West in particular, historians have tended to stress the foresight and wisdom with which the architects of federal government policy carefully devised and then implemented a blueprint for the orderly and stable development of the region. Yet the history of western Canada is tied to other parts of the world that were undergoing parallel changes, for its story echoes that of race relations and colonial dynamics in many countries where the indigenous people also found themselves numerically dominated by another culture. This study introduces a colonial framework through which the history of the Canadian West during these years can be understood. Although the usual images of imperial grandeur are absent from the picture, other features of colonialism were clearly present, including the sharp distinctions between the dominant and subordinate population.

In popular culture as well as scholarship, this era has generally been associated with powerful masculine images: whisky traders, ranchers, cowboys, the North-West Mounted Police, the North-West Field Force, missionaries, farmers, merchants, and politicians. By focusing on women, this study highlights a side to events that is scarcely touched on elsewhere. As in other colonial contexts, white women became essential symbols, or key icons, around which the new society was to be built. White women were the true "empire builders," their children the cornerstone of a strong nation. They were seen as essential to the moral, religious, and economic health of the new region of the nation, as the moral and cultural custodians of the new community.

The idea of white femininity as a racial category, as scholars have argued was the case in other colonial situations, is clear in the context of western Canada in the late nineteenth century. Ideas about the vulnerability of white women helped to create and sustain concepts of racial and cultural difference, to legitimize tough action against indigenous people, and to convey the message of the necessity of policing boundaries between different peoples. The resistance of 1885, and in particular the captivity of Theresa Delaney and Theresa Gowanlock, provide an opportunity to examine the way in which the category of white woman was produced and manipulated. In the Canadian West, ideas about the vulnerability of white women (and the role of white men as their heroic protectors) were drawn not only from British colonial culture but also from the American symbol of white female victimization, the "Indian captive."

The experiences of Delaney and Gowanlock, combined with the alarm raised a few years later over the supposed captivity of other young white women (which turned out to be hoaxes) served to promote hysteria over the issue of the safety of white women in the West and to provide a rationalization for the repressive measures taken against the supposed perpetrators. Through the imagined experiences of Delaney and Gowanlock, hatred against the "enemy" was cultivated and the theme of white female victimization stressed in order to bolster military resolve and national accord. The year 1885 was a time of crisis in the Dominion of Canada's authority over the newly acquired territories of the West, and this crisis was managed in part through the circulation of stories about the unspeakable horrors to which "our countrywomen," or "Ontario's fair daughters," were being subjected.

A theme that emerges in several sections of this study is that women are not always free to project their own images or identities, nor are they free to author their own texts fully. This latter point is most clearly evident with regard to the narratives of Delaney and Gowanlock. They were bound imaginatively by the limited repertoire of behaviour available to white women, by widely held views about Aboriginal people, by conventional ways of writing about "captivities," and by a great variety of other pressures and constraints that operated to alter their story. Although Delaney and Gowanlock emerged from their two months with the Cree in June 1885 to declare that none of the rumours were true – that they had been treated well and had been protected, especially by several Métis families – this was not the central message conveyed in the published account released five months later in the volume *Two Months in the Camp of Big Bear: The Life and Adventures of Theresa Gowanlock and Theresa Delaney*. In the book there was a decided emphasis on their frailty and on the constant threat of the "fate worse than death." The published version advanced the clear cautionary message that a union of white and Aboriginal was an abominable business, especially since such unions had created the menacing Métis. Just as the imagined experiences of the two women were exploited during their months of captivity, so too was their published account carefully constructed to serve certain interests while condemning others. The version of events given in the book was made to conform to already established attitudes towards women and Aboriginal people. Despite the book's subtitle referring to the "life and adventures" of Gowanlock and Delaney, there is little in the narrative about the women themselves. Rather, the book is about regulating race and gender relations in the West, about clarifying and maintaining boundaries between Native and newcomer. Similarly, the captivity hoaxes of the late 1880s and 1890s kept alive the theme of the vulnerability of white women, as well as the suspicion of the "savages." The message was advanced that if white women were to continue to move west and escape the fate of these "captives," relations between the races had to be highly regulated. Non-Aboriginal readers of these stories were drawn into a racist consensus against Aboriginal males, who were perceived as a potential menace to the honour of white women.

In the Canadian West, as in other settings, colonialism also functioned in a gendered way to develop powerfully negative images of the indigenous women, who were projected as being a threat to the white community. They were cast as the complete opposite of white women, as agents of the destruction of the moral and cultural health of the new community. During the months of the resistance of 1885, Aboriginal women were said to be actively participating in violent and brutal acts against white soldiers and to be similarly threatening to white women. In the years immediately following 1885, they were further denigrated in order to bolster the "honour" of the white males of the West, whose behaviour had come under criticism. Aboriginal women were said to be accustomed to being bought and sold by their own elders and to be mistreated by their own men. This fabrication served a double purpose, for elite white men at this time were hoping to marry women of their own race and class, whose children would be their legitimate heirs. It was useful to insist that Aboriginal women, some of whom had married prominent white men, were accustomed to many sexual partners. Their children were not, therefore, to be considered the legitimate heirs. Thus, women in the Canadian West were defined differently according to their race, and the specific image of each was mobilized for particular purposes. These representations of women in the West proved resilient and were pressed into service from time to time well into the present century.

Acknowledgments

I was first inspired to look more closely at the story of Theresa Delaney and Theresa Gowanlock during a spring 1993 visit to Frog Lake and district with rancher and historian Edgar Mapletoft of Frenchman Butte, Saskatchewan. Based on his years of research and his knowledge of the countryside, Edgar was able to tell the complex story of events with sympathy and understanding for all sides and individuals involved. We visited the sites of the settlement of Frog Lake and of the Gowanlock home and mill on Frog Creek, and followed part of the route of the Cree to Fort Pitt and to the still visible trenches at Frenchman Butte. Frances W. Kaye of the University of Nebraska, who visited the University of Calgary as a Fulbright Faculty Fellow in 1995, persuaded me that all of this was material for a book. A great number of archivists provided valuable assistance at the Glenbow Archives, the Saskatchewan Archives Board, and the Provincial Archives of Manitoba. I especially wish to thank Jennifer S.H. Brown of the University of Winnipeg for her perceptive comments on an earlier draft of the manuscript. I am grateful to the Social Sciences and Humanities Research Council of Canada for the research grant that greatly facilitated this project and allowed me to hire Siri Louie and Pernille Jakobsen, fine research assistants and promising scholars. I would like to thank McGill-Queen's University Press, and especially Carlotta Lemieux. The University of Calgary Department of History provided me with the ideal working environment. My husband Walter Hildebrandt provided abundant support and thoughtful criticism, and I also wish to thank our daughter Mary for her fresh ideas and patience.

Portions of this book appeared previously as " 'A Fate Worse than Death': Indian Captivity Stories Thrilled Victorian Readers – But Were They True?" *Beaver* 68 (April/May 1988): 21–8; "The Exploitation and Narration of the Captivity of Theresa Delaney and Theresa Gowanlock, 1885," in *Making Western Canada: Essays on European Colonization and Settlement,* ed. Catherine Cavanaugh and Jeremy Mouat (Toronto: Garamond Press, 1996), 31–61; and "Categories and Terrains of Exclusion: Constructing the 'Indian Woman' in the Early Settlement Era in Western Canada," *Great Plains Quarterly* 13 (Summer 1993): 147–61. I am grateful for permission to reprint this material.

CHAPTER ONE

Introduction:
Defining and Redefining Women

Girls Ho! For the West
(A Reply to "An Ontario Girl's Lament")

We have heard the lament of the Ontario lass
How her lovers forsook her for the far, far West
Left her to sigh in her own native home
While they o'er our boundless prairies roam,
Forgetful of the lone maiden who lingers behind
Breathing the sad refrain of love so unkind.
We admire her candour, but pity her lot;
Her words confirm what we've frequently thought
While visiting the poor bachelor's retreat,
Where hard his couch, and, cold was his meat,
Listening to his story full of despair
How no maiden was willing his lot to share,
That, far away in the land of his birth
Waits the girl who would gladly cheer his hearth.
Thousands of bachelors in this wonderful West
Are anxiously waiting their time to be blest
With the smile of women – the touch of her hand
Would make this an Eden – our glorious land.
Then come all lone maidens – this is your year,
There are plenty of husbands, and naught to fear;
Ontario may send us her daughters so fair,
New Brunswick can contribute a goodly share;
Acadia, too, will spare some of the best

To meet the wants of our Great North-West;
Lands beyond the sea may send all they will,
Our heritage is vast; we'll welcome you still.
                          C.T. Lewis, 5 Feb. 1884[1]

Charles T. Lewis, the genial Canadian Pacific Railway station agent
at Indian Head, District of Assiniboia, North-West Territories, a recent arrival from New Brunswick, was an outspoken advocate of the
importation of young women to "meet the wants of our Great
North-West." A few years after publishing "Girls Ho!" he devised a
scheme that would, he thought, help meet the needs of the hour. In
a brochure entitled *A Revolution: The World's Return Rebate Marriage
Certificate, or the Want of the West,* Lewis described a vast domain, rich
in diversified resources.[2] Yet despite its attractions, he wrote, "the
West has its wants, but we are only dealing with one want. A want
that lays at the very foundation of social life; the first want that
Adam expressed when alone in the garden of innocence; the want
of companionship; the want of noble woman."[3] The question was
one of national importance: "What Napoleon said of France may be
truly said of the West 'What France wants is good mothers and you
may be sure that France will have good sons.'"[4] The problem, as
Lewis saw it, was that there was an abundance of single men on the
prairies who could not afford the expense of a trip east and the subsequent heavier expense of a return trip for two. Lewis proposed
that single males be offered tickets with a return rebate that would
allow the purchaser to travel back to his new home in the West at
very little cost, provided he had a wife with him. A reasonable number of months would be allowed for this hunting trip, and to guard
against an "undesirable" class of immigrants, a marriage certificate
was to be appended to the rebate contract. This certificate was to be
signed by the officiating clergyman and two responsible witnesses.
On presentation of these documents, the railway agent in eastern
Canada would issue two free tickets to the newly-weds.

Lewis's scheme won favourable comments in the western press,[5]
for there was widespread concern about "the want of the West." In
1886 the Canadian Pacific Railway had launched promotional material specifically aimed at women. The pamphlet *What Women Say
of the Canadian North-West,* which was supposedly based on the
actual testimony of women settlers (excluding Aboriginal women),
gave a very positive impression.[6] Women and children were encour-

aged to accompany the "intending settler" rather than waiting until a home was ready for them. It was stressed that there were few hardships or privations to put up with now that the railroad had been completed. It was also emphasized that the women settlers did not "experience any dread of the Indians."[7] To a great many who had hopes, dreams, and capital invested in the West, the mass importation of women, especially women of Anglo-Celtic origin, seemed an urgent necessity.

Of course, there were already many women in the West, a great variety of Aboriginal women. They were vital to the material and spiritual welfare of their own people, and they also assisted the newcomers with their knowledge of medicine and their work as midwives. Many of the earliest non-Aboriginal "bachelors" (including fur traders, whisky traders, North-West Mounted Police, government officials, farmers, ranchers, and missionaries) married Aboriginal women, while others formed relationships of a fleeting, casual nature. It is curious that this era of intermarriage has all but disappeared from the collective non-Aboriginal memory of the prairie past, at least as exemplified in most memoirs, local histories, and museums. There is seldom any recognition of the contribution of Aboriginal women. It is white women who receive all the praise. By the 1920s, tributes were being made to the "Pilgrim Mothers" (a category that did not, of course, include women of Aboriginal ancestry) who had "first braved unknown terrors of a primeval land, a country of snow and ice, hostile Indians, and lack of food and water."[8] Today, a feature of many prairie museums is the homage paid to the "first white woman" in this or that district. Invariably, observers are invited to contemplate the isolation and hardship these women endured in rugged conditions in order to bring "civilization" to an untamed wilderness.

By the late 1870s, and clearly exemplified in the 1880s and 1890s, the emerging elite in the North-West, as well as the advocates of British settlement, were anxious to establish a society that was not founded on any mingling of European and Aboriginal people and culture. There was a concern to forget the past, to present Aboriginal women as a menace to the emerging community, and to encourage and celebrate the arrival of white women. The creation of these patterns of thought was so successful that they were accepted without question in much of the non-Aboriginal community well into this century. It would be profoundly jarring to many non-Aboriginal westerners today to suggest that it is racist or at best Eurocentric to assume that white women brought civilization to the West. Both in the press and in the literature of colonial settlement, white women were projected as essential to the creation and reproduction of the community. They were cast as the moral and cultural custodians of the new community.[9] Their influence was clearly to be seen in "brighter and better homes, a higher standard of morality, and the introduction of the refinements of life."[10] Most of all, they were responsible for reproducing "the race": "Where formerly the Indian, wolf, and coyote roamed free and unmolested, the air resounds with the merry laughter of boys and girls, who love the healthy mountain breezes, and grow strong and ruddy in our western land."[11] Women who produced large numbers of children were often given special mention in the press. For instance, in 1884 a Mrs W. Stafford of Lethbridge was the subject of congratulations. She had married at seventeen and, although only thirty-six, had produced twelve children, ten of whom had survived: "The population of the North-West would be rapidly and materially increased by a few more such women."[12] Western newspapers ran regular features on weddings, births, and other events that provided the opportunity to comment on the importance of the arrival of white women and their vital role as custodians and reproducers of the community. In certain districts their numbers were tracked year by year. In 1889 it was noted in the *Macleod Gazette* that only eight years earlier there had been just seven white women within a radius of one hundred miles, whereas now there were several hundred.[13]

The publications of the missionaries – who were among the most industrious promoters of western settlement – regularly eulogized the virtues of the noble women in their midst, stressing the need for more of their kind. Wives and daughters of missionaries were especially singled out as "women of culture" who were directly involved in the work of "elevating the red men and their families" while surmounting isolation and much suffering without praise or recognition.[14] In the words of John Maclean, the Methodist missionary to the Bloods, they were "the wise women from the east, the magi of modern times, [who] have travelled westward with their gifts of culture, grace and love."[15] Other advocates of western settlement echoed Charles Lewis's call for "noble" women. Journalist Jessie M.E. Saxby, whose book *West-Nor'-West* included a chapter entitled "Women Wanted," made the racial and class dimension much more explicitly than Lewis.[16] She argued that what was needed for the Canadian West was not the domestic servant class but women of the "educated middle class" – girls who "at home go out as lady-helps, nursery-governesses, telegraph clerks, shop girls ... who cannot hire themselves as domestic servants at home because of losing caste."[17] The colonists of western Canada should not have to marry "beneath them," she maintained. Consequently, educated, refined girls should go to the lands where the "manly Titans of the West" needed helpmates. Women had an "absolute duty" in this matter: "We have no right (we women) to encourage our sons and brothers to go away in quest of fortune, if we are not willing to follow them and share their life – whatever it may be. We have no business to let them go from all the sweet, ennobling influences of home life."[18] Saxby urged British women to go "bravely to work with the men in building up those grand young nations of which Britain is so justly proud."[19] She estimated that in the Canadian West there was about one woman to every fifty men, and she believed that the "old country could confer no greater boon upon this fine young nation than by sending it thousands of our girls to soften and sweeten life in the Wild West."[20] Here they would find a race of able, prosperous, handsome men: "Britons of larger body and larger heart than those at home. There is a freedom of gait, a heartiness of manner ... You feel that here is a race of men who must be winners in life's battle." (However, she also stated, somewhat in contradiction, that the absence of a feminine influence tended to make the men "restless, dissatisfied, reckless and godless.")[21]

Mrs George Cran, in her book *A Woman in Canada* (1910), held much the same views about the type of woman needed.[22] In her chapter on the prairies, she argued that it was a place for English women of the middle rather than working class. This was essential for "race making":

The working-class woman does not bring the intelligence to bear on domestic emergencies which a cultured woman can, out of her ignorance how can she reduce disorder to comeliness, and make the prairie home a beautiful thing? It can be done. I have seen it. Then the next generation deserves some attention. If ignorant women of our lower orders go out and marry – as they will – farmers, who are often men of decent breeding, their children will go down, not up, in the scale of progress; a woman of refinement and culture, of endurance, of healthy reasoning courage, is infinitely better equipped for the work of homemaking and race-making than the ignorant, often lazy, often slovenly lower-class woman.[23]

Definite meanings were attached to the category of white woman in the emerging Prairie West of the late nineteenth century. She was to be the civilizer and the reproducer of the race. The wise women from the East would exemplify all the qualities of the ideal Victorian woman, which included purity and piety. At times it proved useful also to emphasize the frailty and delicacy of the white woman, as well as her dependence on males, though these were scarcely the qualities that would ensure stability or success in the Prairie West. How this category of white woman was produced and manipulated can be seen very clearly in the events of 1885. In that year the Dominion of Canada faced a crisis in its authority over the indigenous Métis and Indian population of the recently acquired region. The previous year, because the requests of the Métis of Batoche and St Laurent (in present-day Saskatchewan) for land guarantees had largely been ignored by the Canadian government, the Métis had asked Louis Riel to lead a protest as he had in Manitoba in 1869–70. This led to a skirmish between the North-West Mounted Police and the Métis at Duck Lake in March 1885, with the result that troops were dispatched west – the largest mobilization for war ever to take place on Canadian soil. Meanwhile, the threat of violence towards white women, which was exemplified in the experiences of Theresa Delaney and Theresa Gowanlock, who had been captured by a group of Cree, was exploited to rally consensus around the project of first subduing the indigenous people and then policing boundaries between them and the newcomers.

During the 1885 crisis in authority, powerfully negative and completely fabricated representations of Aboriginal women were circulated. They were cast as actively instigating violence, both by participating in aggressive acts and by inciting the men. Earlier dominant non-Aboriginal images of Aboriginal women as passive and abused slaves to the men of their own society were replaced by these projections of them as instigators of dreadful atrocities. In the years immediately following the 1885 crisis, assiduous efforts were made to cast Aboriginal women as dangerous and immoral, as a threat to the emerging non-Aboriginal community. In the press and other publications, they were presented as the complete opposite of white women; they were agents of the destruction of the moral and cultural health of the new community. At the same time, Aboriginal males were assumed to be a potential menace to the "honour" of white women and girls. These representations, like those of the vulnerable white woman in need of protection, were central to the new notions of spatial and social segregation that were taking shape in the West.

This study focuses on the representations of women more than on what women actually did. It examines a particular system of beliefs, often illusory or false, held by the group that became dominant in the Canadian West in the late nineteenth century. Varied sources have been drawn upon, including newspaper accounts, government reports, early histories, and the writings of missionaries, promoters of settlement, and others who claimed the authority to write and who disseminated information, however misguided and erroneous, and exercised power and surveillance based on that information. This is not to suggest that all the non-Aboriginal public at all times held a particular body of views. There was not a completely unified or essential "colonial discourse."[24] Yet some of these ideas, by virtue of their repetition and promotion, appear to have achieved greater prominence and acceptance than others.

What women in the West actually did and what actually happened to them would be the topic of another study. One of the points raised by this study is that it is difficulty to uncover the "real," since we have access to the "real" only through representation.[25] It is important to consider for a moment, however, the extent to which these representations may have reflected the actual lives of women. It could well be argued that the pioneer white woman on a typical homestead was far removed from the fragile, rarefied, genteel, "civilizer" ideal; otherwise, she would not have survived for long. There must have been a high premium on the opposite qualities: strength, independence, resourcefulness, and resilience. The pioneer farm woman had to haul water and fuel, just like the "drudges" of Aboriginal society who were so maligned in the popular press. She had to cope for long stretches alone or with only her children for company, since husbands and fathers typically worked off the farm, especially during the start-up years. She may well have had to fight prairie fires, find and tend livestock, and put up a sod barn, all without the help of men. The West

wanted women not so much because they were "civilizers" but because of their free labour. The work of women, especially in diversi-
fying the economic base of the farm, was vital on the dry plains,
where the risk of crop failure was high. Similarly, Aboriginal
women would have had difficulty recognizing themselves in the ma-
levolent representations of them that were circulated. Aboriginal
women were vital to the cultural and physical survival of their people at this time when many of the foundations of their society were
being undermined. Far from being a threat to the well-being of the
new communities, they assisted with their knowledge, helping as
midwives and with their medicine.

These late-nineteenth-century representations of women, then,
bore scant resemblance to the real lives of the women. What historian Andrée Lévesque has written about the "normative discourse,"
or canons, regulating the behaviour of women in Quebec in the
mid-twentieth century could also apply to the era and place under
scrutiny here.[26] Norms of femininity are articulated by those who
wield social and economic power. "It is these arbiters of the norm
who elaborate the qualities that define/construct what society rec-
ognizes as 'woman' at a particular moment in history."[27] Actual
behaviour might deviate from the established norm, but "the public discourse on women did not lose its importance in conse-
quence. In its power, it mapped out what was permitted, and what
would be repressed."[28] In the Canadian West of the late nineteenth
century, representations of women as either noble, pure, and fragile or as malign, immoral, and sinister persisted and proved resilient to change. These representations were useful to those who
exercised power and controlled knowledge in the non-Aboriginal
world of the emerging West. They were not unique to the situation
in the Canadian West, however. They mirrored patterns in other
colonial settings at that time.

WOMEN AND THE COLONIAL EXPERIENCE

This study has drawn inspiration from a variety of approaches to
understanding the past. Of particular importance are works that
draw attention to the way in which identities, whether of race,
nationality, femininity, or masculinity, are culturally and historically
constructed categories of meaning. Recent gender histories begin
with the premises that femininity and masculinity are "not cultural

universals but vary with other forms of power and markers of difference," and that these identities were made not in isolation but in
relationships.[29] Race is also a constructed category. Today there is
fairly widespread consensus in the sciences of biology and anthropology that the word "race" refers to nothing that science should
recognize as real.[30] There is no "racial essence" that can explain a
person's intellectual or moral aptitude. Yet while recognizing the
essential unreality of races and the beliefs about them, it must also
be acknowledged that the beliefs about racial categories assume social importance. As Kwame Anthony Appiah has written, "Races are
like witches: however unreal witches are, *belief* in witches, like belief
in races, has had – and in many communities continues to have –
profound consequences for human social life."[31] The latter half of
the nineteenth century was the heyday of dubious assumptions
about race, based on a cluster of biological or historical specula-
tions. British and American anthropologists, historians, poets, missionaries, and comparative philologists created and "elaborated the
myth of the sturdy, freedom-loving energetic Anglo-Saxon race that
entitled them to despise those of 'mixed' or 'lower' origins."[32] Educated English men and women thought of themselves as part of a
race that had inherited certain superior capacities and virtues that
gave them a decisive advantage over other peoples, who were seen
as dogged by grave defects; and the politicians of the day exploited
race pride and race hatred to bolster domestic accord.[33]

Catherine Hall has examined the ways in which the English of
the nineteenth century constructed an identity – that is, "the process of representing symbolically the sense of belonging which
draws people together into an 'imagined community' and at the
same time defines who does not belong or is excluded from it."[34]
Hall argues that white British identities, both male and female,
were forged in relation to sets of assumptions about the colonized,
racialized "others" of the British Empire and the people on the turbulent margins of the United Kingdom.[35] Representations of Eng-
lishness, according to Hall, depended on a series of boundaries,
which differentiated the English from an ever-shifting map of others, who were perceived as threatening and dangerous at different
times in history. Hall has also drawn attention to the idea that race
has shaped the history and identity of white women.

Similarly, a central theme of Vron Ware's *Beyond the Pale: White
Women, Racism and History* is the need to perceive white femininity as

an historically and culturally constructed concept.[36] In wondering why there are so few studies of the racial categorization of white femininity, Ware wrote that this was perhaps because "in a predominantly white society it is hard to get away from the assumption that to be white is to be normal, while to be non-white is to occupy a racial category with all its attendant meanings."[37] White women are typically represented in terms of gender, class, and sexuality, and the dynamics of race are rarely acknowledged. Ware's book is based on "a recognition that to be white and female is to occupy a social category that is inescapably racialized as well as gendered."[38] Her study in part examines the British campaign against lynching in the United States in the 1890s and analyses the racist assumptions about predatory black men and vulnerable white women that functioned to justify lynching, which was a way of reinforcing white supremacy by rule of terror. Ware found that definitions of femininity were inextricably tied to ideologies of race and class, and she effectively argues that different ideas about what it means to be a white female "can play a pivotal role in negotiating and maintaining concepts of racial and cultural difference."[39] Images of white female vulnerability were exploited to convey the message of the necessity of policing the boundaries between black and white. It was important that white women were seen to be not only helpless but powerless, without a voice of their own, and to be the property of white men; thus, according to Ware, "their 'protectors' could claim to be justified in taking revenge for any alleged insult or attack on them."[40] The value and sanctity of traditional domestic arrangements that implied little power or freedom for white women were central to this definition of white femininity of the late nineteenth century. Ware further notes that an analysis of the components of white femininity only makes sense in the context of ideas about black women. The meanings of the different ways of being female were constantly being referred to each other, compared and contrasted.

Ware's study echoes the argument of Hazel V. Carby in *Reconstructing Womanhood: The Emergence of the Afro-American Woman Novelist.*[41] In part, this is an examination of the racially specific gender ideologies and images of womanhood under slavery. Carby acknowledges whiteness as well as blackness as a racial category. According to Carby, stereotypes of white and black womanhood did not exist in isolation and can be explained only in relation to each other. The dominating image was of white southern womanhood against which other women were measured and found wanting. White women were defined as pure, submissive, pious, and domestic, with delicate constitutions. Black women were without any of these qualities; they could not be pure, virtuous, or frail; rather, they were strong and licentious. Despite the fact that these race-specific ideologies of womanhood were at odds with the actual lives of most women, they proved to be persistent and played a powerful role in relegating women of different ethnicities to certain jobs and physical locales. Government as well as police authorities capitalized on these different racial/ethnic images of women, which helped to determine strategies of exclusion and control.

In those colonial settings in which the issue of race did not apply, women were nonetheless polarized into the same two categories – as agents of either the salvation or the ruin of elite men. In her study of women and the colonial experience in sixteenth- and seventeenth-century Ireland, for example, Mary O'Dowd argued that in Irish colonial theory the traditional dual image of the benign and malign powers of women were given this formulation.[42] "While Irish women were portrayed as guileful, deceitful, and licentious creatures who could lead men into 'degeneracy,' English women were seen as nourishing and strengthening the colonial ideal."

Many of the scholars of European women and empire stress that there was often rigid control over the activities of these women and limits to the social space in which they could operate, precisely because they were cast as the guardians and caretakers of the morality of the new communities. Being idealized as the "ideal English woman" who was vulnerable and dependent on male protectors was restricting in a British colony. In her study of eastern Ontario Loyalist women, Janice Potter found that many of those who were loyal to the British during the tumultuous years of the American Revolution performed valuable services and behaved every bit as heroically as their husbands, yet when they reached the British lines they were reintegrated into a paternalistic and patriarchal power structure.[43] They could only fit into this well-entrenched power structure as subordinates, needing care and protection. There was no recognition of their remarkable accomplishments. Many of them were widows who were solely responsible for their children and in need of British support, and they had to stress their dependence and weakness in order to earn this support. "Only their suffering and their husband's service counted with the

British."[44] Heroic women, or even women who simply coped reasonably well, were not as useful to the British military and colonial authorities as suffering, vulnerable victims.

It has frequently been argued for a variety of colonial settings that it was the white women themselves who were responsible for racial segregation and for the polarization of women into the benign and malign. They are depicted as racist and petty snobs who introduced and perpetuated negative attitudes towards Native women. This approach has recently been subjected to considerable scrutiny.[45] Ann Laura Stoler has argued that white women did not create racial tensions, though they may well have exacerbated them and supported racial segregation.[46] Stoler contends that the arrival of white women in colonial settings usually occurred in conjunction with some recently enacted or planned "stabilization" of colonial rule, and she notes that the term "stabilization" is ambiguous since "it may express either a securing of empire or a response to imperial vulnerability."[47] In times of a real or imagined threat to the stability of colonial rule, the arrival and the protection of white women was part of a broader response to the problems of colonial control. In Delhi, for example, in the 1920s, as resistance to colonial rule mounted, the presence of white women was used to legitimize the coercive measures needed for control. White women were made the moral and cultural custodians of the European community, and "any attempted or perceived infringement of white female honor came to be seen as an assault on white supremacy and European rule."[48]

In the colonial settings that Stoler focuses on, including French Indochina and the Dutch East Indies, there were métis populations, and she found that in each case the métis were eventually perceived as a dangerous source of subversion, a threat to white prestige, and a danger to the European community at large.[49] In many colonial situations there was an early phase of intermarriage which produced métis offspring, and in communities as diverse as Mexico, Cuba, India, Indochina, and the American South, the prohibition against intermarriage was a relatively late colonial intervention. Stoler concludes that it was not therefore "interracial sexual contact that was seen as dangerous, but its public legitimation in marriage. Similarly it was not the progeny of such unions who were problematic, but the possibility that they might be recognized as legitimate heirs to a European inheritance. The point is obvious: Colonial control and profits were secured by constantly readjusting the parameters of the colonial elite to delimit those who had access to property and privilege and those who did not."[50]

One common theme that emerges in recent histories of European women and colonialism is that in colonial situations varying in time and geography, protecting the virtue of white women became a pretext for suppressing and controlling the indigenous population. The threat of real or imagined violence against white women was a rationale for securing white control, for clarifying boundaries between peoples. The degree of concern and the nature of the measures taken varied, depending on how secure the colonial authorities felt. During times of upheaval and uncertainty or insubordination, frenzy over the safety of white women dramatically increased, often bearing no relation to the actual level of assault or rape. These events had lasting impact, however, and were reflected in government policy and social relations.

The memsahib figure was one of the British Empire's most powerful symbols. Historically, the word "memsahib" was "a class-restrictive term of address meaning 'lady master,' which was used for the wives of high-ranking civil servants and officers."[51] Throughout the course of British imperial rule in India, the memsahib was popularly represented in a number of different and contradictory guises, though she consistently remained a "lady." By the time of the publication of E.M. Forster's *Passage to India* (1924), she was well established stereotypically as a petty racist snob embodying the worst evils of Empire.[52] However, in an earlier era, when British authority had been tested in the Indian rebellion of 1857, the memsahib (at that time a sacred image of virtuous English womanhood) had been popularly represented as a defenceless and innocent victim of barbaric attacks.

In *Allegories of Empire: The Figure of Woman in the Colonial Text*, Jenny Sharpe argues that this crisis in British authority was managed and British strategies of counterinsurgency introduced through the circulation of stories about the violation of English women.[53] Images of violence towards English women had not been prevalent when there was a belief that the colonial structures of power were firmly in place, but they were assiduously circulated in 1857, transforming an indigenous resistance to British rule into an uncivilized eruption that had to be contained. Sensationalized reports of the rape of English women and invented stories of assault, humiliation, and terror were rife. According to Sharpe, during the earliest days of the rebellion, a strange and horrifying tale took hold of the colonial imagination in Anglo-India and England that the mutineers were subjecting "our countrywomen" to unspeakable torments, systematically raping them and then dismembering their ravished bodies.[54]

Although commissioners and magistrates entrusted with investigating the rumours found no evidence to substantiate such stories, the rebellion remained fixed in memory, in canvas and in ink, as a barbaric attack on innocent white women, an image reinforced in rebellion narratives and given coherence in the Anglo-Indian fiction of the later nineteenth century. The massacre of British civilians at Cawnpore (Kanpur) in July 1857 sealed the blanket image of the rebels as sadistic fiends who desecrated English womanhood. Before an approaching British army, the Hindu leader Nana Sahib ordered the execution of his hostages, including two hundred English women and children. Their bodies were concealed in a well or thrown into the Ganges River. Sharpe writes, "Although Nana Sahib's actions were the exception rather than the rule, the occurrence of even one massacre such as Cawnpore endowed all the terrifying tales with their truth-effects."[55]

Entirely fabricated stories of the murdered women's torments drew on a stockpile of horrors from classical and biblical tradition.[56] These stories functioned to sanction force and violence and to justify the public spectacles of repression that were designed to maximize terror in the indigenous population. Tales of the violation of innocent English women allowed the British strategies of counterinsurgency to be depicted as the restoration of moral order, screening the British campaign of terror waged on the insurgents. Representations of the desecrated English lady played into a code of chivalry that called upon British Victorian males to protect the weak and defenceless – and the English lady was invariably cast as weak and passive; any agency she might have expressed was erased, "for her value to colonialism resides in her status as a defenceless victim."[57] Abused victims were required for heroic avengers. The category of "English woman" did not include those from the working-class, for the chivalric code demanded the victim be a chaste lady. Indian women also did not share the status of innocent victims; indeed, they were depicted in the popular press and in rebellion narratives as inciting their men to the bloodiest acts.

In the aftermath of 1857, English women in India were to a greater extent confined to the domestic sphere, and Sharpe argues that the representation of rebellion as the violation of English women contributed to this confinement. Here the restriction of English middle-class women to the home resembled its English counterpart, but there was an added dimension in the emphasis on the home as a space of racial purity and on the duty of colonial women to maintain the purity of the race.[58]

An example of some of the same forces at work can be seen in the Jamaican "revolt" of 1865 when the British governor, Edward John Eyre, fearing a general uprising against the much out numbered white population after a riot at Morant Bay, declared martial law and sent in troops. The reprisals were exceedingly harsh: 439 killed, 600 flogged, and more than 1,000 huts and houses burned.[59] Eyre was most proud of having "saved the ladies of Jamaica," for this colonial situation, too, was rife with terrifying stories of brutalities to white women, stories that were later shown to have been grossly overstated.[60]

Rape scares were a common phenomenon in racially divided colonial societies, and they emerged when there was a fear of a loss of colonial power, authority, or prestige. In his article "Natal's Black Rape Scare of the 1870s," Norman Etherington argues that the hysteria that gripped the settler minority in Natal was born of a broader fear of losing control.[61] This fear of the rape of white women by African men was not triggered by any specific event, nor was there found to be any confirmed basis for the hysteria in criminal prosecutions. Unease among the white colonists at this time was created by the such factors as the emergence of Africans as formidable competitors in agriculture and transport. Similarly, in India during the 1883 Ilbert Bill controversy, rumours were circulated about the attempted rape of an English woman in Calcutta.[62] This bill would have granted Indian magistrates criminal jurisdiction over Europeans in rural districts. The most vocal opponents of the bill were indigo and tea planters in Bengal, who feared that Indian judges, unlike British judges, might not so easily overlook the mistreatment of workers. Great indignation was expressed, however, about the humiliating prospect of English women having to appear before Indian judges in the event of cases of rape. A much weakened and ineffective bill was passed the following year. According to Jenny Sharpe, whenever the need arose, the Anglo-Indian com-

munity continued to rally around the memory of the rebellion and
the supposed threat Indian men posed to white women.[63] Indeed,
the memory of the Indian rebellion as the violation of English
womanhood could be recalled when the need arose even in the far-
thest corners of empire, including western Canada.

WESTERN CANADA AND
THE COLONIAL EXPERIENCE

Several of the themes and arguments articulated by these writers
are relevant in the context of western Canada. Some of the themes
have been explored with regard to the history of women in the fur
trade and women at the settlement of Red River (Winnipeg) in the
eighteenth and nineteenth centuries, when marriage among fur
traders and Aboriginal women was common. In *Strangers in Blood:
Fur Trade Company Families in Indian Country,* Jennifer S.H. Brown
has described how the criteria of race, religion, and ideas about
respectability relegated women of Aboriginal ancestry to lower
ranks in fur-trade country in the 1820s and 1830s. Many of these
marriages were "unchristianized," and, in British society, women
involved in these unions were regarded as mistresses or prostitutes, not true marital partners. Clergymen at Red River were suspicious of the rank and virtue of the women in these marital
partnerships.[64]

Sylvia Van Kirk has taken a parallel approach when detailing the
way in which the arrival of white women in some of the main centres of fur-trade country brought Aboriginal women into disrepute,
especially the wives of fur traders.[65] Events such as the sensational
Foss-Pelly trial of 1850, in which the part-Aboriginal wife of a chief
factor was accused of adultery, illustrate the way in which categories
of women were created, white women being chaste and pure, while
Aboriginal women were immoral and sinister.[66] Implicit in the attitudes of many of the non-Aboriginal residents of Red River at the
time of the trial, according to Van Kirk, "was the belief that a certain moral weakness was inherent in women of even part-Indian
extraction," and the scandal served to justify the notion that it was
folly for white men to marry other than pure white women.[67] By
the mid-nineteenth century, racial tensions and the categorization
of women had intensified at Red River, the earliest and largest of
the European settlements in the Canadian West.

A similar pattern is traced in a recent article by Erica Smith, who examined another of the scandals that rocked the community in order to illuminate the process through which, as Red River became consolidated and distanced itself from its fur-trade past, "the polarization of women as either promiscuous or pure was made absolute." Like Van Kirk, Smith found that "within the prevailing racial discourse Indian women were agents of men's ruin and white women agents of men's salvation."[68] In 1863 the Reverend Griffith Owen Corbett was accused of having seduced Maria Thomas, a sixteen-year-old girl of part-Aboriginal descent who was a servant in the Corbett household. Corbett was found guilty of attempting to procure an abortion for her and was sentenced to six months' imprisonment. Focusing on the coverage of the three-month trial in the local paper, the *Nor'Wester*, Smith describes how white women, particularly Abigail Corbett, the English wife of the accused, were cast as paragons of virtue, exemplifying "sterling character, noble sentiments, refined emotion, genteel deportment, and most importantly, sexual purity."[69] They were weak, vulnerable, and frail. Women of Aboriginal ancestry, particularly Maria Thomas, were prostitutes who "articulated inappropriate sexual knowledge, and gadded about in public, destroying the domestic happiness of respectable families and the reputations of respectable neighbourhoods."[70]

This present study has a different geographic and chronological focus than these histories of the fur-trade era. It focuses on the western prairies, beyond the region that became Manitoba, and on the last three decades of the nineteenth century. It is appropriate to view this place and time within a colonial framework, recognizing that "colonialism" is a term that refers to a great variety of asymmetrical intersocial relationships and that colonial rule is highly varied in administration and impact. While the Prairie West does not readily conjure up the powerful images of "Empire" – spacious mansions, palm trees, houseboys, and ayahs – nevertheless, the fundamental features of colonialism were clearly present in the extension of the power of the Canadian state and in the maintenance of sharp social, economic, and spatial distinctions between the dominant and subordinate population. Colonial rule involved the domination, or attempted domination, of one group over another. There was a racial dimension and a dimension of inequality, since the colonies were run by whites for the prestige, power, and profit of whites. Colonial administrations facilitated the commercial enterprise of the expatriates, and typically the indigenous people lost a good proportion of their land. When the indigenous people attempted to participate in or compete with these commercial enterprises, their efforts were often thwarted by the combined efforts of entrepreneurs and colonial administrators.[71] Indigenous leadership and authority, along with the independence of the original inhabitants, were thus eroded, and the rebellions that so often resulted were typically met with overwhelming force, especially during periods of social and political uncertainty.

In the late nineteenth century, Canada's North-West Territories were governed as a colonial dependency of Ottawa. In 1870 the Territories had been purchased from the Hudson's Bay Company without consultation with the residents, and consequently there has been none of the Confederation debates that prevailed in other regions. Another difference that set Manitoba and the North-West Territories apart from the provinces was that the control and disposal of public lands and natural resources were under federal jurisdiction. Confirming colonial status, there was no trust of self-government in the Territories. An appointed lieutenant-governor and an appointed council with very limited powers defined by the federal government prevailed until the granting of responsible government in 1897. As historian Lewis G. Thomas wrote, "The relationship of the prairie west to the federal government was to be that of a colony."[72] He further noted that the North-West Mounted Police, like other British colonial police forces, was inspired by the Royal Irish Constabulary, which had been formed to keep law and order in the troubled colony of Ireland. There was, according to Thomas, "uncontrolled and indiscriminate exploitation not only of the physical but also of the human resources of the prairie provinces."[73]

In 1885, when the Dominion of Canada faced a crisis in its authority over the indigenous Métis, there was thought to be the potential for more widespread insubordination. For the past decade, the First Nations people of the West, most of whom were now living on reserves and were in desperate economic circumstances, had protested government indifference and policies, especially the government's failure to help them create an agricultural base, as promised in the treaties. By 1884 the Plains Cree had begun to organize a strong alliance aimed at the revision of the treaties.[74]

Central-Canadian dreams of prosperity and of a nation from sea to sea would lie in tatters if authority was not firmly established over the indigenous people of the West. Although only a handful of treaty people joined the Métis in active resistance, the military was used in 1885 to disarm, impoverish, and subjugate the Cree and to deprive them of their leadership. Eighty-one Indian men were sent to trial, and forty-four were convicted. Cree leaders Big Bear, Poundmaker, and others were sent to Stony Mountain Penitentiary in Manitoba to serve out their sentences, and both died shortly after their release, having contracted tuberculosis while they were incarcerated. In November 1885, the same month that Louis Riel was hanged in Regina, a public spectacle of repression was staged at the North-West Mounted Police (NWMP) barracks at Battleford. Eight Cree convicted of murder, including those at Frog Lake, were hanged in the largest mass hanging in Canadian history.

Indignities to white women in the West were kept before the public eye that November as *Two Months in the Camp of Big Bear: The Life and Adventures of Theresa Delaney and Theresa Gowanlock* was released. Excerpts were published in newspapers such as the *Huron Expositor* of Seaforth, Ontario, which featured the complete account of Theresa Gowanlock on the front page for four successive issues in November and December 1885. Historians who have examined various aspects of the emerging Canadian West in the 1880s, including the behaviour of the press and the NWMP, have detected a significant shift in Euro-Canadian attitudes towards Aboriginal people after 1885.[75] Whereas before then they were regarded as "nuisances" but relatively harmless, afterwards they were depicted as a distinct threat to the property and lives of the white settlers. The anxieties aroused about the safety of white females in the West both reflected and played a role in this significant change in attitude.

In the mid-1880s there were very few white women in the territories beyond Manitoba. Although there were small pockets of Euro-Canadian settlement, the First Nations and Métis population still outnumbered the newcomers. In 1885 in the District of Alberta, for example, the host population was more than 9,500 while the recent arrivals numbered only 4,900.[76] Clearly, Canada's authority could not be successfully extended until there was further immigration, yet this was almost at a standstill. It would be possible to enhance and encourage travel west once the transcontinental railway was completed, but in the early months of 1885 there were still

large stretches uncompleted across Ontario north of the Great
Lakes. In the 1880s, then, the British-Ontarian fragment that constituted the majority of the newcomers felt threatened and vulnerable, and by 1885 this emerging elite was faced with insubordination
from the indigenous population.

The military action taken against the indigenous population of
the Canadian West was a rare and fleeting instance of near national unity between French- and English-speaking non-Aboriginal
Canadians and between the different regions of the new nation.
Expressions of national pride were manifested in the massive re-
ceptions given for the troops on their return home, as well as in
poetry and song, and in newspaper editorials. The euphoria lasted
into the early summer of 1885, when the issue of Riel and his
hanging divided the nation as never before. It is clear from the
rhetoric and propaganda of the military campaign, and from the
verse and song produced in the months of conflict, that efforts to
create a spirit of national unity, to create an imagined community,
were built on a series of negative assumptions about the indigenous people of the West, who were depicted as a cruel, treacherous, subhuman enemy. Typically, a poem by Agnes E. Wetherald
published in the *Week* described them as "Versed in animal cunning, warily waiting in ambush; / Merciless in the purely animal
power to smite ... The heart of our country is beating against the
knife of the savage."[77] Meanwhile, the men who went out to show
the treacherous enemy "British sport" were depicted as gallant
conquering heroes. The indigenous people served as the "convenient other," to use historian Peter Gay's words: an "immensely
serviceable alibi for aggression, solidifying the bracing sense of
one's merits – or assuaging the secret fear of one's imperfec-
tions."[78] According to Gay, politicians were well aware of how help-
ful it was to have a hateful other to hand; they exploited the
knowledge that hatred can be cultivated with a purpose, and they
"constructed enemies in order to bolster domestic concord." At
this time, Prime Minister John A. Macdonald was in need of domestic accord, since he required the funds to complete the Canadian Pacific Railway. The hated other could be made even more
hated if he posed a threat to the honour of white women.

As in colonial situations elsewhere, the threat of violence towards
white women was exploited especially to provide a rationale for
those who wished to secure greater control over the Aboriginal

population. Quite possibly, the historical memory of the presence of white women in other parts of the British Empire helped cement the image of the powerless and vulnerable female. The India of 1857, which had entered the colonial record as a barbaric attack on innocent English women and children, was not as many worlds away from western Canada as one might assume. Major General Frederick D. Middleton, who commanded the North-West Field Force in 1885, had distinguished himself in the "Sepoy Rebellion," having taken part in the famous expedition for the relief of Lucknow as aide-de-camp to General Lugard.[79] Major General Thomas Bland Strange, a retired British officer who commanded the forces that pursued Big Bear with the goal of freeing the captives, was born in India in 1831 and fought in the "Indian Mutiny."[80] Moreover, both men had served together in India.

CAPTIVITY NARRATIVES AND AMERICAN HISTORY

An extensive body of literature evaluating the American "captivity narrative" has also been important to this study. *Two Months in the Camp of Big Bear* is a captivity narrative – in fact, two separate narratives. In the United States, captivity narratives were a popular form of literature from colonial times on. The many studies of this genre attest to the complexity of understanding both the experience and the narration of captivity. As texts that shed light on Aboriginal lifestyles and cultural values, these narratives have generally been regarded with suspicion, for they so often portray Aboriginal people as savage, sadistic, and irrational. The typical American captivity narrative has been described as a device for anti-Indian propaganda. At a time when Indians were an obstacle to frontier expansion, these accounts of atrocities were "shaped by publishers exploiting a mass market that thrived on sensationalism, in a natural alliance with land speculators who wanted to implement a policy of Indian extermination in the interest of real estate development."[81] In the nineteenth century, when war was being waged against the indigenous people of the American West, captivity narratives served to turn public opinion against the "hostiles" and promote sympathy for the victims of these outrages.

Care must be taken, however, in extending broad generalizations to all accounts of Indian captivity in the United States. These changed considerably over time both in their style and content and in the purposes to which they were applied.[82] Certain themes dominated at certain periods, according to the major preoccupations of the day. Those depicting Aboriginal life favourably are rare, but a few narrators expressed sympathy for the Indian or displayed little prejudice. In a recent study, Colin Calloway has argued that some captivity narratives may be seen as rare sources from inside Aboriginal societies and that some eighteenth-century narratives from New England display a keen sense of toleration for cultural differences.[83] Captivity was a point of contact between cultures, and some of the captives gained a unique perspective and knowledge. Some even chose to stay among their captors, marrying and raising children, despite efforts on the part of officials and their kin to lure them away.[84] Thus, formerly distinct and irreconcilable elements were blended together. Those who chose to remain with their captors were less likely to leave written accounts of their experiences, so we know about them mainly from other sources. It is not easy, then, to generalize about the experience or narration of captivity, but it would be safe to say that in the most standard accounts the captives are wrenched from happy homes and are made to suffer intolerably at the hands of "savages" before they are returned or redeemed.

From the time of earliest European settlement in the United States, captivity narratives proved useful; they were exploited for a wide range of purposes and were often edited, adjusted, or meddled with in order to advance certain points more effectively. They were used to rally newly formed communities around their commitment to their errand in the wilderness, their obligation to settle and subdue. These narratives allowed the intruders in Aboriginal territory to appear as innocent victims – the wronged, who were subject to injustice and misrule. They could be used to show the great need for non-Aboriginal settlement and for possession of the land and resources. In *Legacy of Conquest: The Unbroken Past of the American West*, Patricia Limerick wrote: "The idea of captivity organized much of Western sentiment ... It was an easy transition of thought to move from the idea of humans held in an unjust and resented captivity to the idea of land and natural resources held in Indian captivity – in fact, a kind of monopoly in which very few Indians kept immense resources to themselves, refusing to let the large numbers of willing and eager white Americans make what they could of those resources."[85]

Captivity narratives were especially useful when the protagonists were women. Since these accounts tended to stress physical discomfort and distress in a vast, inhospitable wilderness, the female captive was by far the more affecting image, for she appeared more vulnerable than a male captive.[86] The most recent comprehensive analysis of the American captivity narrative from 1607 to 1870 is June Namias's, *White Captives: Gender and Ethnicity on the American Frontier.*[87] Namias argues that the archetype of the frail and vulnerable female captive did not always prevail, for the nature of the narratives changed over time, reflecting prevailing social beliefs about women and the expectations of women. She identifies three female models: the Survivor of the colonial period, the Amazon of the revolutionary era and early republic, and the Frail Flower of the era of western expansion, 1820–70. The earlier literature portrayed women captives as physically and emotionally tough, as symbols of the courage and fortitude they needed for their own survival and that of the civilization they represented amid an alien culture. They were often fierce defending mothers, even warriors. By contrast, the Frail Flower was a poor hapless creature. Shocked, distressed, and disgusted by her capture, she was paralysed and unable to adapt. In the nineteenth century, a culture of delicate and frail femininity had so permeated the ideology of white middle-class womanhood that the loss of a protective husband supposedly left a woman totally defenceless. Through their weakness, women served to define masculine strength and courage. Men alone now had the means of ensuring the survival of their civilization, often through heroic rescues, which were a fixture of many of these narratives. A central point raised by Namias is that the captivity narrative was a popular means of projecting the brutality of Aboriginal people and the threat they posed, especially to the virtue of white women, regardless of the actual data or the first-hand accounts of the captives themselves. The changing editions of popular works reveal the changing purposes of editors and publishers.

In a recent essay entitled "Captured Subjects/Savage Others: Violently Engendering the New American," Carroll Smith-Rosenberg has attempted to trace the process by which white Americans imagined themselves to be the true Americans.[88] To claim the name American, the early British settlers had to wrest the term from the first inhabitants of the continent. Until the late eighteenth century, the English used the word "American" to refer to the First People. An important part of the process of making the white American the true American was through the production of captivity narratives, tales of "tribal atrocities, of savage attacks upon innocent, productive farming families and, especially, upon their women and children."[89] Smith-Rosenberg argues that British-American women played a vital role in the construction of the American Indian as savage and inhuman and the construction of white Americans as true Americans. They did so in three distinct moves: "by assuming the role of innocent victims of barbarous savagery, by assuming the role of authoritative writers, and by authorizing themselves as an alternative white icon for America."[90]

WHOSE CAPTIVES?

American Indian captivity narratives, in which very often the protagonists were women, give us insight into the changing role of white women in America. Most of those who have analysed these accounts recognize that they are making a contribution to an understanding of white society but are shedding little light on the Aboriginal side of the story. Few historians have considered such issues as what Aboriginal Americans thought of these captives or of the uses to which these societies put captivity narratives. The common usage of the term "captivity" is profoundly Eurocentric, for it is almost always understood to mean white captives among Aboriginal societies, when in fact the opposite was a far more common phenomenon. Beginning with the host of captives taken unwillingly to Europe by the earliest European visitors, and including the more recent experiences of whole groups captive on reserves and of Aboriginal children captive in residential schools, the experience of being captured and enclosed within an alien culture was typically an Aboriginal experience, whereas the white captive was always an anomaly. The many Indian "as-told-to" or self-written autobiographies and the accounts of residential school life could be understood and read as captivity narratives.[91]

The whole question of the function of captivity narratives within Aboriginal societies also has received little attention. In a sense, the "stolen women" narratives of many Aboriginal societies are similar to the captivity narratives of Euro-Americans.[92] Both seem to reflect ideals of suitable roles for women, though very different ideals, and both functioned as instructional parables, serving educational purposes that were much larger than that of simply imparting a knowledge of the actual incidents. Some were accounts of authentic experiences, while others were wholly or partly invented. In the "stolen women" narratives, women are abducted or lured away by enemies or supernatural forces. They then use their practical survival skills, their resourcefulness and ingenuity, to outwit their captors and return to their families. These stories were used to educate young women in particular about how problems could be solved, how they could apply their skills to different predicaments, and what pitfalls to avoid; they were expressions of admiration for women who were capable of surviving on their own without the assistance of men. By contrast, narratives such as *Two Months* emphasized the helplessness and vulnerability of women in an inhospitable environment, stressing how they were unable to cope without their husbands since they were entirely lacking in ingenuity and wilderness skills. They had no ability to outwit their captors; they had to be rescued. Although this was not the first impression that Theresa Delaney and Theresa Gowanlock gave to correspondents on the scene in June 1885, it is the image that pervaded their written account.

A very different construction of femininity would likely emerge from a study of narratives told about captive women in nineteenth-century Plains Indian societies. Calf Old Woman, a Blackfoot, was esteemed for her behaviour when captured by the Gros Ventres as a young girl.[93] Her captor, who had killed her father moments earlier, scooped her up on his horse, and while they were riding together she stabbed him with his own knife, tossed his body from the horse's back, scalped him, cut off his right arm, picked up his gun, and rode back to her people. Although chased most of the way, she returned with the three greatest trophies a warrior can wrest from an enemy. She later married a prominent Blackfoot chief and medicine man, Old Sun, and was one of the few women to sit as a warrior in Blackfoot councils.[94] Women taken as war captives often played specialized roles in negotiating matters of war and peace. According to Ojibway oral tradition, a captured Ojibway woman who became the favourite wife of Shappa, a Yankton Dakota chief, arranged a peace between her husband's people and the Pembina band of Ojibway.[95]

The acquisition of captives was a tactic of Aboriginal warfare throughout North America, just as it was (and remains) a function of the warfare of Europeans.[96] In the northeastern United States, adoption and ransom were the Native people's major motives for capture. Gender, age, and health were important considerations in determining the fate of a captive; the elderly and the sick might be killed. Captives were often adopted to assuage the loss of a son or daughter, a brother or sister. Some northeastern people ritually tormented and executed adult male prisoners of war. For women and children, the odds were greater in favour of adoption. There were strong spiritual sanctions against raping women prisoners, for this was thought to rob a warrior of his sacred powers at a time when he was strictly obeying prohibitions against any act that would contaminate the favourable disposition of the spirit world. As a traveller in the later years of New France observed, "Savages have scruples about molesting a woman prisoner, and look upon it as a crime, even when she gives her consent."[97]

CAPTIVITY IN AUSTRALIA: THE ELIZA FRASER STORY

The captivity narrative is often described as being uniquely North American and especially applicable to the United States. Yet as Kay Schaffer, professor of women's studies at the University of Adelaide, Australia, has reminded us, narratives of the captivity of white women at the hands of "barbarous savages" is a structure embedded within the colonial experience of Australia, South Africa, and a great many other colonial settings.[98] Schaffer focuses on the Eliza Fraser story. Fraser was an English woman travelling from Australia in 1836 with her ailing Scottish ship-captain husband, when they were shipwrecked. She and some other survivors spent six weeks on what is now called Fraser Island, and Mrs Fraser became the first white woman to have a close knowledge of the Aborigines and to tell her tale. Fraser has become legendary in the twentieth century, her mythical status bolstered by Patrick White's novel *A Fringe of Leaves*. Schaffer looks at the great variety of nineteenth-century texts that reproduced the story of Eliza Fraser, to examine her construction as a victim of native savagery.[99] Mrs Fraser gave different reports of her ordeal to different audiences. These included an official report, interviews with the local press, and a published account that received widespread coverage in English newspapers. In her first account, which was addressed to an official government audience, there was no mention of the "savagery" and "barbarism" that found its way into subsequent accounts. Her aim with this audience was to relieve her dead husband of any responsibility for mismanagement and to see that certain surviving crew members were punished. Press accounts of her ordeal, based upon interviews, depicted the horrible sufferings of an innocent woman and incited fears of the "savages" at the fringes of the new society. As a result, there were outpourings of generosity and sympathy for the widowed and penniless Mrs Fraser. The lengthy published account was a classic captivity narrative, complete with fabricated tales of torture and cannibalism. Fraser had become the classic vulnerable woman victim of the captivity narrative, and it was her "vulnerability that excites sympathy and incites the instincts of revenge against the barbarous enemy within colonial discourse."[100] Within months, an Americanized version was produced, complete with Indian chiefs, teepees, and tomahawks. Fraser's story had provided "for a widespread Western colonial audience the justification for control by the West over the rest of the world." Schaffer stresses the degree to which the knowledge of Eliza Fraser was manipulated, for the narratives of her experiences were not in fact about Eliza Fraser; they were about regulating race, class, and gender relations and maintaining dominant ideologies of colonialism and Victorian morality.

INDIAN CAPTIVITY IN CANADA

In Canadian history, the experience and narration of Indian captivity has not received the same degree of scholarly attention as it has in the United States. No one has attempted the type of comprehensive survey undertaken by June Namias. This is perhaps partly because there simply were not as many incidents of captivity, for it was generally a function of warfare, and there was less warfare in the territories that became Canada. Yet Indian captivity was a reality in Canada, and it was put to a variety of ever-changing purposes. Jesuit missionaries in New France may be seen as the earliest authors of the captivity narrative in Canada. Like the Puritans and Quakers of the New England colonies, the Jesuits interpreted Indian captivity primarily within a religious framework. *The Jesuit Relations* – reports from the missionaries in New France that were carefully edited in Europe and then read by an eager public – contained accounts of priests held captive by Aboriginal people and subjected to hideous torture. Captivity was a manifestation of God's providence in the testimony of captive Jesuits. Their harrowing accounts elicited sympathy in Europe for the work of the missionaries.

One group of captives who have been examined in some detail, though most often by American scholars, are the New Englanders who were taken to New France in the seventeenth and eighteenth centuries.[101] It is estimated that during what the Americans call the French and Indian Wars as many as two thousand captives from the British colonies may have been taken to New France.[102] Some were prisoners of war of the French, but others had been taken by their Aboriginal allies; some began as prisoners of an Aboriginal group and were subsequently purchased by French families or individuals, or were placed in convents and seminaries. A great many eventually made their way back to New England. The narratives written by some of these people convey multiple messages, including in some cases the horror of being subjected not only to "savage" captors but to French and Roman Catholic overseers. These narratives were clearly used for the purpose of anti-French war propaganda. On the other hand, the accounts of some of the captives described kind treatment which the French had bestowed on them.[103]

Quite a number of the captured New Englanders remained in New France, adopting the Canadian language, culture, and religion. Some joined religious orders, refusing to return even when given the opportunity. While the Canadian accounts depict the women as choosing of their own free will, the New England accounts stress coercion or state that the girls were indoctrinated at an impressionable age. Esther Wheelwright, for example, who became mother superior of the Ursulines of Quebec, was captured at the age of seven in 1703 from her home in Deerfield, Massachusetts.[104] She spent six years with the Abenaki until she was purchased by a priest and placed in the boarding school of the Ursuline convent. According to Ursuline accounts, Esther early on expressed a strong desire to become a nun, and she "took the white veil" in 1713. Although she received letters from her Deerfield family imploring her to return home, and although special ambassadors working for a general exchange of prisoners demanded her release, Esther resolved to remain a nun. The suspicion remained, however, that she had been coerced into this life, and her term of probation was shortened by the Ursulines in case she was tempted to return to her family. She was elected superior of the Ursulines in December 1760, the same

year that British authority was established following the conquest of
Quebec, and she was re-elected in 1769. Other New England captives who joined the Ursulines include Mary Anne Davis and
Dorothy Jordan.[105] Mary Silver, captured at Haverhill, Massachusetts, in 1708 when she was fourteen, was placed in the charge of
the Sisters of the Congregation of Montreal.[106] Baptized and given
the name Adelaide, she joined the Sisters of the l'Hôtel-Dieu at the
age of eighteen, much to the distress of her Puritan mother.
Although her mother entreated her to return to New England, convent sources suggest that she preferred to remain in Canada. She
died in 1740 after thirty years of convent life.

Some New England captives remained in Aboriginal society,
absorbing the language, culture, and religion. The most famous of
these is undoubtedly Eunice Williams, who has been the subject of
many studies, including the recent award-winning book by John
Demos, *The Unredeemed Captive: A Family Story from Early America.*[107]
Eunice Williams was seven years old in February 1704 when she
and her family were among the Deerfield settlers who were
attacked and captured by a *Canadien* and Mohawk war party.
Although the other surviving members of her family were eventually "redeemed" and returned to New England, Eunice remained
behind. Her father, an eminent Puritan minister, published an
account of his captivity and his efforts to have Eunice released from
her Mohawk and Jesuit captors: *The Redeemed Captive Returning to
Zion.* Eunice was adopted by a Mohawk family of Kahnawake, which
was a Jesuit mission community. She was baptized into the Roman
Catholic Church, taking the name Marguerite, and was also given
the name A'ongote, meaning "they took her and placed her as a
member of their tribe," indicating a level of incorporation into the
Mohawk world.[108] She married a Mohawk called Arosen, with
whom she had several children. There were efforts to ransom her
from her captors, as well as other attempts to redeem her, but they
all failed, and by 1707 Eunice was reported to be "unwilling to
return."[109] She made several trips throughout her long life to visit
her family in Massachusetts, and her relatives never gave up hope
that they could persuade "their poor captivated sister" to settle
among them, but she always refused. She lived to be over ninety
years old and died at Kahnawake. Her daughters married Mohawk
men who became prominent in their community.[110] The descendants of Eunice Williams and Arosen, who retained the name

Williams in accordance with Mohawk matrilineal society, are still to be found among the people of St Regis and Kahnawake. Their descendants continued to visit relatives in Massachusetts well into the nineteenth century.

The experience of Eunice Williams was not unique. It is known for certain that five girls, who were between the ages of six and eleven when they arrived as captives from Deerfield, remained at Kahnawake and became fully integrated, marrying and bearing children, and there may have been at least four others who remained there permanently.[111] Others stayed for lengthy periods, some for as long as twenty-five years. One Deerfield captive, Joanna Kellog, subsequently married a Kahnawake chief.[112] But the experience of Eunice Williams continues to intrigue and fascinate. Historians know more about her than the other captives, for she was something of a sensation in her time; yet she left no account of her experiences, and because of this her behaviour has remained a puzzle and open to much interpretation.

Eunice Williams was still firing the public imagination in 1897 when Clifton Johnson published *An Unredeemed Captive*.[113] In this slim volume, her behaviour is at best depicted as odd. An unflattering portrait of an anonymous Aboriginal couple and child on the cover of the book would have caused readers to assume that she surely could not have chosen this life for herself. The man stands in proud ownership over his clearly subordinate wife, who is seated on the ground. The book concludes that we will never know whether Eunice was "a savage from choice or lived her long life in repression and unhappiness."[114] In the more recent book by John Demos, which bears almost the same title, readers would be more likely to conclude that it was not surprising that Eunice decided to stay with the Mohawk after an initial period of feeling unhappy and homesick. Demos has included lengthy passages that display sensitivity to the life Eunice would have enjoyed at Kahnawake. As a child, she probably experienced a milder, less regulated regime than that of children raised in accordance with Puritan norms.[115] Women had considerable power and influence in Iroquoian society (in contrast to the prevailing European views of the time, which insisted that Aboriginal women occupied the status of slaves). Demos suggests that one way to explain the large number of women who chose to remain with their captors – a far larger number than that of the men who chose to remain – is that women enjoyed a degree of authority, prestige, and power which they would not have had as members of a Euro-American colonial society.[116]

The Englishman John Jewitt certainly did not wish to remain a captive. On Vancouver Island in 1803, Jewitt and his shipmate John Thompson were captured by the people of Nootka Sound when the American trading ship *Boston* was attacked and destroyed in retaliation for a long series of insults and murders suffered by the Nootka. The rest of the crew were killed. Jewitt kept a journal during his two years of captivity, and this was published in 1807. His account was not as popular as the story of his experiences told by a professional writer, Richard Alsop, who drew on the journal and interviews with Jewitt to produce *Narrative of the Adventures and Sufferings of John R. Jewitt* (1815), which was reprinted at least eighteen times in the nineteenth century. Jewitt, who spent most of his life in New England after his release, sold copies of the *Narrative* door to door and also performed in a play recreating his life as a captive.[117]

INDIAN CAPTIVITY IN THE
CANADIAN PRAIRIE WEST TO 1885

Until *Two Months in the Camp of Big Bear* appeared in 1885, almost no captivity narratives involving Euro-Canadians emerged from the Canadian Prairie West. *A Narrative of the Captivity and Adventure of John Tanner* (1830), often claimed as an American tale, took place primarily in the land that became southern Manitoba. Tanner was a Kentucky boy who, after being captured, chose to live for thirty years among the Ottawa and Ojibway people. His story is regarded as highly unusual in the captivity genre and is perhaps more rightly classified as an as-told-to autobiography. Native American author Louise Erdrich wrote in the introduction to a recent reprint of his book that it is one of the few captivity narratives that appeal strongly to Native Americans because "John Tanner was culturally an Ojibway, and as such he is claimed by many to this day, for he lived as an Ojibway, married an Ojibway woman, cared devotedly for his mixed-blood children, and was never able to accommodate himself to a non-Indian life."[118] There was never any question of ransoming Tanner from his Ojibway family; he had no desire to return to his non-Indian life until he reached middle age.

In British North America, in the western lands that had been claimed since 1670 by the Hudson's Bay Company, the indigenous people first met the newcomers as fur traders. Consequently, it was not such a conflict-ridden region as the contact zone in the western United States. For nearly two hundred years, a relatively peaceful "middle ground" prevailed in which European and Canadian fur traders remained at the periphery of Aboriginal life, especially with respect to the plains buffalo hunters. Where the two sides met, a set of cultural accommodations arose because it was in the interests of both groups to cooperate. Marriages between European fur traders and Aboriginal women, with the attendant production of children and kinship networks, characterized this middle ground. The practice was so common that in the nineteenth century, the offspring of the marriages of French-Canadian fur traders and Aboriginal women proudly defined themselves as a "new nation."

The arrival of women from eastern Canada and overseas to the Red River Settlement in the early nineteenth century did not usher in an era of Indian captivities. It is interesting to note, however, that many Euro-Canadian women harboured the notion that their children were in danger of being taken captive by hostile or, more often, curious Native people. This idea prevailed until the end of the nineteenth century. Marie-Anne Gaboury, wife of Jean-Baptiste Lagimodière, is renowned as the first Canadian woman in the West, having arrived in 1806. She was at Fort Edmonton shortly after the birth of her second child, Laprairie, a "pretty little baby with a fresh complexion, blue eyes and fair hair."[119] According to a story that became part of Red River folklore, a Blackfoot woman was envious, and one morning while Madame Lagimodière was fetching water, the woman managed to spirit the child away. When Madame Lagimodière learned from the factor that a Blackfoot woman had gone off with her child, she ran after her and demanded the baby back. "The squaw did not understand the words, but she knew what the gesture meant though she made believe not to understand and pretended to be very much astonished, as thieves do when accused."[120] Madame Lagimodière opened the hood that concealed the baby, and there was her little child. The Blackfoot woman then claimed that she was only carrying the baby to play with him and never had any intention of stealing him. (This may well have been the case; there was considerable room for misunderstanding, for it is unlikely that Madame Lagimodière spoke much Blackfoot.)

Painting of the 1823 attack on the Tully family by a party of
Sisseton Dakota near present-day Grand Forks, North Dakota.
The Tullys were Red River colonists who were travelling to St Louis,
Missouri. The painting is by the Swiss-born artist Peter Rindisbacher,
who spent five years in the Red River Settlement. Such pictures of brutal
attacks on women and children did not, as in the American West, become
a staple of the popular literature. There were no such attacks
in the territory that became western Canada.
(West Point Museum, U.S. Military Academy)

Although later generations of women newcomers to the prairies
would also be convinced that their children were in danger of being stolen by Indians, there is no documented case of such an event
in the territory that became the Canadian West. In contrast to the
American West, pictures of savage attacks on helpless women and
children did not become a staple of nineteenth-century popular
histories or fiction about the region.[121] Peter Rindisbacher's painting of an 1823 attack by a party of Sioux on the Tully family of the
Red River Settlement may be alone in this category.[122] To be pre-
cise, however, the attack occurred near present-day Grand Forks,
North Dakota. David Tully was a blacksmith in the Red River colony, and he and his wife Elliston Tully had baptized their children
Andrew (1821) and Jane (1823) in the colony's Anglican
church.[123] They also had an older son named John.[124] The Tullys

had left the Red River Settlement and were on their way to
St Louis, Missouri, when they were attacked. David, Elliston, and
Jane were killed. The boys John and Andrew were briefly taken by
the Sioux but were rescued by Colonel Snelling.

In the Red River press, great interest was expressed in stories of
"white captives among the savages," especially the Dakota Sioux, just
to the south. According to the *Nor'Wester*, in the summer of 1860 the
Métis of Pembina were at the Yankton camp on the plains and saw a
"poor hapless woman in the wigwam of her captors. They say that
they conversed with her, and that she was anxious to get away but
was unable to effect her escape."[125] The American government was
called upon to rescue the woman from a "position of misery and
degradation which she must feel to be worse than the cruelest
death." Such sightings increased following the Minnesota Uprising
of 1862, when some Dakota sought refuge across the border, in
British territory. In 1865 a Mr Edward Harriot was with the White
Horse Plain brigade of buffalo hunters when they camped near a
number of Dakota lodges. He was spoken to by "a young girl of sixteen, of medium size, light complexion, handsome [*sic*] dressed in
leather and apparently anything but satisfied with her position."[126]
Harriot learned only that her parents lived in St Paul and that she
had attended boarding school there, but their conversation was
brief because her old guardian was watching with angry glances. An
effort on the part of the Métis to purchase the young woman was un-
successful because they did not have the required items, which included a puncheon of rum, a chest of tea, two horses, and powder
and ball. The following year the woman was sighted again, and this
time twenty buffalo-running horses were demanded. The *Nor'Wester*
began a subscription list to raise twenty pounds sterling "to be
offered as a reward to any person who will rescue and deliver at Red
River Settlement a white woman, now a prisoner among the Sioux
Indians."[127] It is not known whether this campaign was successful.

Curious rumours about captivities emerged from time to time, as
will be discussed in greater detail in chapter 4. In 1885, for example,
it was alleged that a Quebec farmer by the name of Edward Lambert
had been captured by the Cree more than twenty years earlier. It was
further alleged that the "troublesome" Chief Big Bear was none
other than Mr Lambert.[128] A Mrs Michael Dubois of the St Sauveur
suburb of Quebec claimed to be the first cousin of Lambert and
therefore of Big Bear. Her story was that Lambert had disappeared

while visiting the United States and that now, twenty years later, the family had at last received a letter from him. Lambert explained in the letter that he had been captured by Cree but had been unable to write because he was so closely watched. He said that because of certain acts of bravery on his part, he had been compelled to marry the daughter of a chief, and upon the death of this chief he had been chosen to succeed him. Subsequently, one of Lambert's brothers visited him and verified that he was indeed a Cree chief. He was said to be rich, with two daughters being educated in a convent. Apparently, the family was certain that the Cree chief they knew as Edward was the same man as Big Bear because of a wen, or mark, which was said to identify him unmistakably.

A CANADIAN CAPTIVE IN THE AMERICAN WEST: FANNY KELLY

Evidence that tales of Indian captivity were popular with the Canadian reading public in the later nineteenth century can be found in the fact that several Canadian editions were published of Fanny Kelly's *Narrative of My Captivity among the Sioux Indians*.[129] Kelly's story is told here at some length because it mirrors some of the themes that will be introduced through the story of Delaney and Gowanlock. One of these themes is that accounts of Indian captivity were altered, often dramatically, depending on the intended audience. Various alterations and additions were made when preparing the account of Kelly's experiences for the Canadian reading public. (The story of the "purloining" of the manuscript and the legal battle that followed indicate the potential monetary value of tales of Indian captivity, and apparently Mrs Kelly eventually became a wealthy woman.) The shadowy presence of ghostwriters is also a theme that is introduced through the story of Fanny Kelly. A ghostwriter was clearly the author of the now rare account of Kelly's fellow captive and later nemesis, Sarah Larimer; and the fact that Kelly married a Washington ghostwriter raises the possibility that he may have been involved in the production of her narrative.

Canadians could and did call Fanny Kelly their own. She was born Frances Wiggins near Orillia in 1845, the daughter of James and Margaret Wiggins.[130] Her father owned one hundred acres and farmed eighteen of them on lot 10, concession 2, South Orillia.[131] It did not matter that Frances moved with her family to Geneva,

Kansas, at the age of twelve in 1857, for she had "passed the happy days of early childhood" on the shores of Lake Simcoe, near Orillia, Canada.[132] James Wiggins had decided in 1856 to join a New York abolitionist colony that was determined to establish a community at Geneva.[133] He went back for his family the following year but died of cholera during the return trip. Nevertheless, Margaret Wiggins and her children continued on and settled in Kansas. Some years later, Fanny married Josiah S. Kelly of Kansas. Because of his poor health, the couple resolved upon a change of climate and headed west in May 1864 with a party of six, which included their adopted daughter, Fanny's sister's child. The Kellys carried with them a substantial consignment of trade goods, including flour, coffee, dried fruit, kegs of alcohol, whisky, and brandy, and they drove a herd of fifty milk cows and twenty-five calves.[134] Subsequently added to the party were William J. and Sarah Luse Larimer and their son Frank, also from Kansas. Their destination was Bannack City (today, one of the most remarkably preserved ghost towns in the American West) in the new Territory of Montana. They were among 40,000 newcomers who travelled that year along the North Platte route, part of the Oregon Trail; yet when their small wagon train approached Little Box Elder Creek in Wyoming, they were attacked by a party of Oglala Lakota, or Sioux. These plains buffalo hunters had been growing increasingly alarmed at the great surge of settlers and miners rolling through their territory. Moreover, the Sioux were at that time being pursued by the American army in the aftermath of the 1862 Minnesota Uprising, in which more than seven hundred white settlers had been killed. Sioux skirmishing had increased in 1863 and 1864 with the opening of the Bozeman Trail, a short-cut to the goldfields of Montana.

In the attack on the Kelly wagon train three men were killed and two others wounded. Josiah Kelly, who was some distance from the scene when the shooting began, successfully concealed himself and escaped. William Larimer ran towards some neighbouring timber and survived, although wounded by an arrow in the leg. Sarah Larimer, Fanny Kelly, and their children were carried away. Larimer and her son escaped after one night, but Fanny Kelly remained a captive of a group of Lakota for the next five months, until her ordeal ended safely at Fort Sully, in Dakota Territory. On the first day of captivity, Kelly instructed her daughter to conceal herself and find her way back to the emigrant train. She never saw the girl again. There are several conflicting reports of different parties finding and burying the girl's body.

Fanny Kelly's book is a chronicle of marches through the wilderness, of hunger, thirst, and long days of privation and suffering, of foiled attempts to escape, and of being compelled to join in "orgies" of "savage exultation." Kelly claimed in the book not to have suffered "the fate worse than death" because her captor, Ottawa, the head chief, was aged and infirm and because he appreciated her skilful nursing more than anything else. She mentioned, however, that other white women captives whom she met or heard about were not as fortunate. For instance, Mary Boyer of Spirit Lake, Minnesota, became the "unwilling wife of a brutal savage, and subject to all the petty malice of a scarcely less brutal squaw."[135] Nevertheless, the book is by no means a complete denunciation of the Lakota; there are occasional references to the kindness of certain individuals, and Kelly wrote that during her last few weeks in particular "the Indians had done all in their power for me, all their circumstances and conditions would allow, and the women were very kind."[136]

According to Kelly's narrative, in the final days of her captivity she warned Captain James Fisk, the commander of Fort Sully, that an attack was imminent and thus saved the fort from capture. She claimed that her warning, delivered by a Black Feet Lakota named Jumping Bear (who earlier had saved her life), prevented the Lakota from attacking the fort as they had planned to do, using her as a decoy. Although Kelly's account of the proceedings cannot be reconciled with those of others involved, it seems clear that she was escorted to the gates of Fort Sully and conducted into the fort. There her husband, who had attempted on several occasions to ransom her by sending messengers bearing money and horses, was reunited with her, and together they returned to their former Kansas home. En route to Kansas, crowds of visitors flocked to see the white woman who had been a captive of the Sioux.

Fanny Kelly's trials were far from over, however. She and her husband operated a rooming house in Ellsworth, Kansas, until 1867, when Josiah died of cholera. On the day of his death, his body was robbed of the sum of five hundred dollars. A few days later, Fanny Kelly gave birth to a son, but then she too fell seriously ill with cholera, though she survived the disease. She was in the process of preparing a manuscript about her captivity when she was contacted by the Larimers, the family who had shared part of the same ordeal. They asked Fanny and her infant son to make her home with them at their new location of Sherman Station in Wyoming Territory. Fanny accepted, for she had no means of making a living.[137] The Larimers were trying to make a go of the photography business, and they also ran a general store and bought and sold railroad ties and cordwood. Fanny worked for them as a washerwoman. Then, about a year after her arrival, she went to Washington to urge a claim from the government for restitution of her loss in the attack on the wagon train and for her services in saving Fort Sully.[138] While in Washington, she met with Red Cloud and a delegation of chiefs of the various branches of the Dakota, who assisted her in her claim for compensation, with Red Cloud speaking in favour of the government's reimbursing her for the property lost during the raid.[139] As a result of these efforts, in 1870 Congress voted Kelly $5,000 for warning Captain Fisk and Fort Sully, and two years later she was awarded an additional $10,000 for full payment of the property taken from her and destroyed during the attack on the wagon train.[140]

In 1870 Kelly also filed a lawsuit against both of the Larimers, her "false friends," in the court of Allen County, Kansas. This case has been described as "one of the most fantastic cases in legal and literary history."[141] Fanny Kelly alleged that in 1865 she and Sarah Larimer had agreed that they would jointly prepare and publish a narrative of their captivity, but in 1869 the Larimers had together conspired to secrete the manuscript away to Philadelphia and had had it published as Sarah Larimer's work alone. Mrs Kelly was thereby deprived of her rightful share of the profits.

Sarah Larimer did indeed publish a book in 1870. It was entitled *The Capture and Escape; Or, Life among the Sioux.*[142] This book, now extremely rare, contains only a few pages about Larimer's captivity. The rest is "filler" – descriptions of the experiences of other captives, an account of "Indian customs," and a good number of religious platitudes. (As part of the evidence brought to bear during the proceedings, it was deposed that the greater part of Larimer's book was in fact written by a Mrs Margaret Hosmer of Philadelphia, who wrote for the Presbyterian Board of Missions.)[143] In her concluding remarks in the book, Mrs Larimer stated that she could not include the experiences of Mrs Kelly because of the constraints of space but that these would soon appear in a separate volume – also authored by Sarah Larimer. Her Philadelphia publishers, Claxton, Remsen and Haffelfinger, had apparently already printed a book under Larimer's authorship entitled *Mrs. Kelly's Experiences among the Indians*, though they had not yet bound it. As a result of Kelly's eventually successful lawsuit, all the copies were destroyed.

The case was bitterly contested until 1876, and there were several hearings in the Supreme Court of Kansas. Sarah Larimer maintained that Fanny Kelly had lost her manuscript in a fire back in Kansas and that Kelly had subsequently "feloniously abstracted and purloined" her own book, which was then in the proof stage.[144] As one of their defences, the Larimers claimed that Kelly could not enter into a valid legal contract because she was a *femme couvert* (a married woman without a trade or business at the time of the agreement). A first verdict favoured Mrs Kelly, who was awarded $5,000, but the Larimers appealed and the decision was reversed. At the next hearing Mrs Kelly won again, though the judgment was for only $285. The Larimers appealed once more, on the grounds that one of the jurors had been drinking alcohol on the morning the verdict was brought down. The two parties finally reached a private settlement in 1876, when the case was dismissed at Kelly's costs, which were estimated to have been $2,000. These costs, however, were never paid.[145] One result of the legal battle was that William J. Larimer was moved through this experience to study law, and he was subsequently admitted to the bar, setting up business in Lead City in the Black Hills of Dakota Territory.[146] The Larimers were separated and Sarah was living in Tacoma, Washington, in 1888 when she was finally successful in persuading Congress that she too deserved compensation for her services in giving information to the army in 1864 with regard to the "evil designs of hostile Indians." She was sent a cheque for $5,000.[147]

Fanny Kelly's *Narrative* was first published in 1871 by a Cincinnati publisher and, in the same year, by a publisher in Hartford, Connecticut. To date, the book has gone through eleven American editions or printings. Kelly also wrote a sequel, *Afterwards; Or Life and Trials Subsequent to My Captivity among the Sioux, with an Account of the Litigation Concerning My History, in which Truth is Stranger than Fiction*.[148] Although this book was registered with the Library of Congress Copyright Office in 1871, it was never published. However, in the introductory remarks to her *Narrative*, Kelly had included some of the history of its writing – how she had completed a

work that was "purloined and published," how she had had to sur-
mount many obstacles to gather the scattered fragments, and how,
with the aid of memory, she had been able to place these results
before the public.[149]

Fanny Kelly moved to Washington, DC, where she found employment with the Patent Office. She met with some of her former
Lakota acquaintances on at least one other occasion, in September
1877, when a delegation arrived from the West to meet with the
president. (It is curious that the same day the delegation arrived,
there was a serious fire in the Patent Office in Washington.)[150] In
1880 Fanny Kelly married William F. Gordon, a journalist who specialized in ghostwriting for prominent people. The proceeds from
her book must have been considerable, for she invested heavily in
real estate, which included a mansion in Maryland that had once
belonged to the son of the sixth Lord Baltimore.[151] She died in
1904 and was buried in Washington, DC.

There were, it seems, four Canadian editions of Fanny Kelly's
Narrative. Although the text of the book appears to be essentially
the same in both the Canadian and American editions, the Canadian editions contain different introductions and an extra explanatory footnote, intended to convey particular messages to the
Canadian reading public. In the first Canadian edition, Kelly's original introduction is followed by a "Preface to the Canadian Edition."[152] The purpose of this preface was to point out that because
of the superior form of government in Canada, it would be unheard of for such a situation ever to arise here. Readers should be
thankful that they lived in Canada. Here there was greater equality
between people, who were all well treated. Such a refined and
"carefully reared" lady would never fall into the hands of "merciless
savages" in Canada. The unknown author of the preface asked
readers to imagine how the heroic authoress must have longed for
her Canadian home during her trials among the "loathsome, sick-
ening, debasing life of the wildest savages": "Imagine her longing,
mourning retrospect during those dreary months – cold, in a starving condition; her dreams of a happy childhood and joyous youth
on the romantic shores of Lake Simcoe, where, under the best
form of government now in existence, she had doubtless mingled
with the Indians who dwell there on an equal footing with all other
nationalities, creeds, and colors, 'no one daring to make them
afraid,' and be thankful that the lines have fallen to you in pleas-

anter places."[153] Like Eunice Williams, the Americans' long-gone but still well-remembered captive in Canada, Canada's Fanny Kelly was doubly a captive, of both the Indians and the Americans.

In an explanatory footnote at the end of chapter 1 in the Canadian editions (which readers would assume to have been written by Kelly herself), American Indian policy is harshly criticized and unfavourably compared with the kindness and benevolence of the Canadian system:

In view of the steady exterminating policy of the Americans toward the Indians, the cold-blooded butcheries perpetrated upon them by soldiers, settlers, trappers and adventurers, and remembering that the savage knows no "higher law," can we wonder that he in his turn should pay his enemy in kind; and here it may not be inappropriate to mark the contrast between our system and theirs. Although our Dominion is greater in extent than the "Great Republic," with large numbers of Indians in every quarter, yet there is not a tribe, perhaps, in the whole vast domain that would not freely take up arms in our cause; should we ever, unfortunately, be dragged into war by our restless cousins.[154]

The fourth Canadian edition (1878) featured a new frontispiece, with the familiar photograph of Fanny Kelly but bearing the inscription "The Queen of the Sioux. 'A cultured Canadian Lady, once their captive drudge, now their idol.'" In the introduction to this edition by an anonymous "Washington correspondent," it was explained how in 1877 Fanny Kelly met the train of the Sioux delegation as it arrived in Washington, stepping forward and saluting one of the visitors "in a strange outlandish tongue for one who seemed so thoroughly the refined type of American civilization."[155] The correspondent described the scene that ensued: "An exclamation of surprise and pleasure, a deep, quick, guttural note that called the whole band together, and Mrs. Fanny Kelly, a lady born at Orillia, Canada, stood once more among the savages who had once held her a prisoner, but now surrounded her with an enthusiasm of delight akin to reverence."[156] The correspondent then summarized Kelly's story, touching on the privations and harshness she had endured, including having her life threatened by both men and women on several occasions. This, however, was not the message with which the readers of the introduction were left. When asked how she could harbour any feelings but bitter ones for these

THE QUEEN OF THE SIOUX.

"A cultured Canadian-Lady, once their captive drudge, now their idol."

Respectfully
Fanny Kelly

Frontispiece to the fourth Canadian edition of Fanny Kelly's *Narrative*. None of the American editions bore the inscription "Queen of the Sioux," but Canadian readers were expected to take pride in the Sioux's supposed admiration for Mrs Kelly. (Fanny Kelly, *Narrative of My Captivity among the Sioux* [Toronto: Maclear, 1878])

men, Kelly was quoted as saying that they grew to regard her with great affection and had shed tears on her departure. They had learned that she had much to teach them and were docile learners. She had sung to them, and they had listened hour after hour without any weariness. They had learned of her religion and respected her for it. Kelly added, "with a twinkle of the eye," that she had a "genuine lover among them." Jumping Bear would have risked his life for her and was "a much better Christian and gentleman" than some "married men in Washington … who think it no harm to carry on a flirtation with single ladies."[157] Kelly said that just the other day she had received a letter from a friend at the Cheyenne agency who expressed sorrow that they had originally treated her so badly, "and they all wish I would come out there and teach them and them." They wanted her to be their "big chief," she said, and one member of the Washington delegation had wept "because I would not promise him to go back with them, and another because I declined, in a kind and respectful way, to go to the theatre with him." She believed that they would treat her kindly if she did go back: "I really think the Indians have been in many instances treated unjustly and cruelly by the whites." The introduction to this fourth Canadian edition concluded with the words, "But the Indians still insist that she ought to return, and as their part of the compensation they will give her horses, honours and lands, and make her 'QUEEN OF THE SIOUX.'"

In the American editions of Kelly's book there is no mention that she was now Queen of the Sioux – once their drudge, now their idol. That she had taught them and sung to them is not mentioned either, nor is Jumping Bear depicted as a better Christian and gentleman than many men in Washington. Distinct strategies were targeted at Canadian as opposed to American readers. At this time, a self-congratulatory feeling about the wisdom of Canadian Indian policy compared with the American policy was at a new high. In 1876 Sitting Bull and his followers had sought asylum in Canada from the American military, and their treatment at the hands of the Americans was a convenient foil with which to highlight the comparative wisdom of the Canadian approach.[158] Since 1874 the Canadian approach had involved a small contingent of police, who had been sent west to keep the peace, and a policy of treaty making with the plains people that was carried out well in advance of any intensive settlement or railroad building. In the fall of 1877 the process of treaty negotiation with the plains people had been completed with Treaty 7 at Blackfoot Crossing, a treaty made with the Siksika, Kainah, Peigan, T'suu Tina, and Stoney nations. The "Queen of the Sioux" seemed to symbolize the innate trust the indigenous people of the plains had in Canadians – a sentiment they could not display towards Americans. To Canadian readers, Fanny Kelly could appear as a beloved teacher sympathetic to the mistreatment experienced by the Indians of the American West. To an American reading public, it was important that Kelly appear as another helpless woman victimized by savage assailants.

Those who have studied Kelly's narrative carefully and compared it with other accounts have found that there are some inconsistencies and inaccuracies. There is considerable confusion of time and place, though this is understandable when one considers that she had no knowledge of the terrain over which she was taken.[159] Also, she claimed to have kept notes during her captivity that were destroyed before she left to live with the Larimers in Wyoming. Her "purloined" manuscript was based on these notes, while her subsequently published narrative had to be drawn from memory. Kelly cast herself in a central role in saving Fort Sully from an Indian attack, but there is good reason to believe that the fort was never in danger at that time.[160] A Black Feet Lakota man named Crawler, who was interviewed in 1908, told how he had been sent by Major House of the U.S. Army to purchase Mrs Kelly and bring her to Fort Sully. Horses were given to the Hunkpapa Lakota in exchange for Kelly, and Crawler said that many warriors decided to accompany her to the fort in order to enjoy the free food that would be passed out there in payment for restoring her. According to Crawler, Fanny had not understood the reason for her large escort and had mistakenly concluded that they intended to attack Fort Sully.[161] Other Aboriginal sources assign Sitting Bull a significant role in effecting the release of Fanny Kelly, yet he was not specifically mentioned in her narrative.[162] One other discrepancy is that in the earliest of her petitions to Congress, Kelly clearly suggested that she did indeed suffer the "fate worse than death." She wrote that she was "forced to become the squaw of one of the O-gal-lal-lah Chiefs, who treated her in a manner too horrible to mention, and during her captivity was passed from Chief to Chief, and treated in a similar manner."[163] As mentioned earlier, she stated in her published narrative that she had not been so abused.

The point here is not to test the accuracy of Kelly's narrative or to diminish its value as a source, but simply to point out that women in her position were called on to change their story to fit the intended audience, or that the story was altered for them. For an American reading audience, it would not be appropriate to mention being "Queen of the Sioux" because the military conquest of the Sioux was at that time being aggressively pursued, culminating in the tragedy at Wounded Knee Creek in 1891. An account stressing white female victimization justified this military aggression and the appropriation of Lakota land. Obviously, the notion of friendly relations between the former captive and her captors would have detracted from these themes. On the other hand, Canadian editions would prove popular if they carried messages about the mistreatment of Native people under the American system of government. Yet another approach was appropriate for Fanny Kelly's Congress audience. In order to get compensation from the government, she emphasized the valuable service she had performed, sacrificing her comfort and endangering her life for her country. That she was "passed from Chief to Chief" could be included in a private petition intended for Congress, but for the reading public she would have wished to affirm her chastity. Thus, there was a wide variety of pressures upon a widowed captive such as Fanny Kelly to present her experience in a certain light. Captivity narratives are not reliable unproblematic representations.

The story of Fanny Kelly indicates there was an audience for captivity narratives in Canada. But in the Canadian editions, citizens of the dominion were asked to take great pride in the fact that such events could not occur on their soil. They may not have been prepared, then, for the events of 1885 and the captivity of "our countrywomen" in the far reaches of the Canadian North-West. This brought a very different reaction. Theresa Gowanlock and Theresa Delaney were certainly not depicted as "Queens of the Cree."

CHAPTER TWO

"The Honour of a White Woman Is Sacred":
The Exploitation of the Experiences of
Theresa Delaney and Theresa Gowanlock

"A thrill of pleasure will influence every Canadian man and woman on learning that Mrs. Delaney and Mrs. Gowanlock have escaped from the Indians safe and uninjured. The news will give as much genuine cause for congratulation as that of the success at Batoche." The same day that this item appeared in the Ottawa *Free Press*, 8 June 1885, two telegrams from the North-West were read in the House of Commons conveying the glad tidings of the safety of the prisoners recently in the custody of Big Bear.[1] As though returning to a close and affectionate family circle, the widows were sympathetically greeted, especially by women well-wishers, at the various stops along their trip east from Swift Current, and on their arrival in Toronto in mid-July they were "treated with the consideration and attention which might be awarded to honoured rulers in the land." It was proclaimed that the women had endured "for nearly three months the severest trials of any concerned in the whole of the rebellion in the North-West."[2]

During the events of the spring of 1885 that became known as the Second Riel Rebellion and the North-West Campaign, national attention was riveted on the fate of these two women, whose husbands were among the nine men killed on 2 April at Frog Lake (Alberta). During their two months with the Cree, rumours that they had been ill treated and killed served a wide range of often contradictory purposes. After their release, the news that the women had not been harmed was put to a variety of other uses. The November 1885 book *Two Months in the Camp of Big Bear: The Life and Adventures of Theresa Gowanlock and Theresa Delaney* was proclaimed as a truthful and accurate rendition, but it too was carefully constructed to serve certain interests while condemning others. The original statements that the women made describing their experiences differ in important respects from the version that appeared in their book. What was stressed in particular was the frailty and vulnerability of white women in a menacing environment, an environment that could once again explode into violence unless steps were taken to ensure that the insubordinate were repressed. Boundaries between the indigenous people and the new arrivals needed to be clarified, and a book like *Two Months* helped to establish the imaginary boundaries defining who was "one of us" and who was excluded. Another message conveyed in *Two Months* was that the government administration of Indian affairs was generous and benevolent, though this had not been clearly reflected in the original statements the women made to the press. Several of the Métis whom the two women praised for their conduct immediately on their return from the Cree appear in a sinister light in the written account. An enormous amount of money had been spent and young lives lost waging war on the Métis, and images of Métis heroes were not especially palatable. The book's emphasis on the constant threat of the "fate worse than death" carried the clear cautionary message that unions between white and Aboriginal were abhorrent, particularly as such unions created the menacing Métis.

FROG LAKE

The two women who emerged so dramatically from obscurity in the spring of 1885 had been the only white women from eastern Canada in the village of Frog Lake, about thirty miles from Fort Pitt, ten miles north of the North Saskatchewan River. Theresa (Fulford) Delaney had arrived in the settlement in August 1882 as the bride of the government farm instructor, John Delaney. She was the daughter of J. Marshall and Bridget Fulford and was from the lumbering and farming community of Aylmer, Quebec, not far from Ottawa. Until her marriage, she had lived at the farm established around 1812 by her grandfather, who was originally from Connecticut.[3] Theresa Delaney was the eldest of a family of five boys and four girls, and was thirty-six years old in 1885. Her husband was from Nepean, Ontario, and had worked as a foreman for different lumber firms before his appointment as farm instructor in

Left: Theresa Delaney. As seen here her pose, dress, and hairstyle are remarkably like those in the drawing of Fanny Kelly, Canada's most famous Indian captive at that time (see p. 44). *Right:* John Delaney (Theresa Gowanlock and Theresa Delaney, *Two Months in the Camp of Big Bear* [Parkdale: Times Office, 1885], facing 83 and 91)

"Frog Lake Settlement – Mr. Delaney's house, etc."
(Gowanlock and Delaney, *Two Months*, 106; Glenbow Archives, NA-3988-3)

1879. As the wife of the farm instructor, Theresa Delaney was assigned duties as "farm instructress," and she gave lessons to the women in baking, milking, churning, making butter, knitting, and dressmaking.

Theresa Mary (Johnson) Gowanlock had arrived at Frog Lake Creek, two miles from the settlement of Frog Lake, in December 1884 following her marriage in October of that year to John Alexander Gowanlock, who had secured a government contract to build a combined saw and grist mill.[4] She was a daughter of Henry and Martha (Upper) Johnson and had been born at Tintern (Lincoln County), Ontario. She was nineteen years old in 1885.[5] John Gowanlock had been born in Stratford, Ontario, in 1861. He had somewhat prominent connections in the Toronto area. Two of his brothers, Andrew and James, owned the Parkdale *Times* newspaper, book, and publishing office at 24 Queen Street, the main street of the village of Parkdale, which was absorbed into Toronto in 1889. Published every Friday, the *Times* advertised itself as an excellent newspaper devoted to the family.[6] John Gowanlock's aunt was Dr Jenny Kidd Trout of Toronto, who had graduated in 1875 from the Woman's Medical College of Pennsylvania and was the first woman licensed to practice medicine in Canada.[7] It was on her advice that John Gowanlock left for the West, for he was in ill health and required a change of climate. He worked as a farmer, speculator, surveyor, and storekeeper in the Battleford district before securing the contract to build and operate the Frog Lake mill. When he returned briefly to Ontario after eighteen months, he was in exceedingly good health. It is likely that he met Theresa Johnson on a visit to his sister, Mrs Daisy (Elizabeth) Huntsman of Tintern. The Gowanlocks spent the first months of 1885 on the construction of the sawmill, assisted by some Cree (who had been assigned this among other work in return for their rations) and by some Métis labourers. The Frog Creek mill was the scene of a tragic accident that winter when a Métis labourer, Guillaume Rocheleau, was killed – crushed when some machinery that was being installed fell on him.

Although generally presented in contemporary non-Aboriginal accounts as a remote, isolated village, Frog Lake and district were relatively well populated, being in the heart of Woods Cree territory. There were three reserves nearby, and indeed the settlement existed only because it served the neighbouring Aboriginal population. Frog Lake appears on Captain John Palliser's map of 1859,

John Gowanlock
(Gowanlock and Delaney,
Two Months, 67)

Theresa Gowanlock, seen in Ontario
before her 1884 marriage and her move
to western Canada (National Archives
of Canada, C-28218)

The Gowanlocks' home at Frog Lake as portrayed in *Two Months*.
This idyllic scene, drawn by F.W. Sutherland, bears little resemblance
to the terrain at the site of the Frog Creek mill. Theresa Gowanlock never
saw the place in summer as shown here. (Glenbow Archives, NA-3988-2)

and the name of the lake is a translation of the Cree "Ah-Yik sa-kha-higan."[8] The settlement grew up around a Hudson's Bay Company trading post founded in 1883, and by 1885 the village consisted of the HBC post, the buildings of the Indian agency, the Roman Catholic mission, the store of the "free" trader George Dill, and a six-man North-West Mounted Police detachment. Although it has often been portrayed in non-Aboriginal histories as a "white" enclave in the wilderness, this was not in fact the case. Frog Lake was settled by people from a variety of backgrounds. One of its residents was John Pritchard, the Métis interpreter for the government Indian agency. Interpreters were vital at these Indian agencies because employees such as John Delaney, sent from the east, could not converse with the people they were supposed to instruct. Pritchard was fluent in English and French as well as Cree and several other Aboriginal languages. His family consisted of his wife Rose (Delorme) and their eight children: Salomon, John, Marie Rose, Amelia, Adeline, Ralph, Alfred, and Margaret. The Pritchards also kept a rooming house and store.

John Pritchard looms large in this story. Born at St François Xavier, Red River, in 1840, he was raised in the Fort Ellice, St Lazare, and Spy Hill areas.[9] His grandfather, John Pritchard of Shrewsbury, England, had come to the Canadian West in 1801 as an employee of the New North West Company. The elder John Pritchard's nickname was Cheepi, an Assiniboine word for corpse; he had been lost on the prairies for forty days in the summer of 1805 and had looked very corpselike when a group of Assiniboine found him.[10] Employed at Fort la Souris on the Assiniboine River, he had left early in June in search of some stolen horses but had soon lost his bearings. Subsisting on frogs, eggs, and magpies, his body became entirely wasted, and he suffered greatly from mosquito bites and spear grass, which gave his legs the appearance of a porcupine. He was rescued at last when he managed to signal to a party of Assiniboine by raising his shoe on a stick. His experience indicates how difficult it was for Europeans to function without the help of the residents of the area.

This elder John Pritchard became prominent in the business, educational, and religious life of the Red River Settlement. His first wife was an Aboriginal woman, and their son William and William's wife Marie Fleury were the parents of the John Pritchard of this story. At Red River, the young John Pritchard was educated for the ministry of the Anglican Church, and although he did not follow

John Pritchard (Saskatchewan
Archives Board, R-A5656)

this calling he remained devoutly religious. As a young man he
worked in the offices of free trader Urbaine Delorme, and it was
Delorme's daughter Rose whom Pritchard married at St François
Xavier in 1863. Pritchard was employed by the Hudson's Bay Company at Rocky Mountain House, Fort Carlton, and Fort Edmonton.
In the early 1880s he sought employment with the Indian Department, and in 1884 he and his family moved to Frog Lake, where he
was employed by the department as interpreter to Thomas Quinn.

The HBC trader James K. Simpson and his wife Catherine also
lived at Frog Lake, as did Catherine's grown-up sons, Louis and
Benjamin Patenaude. Simpson was a son of Sir George Simpson
and Mary Keith, and Catherine is reported in some accounts to
have been a sister of Gabriel Dumont.[11] All these people were
among the many captives in 1885, as were the wife and daughter of
subagent Thomas Trueman Quinn. Quinn, who was part Dakota,
was married to a woman from Big Bear's band named Owl Sitting
(also known as Jane Quinn after her marriage). There was also a
"poor house" or old people's home at Frog Lake, possibly attached
to the mission, a small one-room shack into which nineteen persons were crowded.[12]

This was the parkland belt, where the Woods Cree met the Plains Cree, and where many groups before the 1870s had developed a transitional economy that had drawn on the resources of both plains and parkland. There were three bands of Woods Cree in the Frog Lake district in 1885, those led by Mahkayo, Oo-nee-pow-o-hay-oos, and Pus-kee-ah-kee-he-win.[13] In the early 1880s these groups planted wheat, barley, and root crops but had limited success, and well over half the population regularly fished and hunted off their reserves. These people were all part of Treaty 6.

In the fall of 1884 the population of the Frog Lake district was augmented and the resources considerably strained by the arrival of Big Bear's band of Plains Cree. The new arrivals numbered 504, almost equalling the combined population of the reserves at Onion Lake, Frog Lake, and Long Lake.[14] Big Bear, a chief of the Fort Pitt district renowned for his visions, medicine, and political skill, had refused to sign Treaty 6 in 1876 and had pursued a strategy aimed at preserving the autonomy and integrity of the Cree and securing better treaty terms.[15] After several years of severe hardship for his followers, first in the United States and then in the vicinity of Fort Walsh in the Cypress Hills, Big Bear's authority and stature among his people was considerably diminished, for his followers were not eligible for the rations and supplies that were given to the treaty bands. In 1882, faced with the anger and impatience even of his own family, Big Bear had no choice but to accept the treaty, otherwise his followers would have starved. As his last negotiating point, he refused to select a reserve site for his band, for he believed that the government officials would have to meet with him as long as he held out. But this tactic, too, generated anger and discontent among many of his followers. A reserve site was under negotiation in the district of Frog Lake in the fall of 1884, but Big Bear delayed moving there when his requests for extra rations were turned down. The government officials also favoured the delay, for they wished to assess the reserve land.[16] That winter the band received some rations in return for work such as cutting cordwood, but it was a time of great hardship. Many members of the fractionalized band were angry to learn that they would be without a reserve and the promised extra rations that winter. The Frog Lake district was almost entirely devoid of game that year, and it was an extremely cold winter with deep snow. Moreover, these predominantly plains people could not take advantage of whatever resources the country

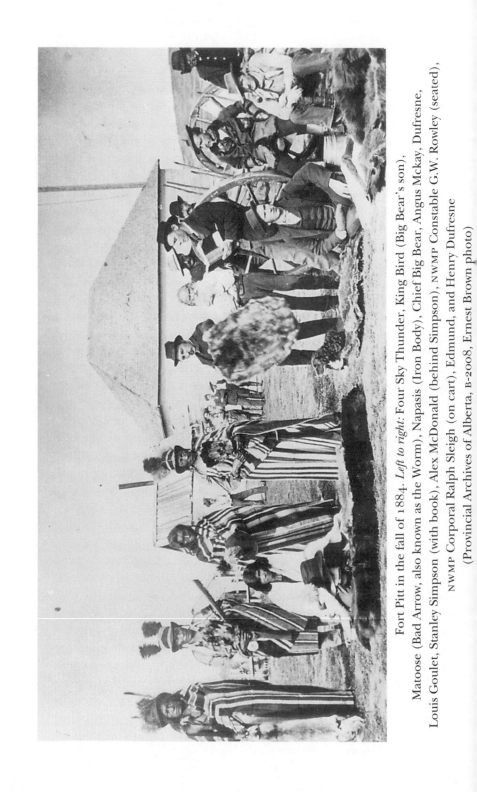

Fort Pitt in the fall of 1884. *Left to right:* Four Sky Thunder, King Bird (Big Bear's son), Matoose (Bad Arrow, also known as the Worm), Napasis (Iron Body), Chief Big Bear, Angus Mckay, Dufresne, Louis Goulet, Stanley Simpson (with book), Alex McDonald (behind Simpson), NWMP Constable G.W. Rowley (seated), NWMP Corporal Ralph Sleigh (on cart), Edmund, and Henry Dufresne (Provincial Archives of Alberta, B-2008, Ernest Brown photo)

offered in the same way as the Woods Cree, for they knew little about trapping and fishing. To make matters worse, it was just at this time that officials of the Indian Department were instructed by Ottawa to cut costs and reduce rations.

The events that took place at Frog Lake in the spring of 1885 have been told in great detail in many accounts, reflecting a wide variety of perspectives.[17] The earliest contemporary non-Aboriginal accounts tended to stress the innocence, good intentions, and martyrdom of the Euro-Canadians at Frog Lake. Thomas Quinn, for example, was depicted in an 1885 history of the North-West as "a fine specimen of humanity: he was a thorough frontiersman, an accomplished horseman, and an expert canoeist. He is said to have laboured long and zealously for the conversion of his Pagan brethren, and to have earnestly sought the amelioration of their condition. His fate at the hands of those to whom he had been kind is a grim commentary on the results anticipated from Indian evangelisation."[18] In these non-Aboriginal accounts, blame was laid variously on the nefarious influence of Louis Riel and his Métis messengers; on the fierce, unpredictable, and savage temperament of Aboriginal people, who could not resist the contagion of revolt; on the notorious Big Bear and his malign influence on the whole district; on the perfidy and collusion of the Hudson's Bay Company; on the critics of the government who pandered to Aboriginal people in their outrageous demands and misguided ideas; and on the maladministration of Indian affairs in the North-West.

Accounts from the perspective of Aboriginal people stress the frustration with government policy and government employees, as well as the conditions of poverty and starvation in the district and the multiple tensions that had built up in the community. There was never enough food that winter, and in order to receive the meagre rations, debilitating work had to be performed in subzero temperatures and in threadbare clothing.[19] Thomas Quinn was inflexible, lacked tact, and had an explosive temper. Despite his Cree wife, Quinn regarded the Cree with contempt and enjoyed saying no to all their requests.[20] Quinn's parents were said to have been killed during the 1862 "Sioux Uprising" in Minnesota, and it is ironic that his behaviour so closely mirrored that of the hated Indian agent there who told the Santee that they could eat grass. John Delaney, too, was disliked by many. In 1881 a man named Sand Fly had accused Delaney of stealing his wife, whereupon

Delaney had charged Sand Fly with assault and then theft. The result was a prison sentence of two and a half years, which was generally seen as an action taken by Delaney so that he could cohabit with the prisoner's wife. Delaney, along with Quinn, was also thought to have deliberately persecuted Big Bear's band because they were camped on land from which the two men had hoped to profit.[21] Mary Dion, a young Métis girl living in Frog Lake in 1885, recalled many instances of the casual cruelty of the white people, their disdain and contempt, and their merriment at the sight of human misery. It would be a mistake, however, to paint a completely demonic portrait of such people as John Delaney, for even he was not disliked by all. In 1881 he had been reprimanded by his superiors for issuing farm implements too generously and not in accordance with treaty stipulations.[22]

News of the confrontation at Duck Lake between the Métis and the NWMP on 26 March, during which seventeen people died, excited a few of the young men in Big Bear's camp who were impatient with his leadership. Louis Riel had proclaimed a new Métis provisional government in mid-March 1885 and had then moved to seize arms and ammunition at the store at Duck Lake. The clash occurred when the police rode out to prevent Riel's action. In the aftermath of Duck Lake, Inspector Francis Dickens of the NWMP at Fort Pitt suggested that the non-Aboriginal people at Frog Lake ought to move to the safety of the fort. This proposal was rejected. However, for reasons that remain obscure, it was decided that the police should evacuate Frog Lake. The little settlement was thus left unguarded. On the morning of 2 April, under the leadership of war chief Wandering Spirit and Ayimasis, one of Big Bear's sons, some of the Cree began to remove items from the stores at Frog Lake and to round up prisoners, including Quinn and the Gowanlocks, Delaneys, and Pritchards. The prisoners were ordered to move with the Cree to a new camp on Frog Creek – an action that had Big Bear's agreement, but only on condition that the whites would not be harmed. Quinn adamantly refused, and he was shot in the head by Wandering Spirit. In short order, Charles Gouin (the Métis Indian agency carpenter), John Delaney, John Gowanlock, Father Adélarde Fafard, Father Félix Marchand (visiting from Onion Lake), John Williscraft (Fafard's lay assistant), George Dill, and William Gilchrist (Gowanlock's clerk) all met the same fate.

Frog Lake, 2 April 1885. This drawing in the *Canadian Pictorial and Illustrated War News* clearly conveyed the image of a brutal and cowardly attack on innocent victims. The visual images produced in 1885 invariably present a one-dimensional and problematic version of events. (University of Saskatchewan Archives, Special Collections)

Scene from *Two Months in the Camp of Big Bear*. The message conveyed through this drawing is of the destruction of the tranquillity of an idyllic setting. The murders are taking place on the hill at the far left. (Gowanlock and Delaney, *Two Months*, 2; Glenbow Archives, NA-3988-1)

Considerable confusion remains to this day over who actually killed the people, and there is speculation that there may have been others who died at Frog Lake on that day. In a recent article Allen Ronaghan has convincingly argued that there was a tenth victim, a Mr Michaux, a lay brother schoolteacher who had been sent to Frog Lake in November 1884 by Bishop Vital-Justin Grandin.[23] The number of bodies actually found at Frog Lake is impossible to determine, since so many people claimed to have found and buried the victims. As historian Hugh Dempsey wrote, "If everyone is to be believed, the nine victims at Frog Lake must have been buried more often than a dog's favourite bone."[24]

IN THE CUSTODY OF THE CREE

Among the people who survived that day in Frog Lake were William B. Cameron, an HBC assistant to James Simpson, and the widows of Gowanlock and Delaney. Catherine Simpson was credited with the survival of Cameron, having disguised him with a blanket. Mrs Gowanlock and Mrs Delaney were hastily and unceremoniously pulled from their dead husbands, most likely in the interests of saving their lives.[25] From this point on, it is impossible to know precisely why the two women were spared or indeed whether their lives were ever in danger. According to George Stanley (Musunekwepan), a Woods Cree, the terrified and distraught women were first taken to the teepee of his father, Oo-nee-pow-o-hay-oos, who assured them that they would not be harmed and whose wife gave them water.[26] Stanley remembered that his father told Cameron, "Neither you nor these two women shall be killed. I will speak for you."[27] Big Bear set aside a tent for the women, and he ordered John Pritchard and another Métis interpreter – Stanley, identified as Budreau – to keep watch over them. At a meeting of Woods and Plains Cree, both Oo-nee-pow-o-hay-oos and Big Bear warned of the dangers that might be incurred if the prisoners were harmed, and it was decided that a close guard should be kept over them by Pritchard and Budreau, as well as by Isadore Moyah, John Horse, and Yellow Bear. Other Aboriginal accounts credit the persuasive skills of the Woods Cree for arranging that the women prisoners be placed in the safe custody of John Pritchard and the other Métis.[28] In fact, the Woods Cree were prisoners as well, although many non-Aboriginal accounts questioned this or failed to recognize it. The Plains Cree placed

Stanley's family tent in the centre of the camp circle. The "holy stem," used by those who had made Treaty 6, was placed outside to signify that they were prisoners.[29]

According to Jimmy Chief, a grandson of Seekaskootch, it was Little Bear (who, Chief claimed, was wrongfully accused and hanged for the murder of George Dill) who brought both of the widows to the safety of the Métis tent and told the Métis to take care of them. According to Chief, Mrs Delaney thanked Little Bear "and told him that she would give him a paper she would write that would help him when the trouble was over. She never did give him that paper."[30]

In W.B. Cameron's first statements to the press, he too credited the Woods Cree with saving the women. But in the account he published years later, *Blood Red the Sun* (1926), he gave a lengthy description of how Pritchard and Adolphus Nolin had cleverly outwitted the Cree and purchased Mrs Delaney from her Cree captors; he also said that Pierre Blondin had played a role in securing the safety of Mrs Gowanlock, though Blondin's later conduct had not been praiseworthy.[31] The memoirs of the Métis Louis Goulet gave much the same story, stating that he had persuaded Pierre Blondin to assist him in the purchase of Mrs Gowanlock by donating his horses and that Goulet had then left her in the care of Pritchard. Similarly, when the two women first emerged from their ordeal, they credited Pritchard, Nolin, and Blondin for their safety. But in the written account, Blondin appears as a villain – responsible, it is suggested, for some of the murders at Frog Lake, interested in acquiring Mrs Gowanlock only for his own sinister purposes, and in the habit of parading before her wearing her dead husband's clothing.[32] It is far from certain, then, just how the women came to be in the protective custody of John Pritchard, but it is clear that they were assisted by several Métis and remained with the Pritchard family for the rest of their captivity.

For the next three months this group of Cree – more aptly described as fugitives than warriors – and their white, Métis, and Aboriginal hostages attempted to avoid capture by the troops by following an exhausting routine of travel through swampy and bushy country. It appears that the function of the captives, or hostages, was to help ensure the safety of the group and perhaps win better peace terms. After the fall of Batoche and Riel's surrender by mid-May, there were four footsore and weary columns in pursuit of Big Bear, struggling across creeks and sloughs, dragging

Hudson's Bay Company
Chief Trader W.J. McLean,
who took charge of Fort Pitt
in October 1884. McLean,
his wife Helen, and their
eight children were among
the forty-four people from
Fort Pitt who were with Big
Bear's moving camp for
nearly two months. They
could have evacuated Fort
Pitt for Battleford but
opted instead to accept the
protection of Big Bear.
(Western Canada Pictorial
Index, 0248-07923)

their heavy guns and wagons. The troops found this last phase of
the North-West Campaign exhausting, and they were galvanized
only by reminders of the white prisoners.[33] As it turned out, none
of the hostages were heroically rescued by the North-West Field
Force or by the NWMP. They either escaped in groups or individu-
ally, or were allowed to leave. Nor was Big Bear ever captured. (He
was depicted in the press as the Artful Dodger, after the *Oliver
Twist* character created by the novelist father of the NWMP's Inspector Francis Dickens.) Big Bear finally surrendered of his own
accord at the HBC post Fort Carlton on 2 July, 1885, about a
month after Major General Middleton had abandoned the blun-
dering pursuit.

FORT PITT AND THE McLEANS:
HOSTAGES OR REFUGEES?

In mid-April, being in need of supplies, wagons, and other equipment, some of the Cree at Frog Lake (though not the hostages or
most of the Cree women and children) went to the Hudson's Bay
Company's Fort Pitt, which was under the supervision of Chief
Trader W.J. McLean. Born in Scotland, McLean had served twenty
years with the company at Fort Qu'Appelle and Île à la Crosse. His
wife Helen was the daughter of Alexander Hunter Murray, the
founder of Fort Yukon, and of Anne (Campbell) Murray, the daughter of Chief Trader Colin Campbell of the District of Athabasca.[34]
Anne Campbell had been born at Fort Dunvegan in 1822 and was
partly of Aboriginal ancestry.[35] Helen McLean was in her mid-
thirties in 1885; she was the mother of eight and was expecting
another child. The three eldest McLean sisters, Amelia (aged eighteen), Eliza (sixteen), and Kitty (fourteen), were well educated,
having attended boarding school, and were said to be musical. They
could also ride and shoot, and were fluent in Cree and Saulteaux.

Besides the employees of the Hudson's Bay Company, there were
twenty-three NWMP stationed at the fort under the command of
Francis Dickens. Fort Pitt was little more than a huddle of five
buildings arranged in a square and was without a palisade. It was
not strategically located to withstand a siege, for it was built on a
flat and surrounded by hills. Nonetheless, many people sought refuge there after the events at Frog Lake, some with the assistance of
Aboriginal friends. In total there were forty-four civilians as well as
the twenty-three NWMP. Among the new arrivals were the Reverend
Charles and Mrs Quinney, an English couple who had been married in Malta in 1872, where Quinney had been an army Scripture
reader.[36] Quinney had since become the Church of England missionary at Onion Lake, and the morning after the killings at Frog
Lake (Good Friday), their house had been surrounded by "their
Indians," and they were detained while Seekaskootch and his coun-
cillors discussed how to ensure their safety, for some of the Onion
Lake people had become excitable on hearing the news from Frog
Lake.[37] It was decided to escort the Quinneys to Fort Pitt, where
they arrived safely, having been met along the route by William
McLean and the police. The Onion Lake agency farm instructor
George Mann, his wife Sarah, and their three children Blanche,

Helen (Mrs W.J.) McLean. She was pregnant with her ninth child during her travels with the Cree camp. (Western Canada Pictorial Index, 0631-19534)

The McLean family *c.* 1895.
Left to right, top row: Helen (Sapomin), Duncan, Kitty, William;
middle row: Freda, John, Eliza, Angus, Amelia;
bottom row: Murray, Lillian, Lawrence.
(Western Canada Pictorial Index, 0248-07942)

Three McLean sisters took turns on sentry duty
at Fort Pitt in early April 1885. The original caption was
"Noble Women on the Defensive: The Misses McLean
show great courage, each one rifle in hand,
stands at a loophole." (*Montreal Daily Star*, 23 May 1885)

Louise, and George also took refuge in Fort Pitt. They, too, had
been warned of danger and escorted by people of the Onion Lake
Reserve who feared for their safety.[38] The refugees could have evacuated Fort Pitt for Battleford – Seekaskootch urged them to con-
struct rafts and leave by the river – but they opted to stay.
Accordingly, steps were taken to barricade the fort. Sentries were
posted in each of the five buildings, with the McLean sisters taking

their turn on duty. This routine lasted almost two weeks. It was while she was on sentry duty that Elizabeth McLean spotted young Henry Quinn, a nephew of Indian agent Quinn of Frog Lake, who had managed to escape from the Cree and had travelled about thirty-five miles on foot to reach Fort Pitt.[39]

On 14 April the Cree party from Frog Lake assembled on a ridge overlooking Fort Pitt. They first shot several of the HBC cattle and then made fires for cooking. Through a messenger, W.J. McLean was asked to meet with some of the head men at their camp, and he agreed. McLean was well acquainted with Big Bear, for they had met that winter on several occasions. But negotiations broke down on the second day when two NWMP scouts, who had been sent out the day before to locate the Cree, were sighted returning to Fort Pitt. Believing they were under attack, the Cree rushed on the unfortunate scouts. Constable David Cowan was killed, and Constable Clarence Loasby was seriously wounded but was brought into Fort Pitt when Amelia McLean and others provided covering fire. Three Cree were also killed during this confrontation. The terms eventually agreed to by McLean and Wandering Spirit were that the civilians would join the Cree camp and that the police would be allowed two hours to evacuate the fort, leaving behind their weapons, ammunition, horses, and supplies. McLean decided that he was willing to accept the protection of Big Bear for all of the civilians. As these details were being worked out, Amelia and Kitty walked into the Cree camp unescorted. They had simply left the fort and walked up the ridge. While their mother and their sister Eliza tended to Loasby's wounds, they wanted to ensure that their father was being well treated. According to Duncan McLean, their bravery astonished the Cree. When the sisters were asked if they were afraid, Amelia replied, "Why should we be afraid of you? We have lived together as brothers and sisters for many years. We speak the same language. Why should we be afraid of you?"[40]

The other occupants of Fort Pitt also accepted Big Bear's protection. The Manns were at first urged by the Quinneys to accompany the police, since it was known that Mann was "not in favour with the Indians." The Quinneys then sent for the advice of Seekaskootch, and he assured them that the Manns would be placed under the care of Loweso and the Quinneys with Nanesso. Thus, they decided to join Big Bear, trusting Seekaskootch's judgment and influence. (In early June, Seekaskootch was shot and killed by Major Sam Steele's scouts at Loon Lake.) The civilians did not leave Fort Pitt until the police were well down the river, and this took some time because of the poor condition of the scow. Eventually, under the cover of darkness, the police escaped on the scow amid the ice floes of the North Saskatchewan River. Although a few shots were fired after them, none met their mark. The people of Fort Pitt then gathered their belongings and left for Big Bear's camp. It was an intensely cold night and soon developed into a blinding snowstorm. As the McLean's neared the camp, some of the Cree came out to meet them and, according to Elizabeth McLean, showed her mother the greatest respect: "They gave a hand in setting up the tent which she had sent out ahead of her, and rendered very useful little services in view of the impending snowstorm, which came upon us during the night as expected."[41]

The number of people in Big Bear's camp was considerably augmented after the events at Fort Pitt. As well as the Quinneys and the large families of McLeans and Manns, they included a cook, a clerk, and three "servants" of the Hudson's Bay Company, Rabisco Smith and his family of six, and Henry Dufresne along with his wife, three children, and "old Mrs Dufresne." A list that William B. Cameron drew up in later years also named the following among the prisoners: "Na-co-tan and family, three friendly Indians, three squaws, friendly, Penderun and family of six."[42] These were added to the Frog Lake group of Mrs Delaney and Mrs Gowanlock, Peter St Luke and his family of five, James Simpson and his family of three, the John Pritchard family, William Cameron, Otto Dufresne the Indian Department cook, the Métis men Louis Goulet, Adolphus Nolin, André Nault, and Pierre Blondin, and the Indian agents J. Fitzpatrick and Henry Halpin.

On 17 April this large party began to move back to Frog Lake, where most of the people had left their families. They covered a distance of thirty miles in two days and arrived at a campsite near Frog Lake, where they remained for the next two weeks. During this time a group of Saulteaux from the Riding Mountain area, who were travelling to visit relatives near Edmonton, were compelled by the Plains Cree to join their group. William McLean was acquainted with these Saulteaux, for he had been in charge of the Swan River District for ten years, and the McLean girls were delighted to converse in Saulteaux with them.[43]

FIRST RUMOURS OF THE FATE OF THE CAPTIVES

It took eight days for news of the "massacre" at Frog Lake to reach a wider public, and for most of April details remained sketchy about what had happened, who had been killed, and exactly who was part of the fugitive Cree camp. Even as late as 23 April there were "authoritative" claims that the massacre was a "canard."[44] The earliest reports included the name of Mrs Gowanlock among the dead. She was described in one account as having pinioned the arms of the man who had killed her husband as he aimed his rifle at another; the man was said to have shaken her off and fired, killing her instantly.[45] (This is the story that survived in the novels of Edmund Collins.) The sad fate of the Gowanlocks was lamented across the nation. In the Charlottetown *Daily Patriot* on 14 April, their story was described as "the most touching of all" because they were newly-weds, working chiefly for the benefit of the Indians: "Their death now at the hands of the Indians is unspeakably sad, but not so horrible probably, as the fate of Mrs. Delaney, wife of the murdered farm instructor, who was carried off a prisoner by the blood-thirsty fiends."[46] A letter from Mrs Gowanlock's father, Henry Johnson, was published that April.[47] Believing that his daughter had been killed, he railed against all who were sympathetic to "half-breeds" and Indians and who did not care "about the wrongs sustained by innocent, civilized people that have been induced by the Government to settle in that country, unprotected from those savage hordes." He expressed anger at Sir John A. Macdonald who had allowed Riel, the murderer of Thomas Scott, to go free and who had even rewarded him with $1,000 to leave the country, thereby enabling him to return and stir up wild hordes to do wicked deeds. "Feeling safe under British rule," wrote Johnson, "I allowed a dear girl to go into that country, and she with some kind friends has had to suffer a cruel death ... When will the people quit harping about the wrongs of the Half breed and Indians, and place a force in that country sufficient to protect all parties in their rights? Innocent settlers should not be left to the mercy and the whims of barbarians."

It was the NWMP from Fort Pitt who first reported that Mrs Gowanlock was alive and with the Cree.[48] The sorrow of her situation was little diminished, however, when it was recalled that she had left full of hope as a young bride only nine months earlier. Theresa Gowanlock's last letter from Frog Lake, dated 3 March 1885, was published in several papers. Written to her younger sister Effie, it described the beautiful weather, a dinner with the Delaneys, and the nice frame house they would have in the fall. Theresa had included some words in Cree and said that the local women brought them large white fish all cleaned nicely. There were many references to Johnny and the plans they had made together: "Johnny says it would take a life time to make a home in Ontario, and then it would not be as good as we would have here in two years."[49] It was very sad for readers then (and today, too) to reflect that all these hopes and plans lay in ruins and that her dear Johnny lay dead.

It gradually became evident that a great number of people from a variety of backgrounds – Euro-Canadian, Métis, and Aboriginal – were part of Big Bear's camp. At first, there was some uncertainty over whether the people from Fort Pitt, especially the McLean family, could be described as prisoners, for word came out that they had opted for the protection of the Cree. The police who had effected their plucky escape from Fort Pitt reported on arrival at Battleford that William McLean and his family had "insisted upon giving themselves up to Big Bear."[50] A letter also came to light in which McLean asked his wife and children to join him in the Cree camp, and this did not match the public image of white people being dragged from burning homesteads.[51] It may well have been because of the McLeans' ambiguous status as prisoners or as people who had chosen the protection of the Cree that public attention focused very little on the captive McLean women. There was also the fact that Mrs McLean and her children were known to have some Aboriginal ancestry. When the family arrived at Battleford after their travels with the Cree, a policeman described Helen McLean as "a thin woman with Indian blood in her veins."[52] There were thus few expressions of concern about the fate of Mrs McLean and her daughters. Nor was there much concern for Mrs Quinney or for the widowed Mrs Gouin, the widowed Jane Quinn and her daughter, or any of the other Métis or Aboriginal women. Indeed, Jane Quinn was suspected of having been cognizant of the intended murders at Frog Lake.[53] Thus it was that frenzy about the captives came to focus solely on Mrs Gowanlock and Mrs Delaney.

MISREPRESENTATIONS OF MÉTIS AND INDIAN WOMEN, 1885

In May 1885, when Major General Middleton led the North-West Field Force in a major assault on their settlement, the Métis women and children of Batoche experienced death, hardship, and hunger, as well as the loss of their property and belongings because of the field force's looting. Yet these women never became objects of public concern. At the end of June, after hostilities had ceased, the *Manitoba Daily Free Press* gave but one example of the "horrors of war" by reporting on the sufferings of the Tourond family of Fish Creek, who were originally from the parish of St François Xavier, Manitoba.[54] Madame Tourond was a widow with a family of five boys and two girls. During the fighting, their home had been attacked by cannon and sacked by Middleton's troops. Fearing for their lives, the two Tourond girls, aged eighteen and twenty, had escaped into the woods with a Miss Gervais. They were never seen again. Without doubt, they perished from cold and hunger. Two of the Tourond boys died at Batoche, another was seriously wounded, and the remaining two were prisoners at Regina. It was reported that Madame Tourond was alone without a dwelling or any means of subsistence.

An appeal for the "starving halfbreeds" from Alexis André, OMI, superior of missions in the District of Carlton, did not receive wide coverage in the press. Only a few papers published his letter of 24 June which asked people to plead the cause of the Métis, as "they are human beings, and surely this Christian country will not let them die."[55] Father André described a visit to St Antoine de Padoue (Batoche), where most of the houses had been burned to the ground, fields and gardens laid waste, and everywhere there was the utmost poverty: "Who could help not to be moved to compassion in seeing those poor and unfortunate women surrounded by their children coming to meet me and to shake hands with me? They formed a perfect picture of squalor and desolation, in tatters and broken hearted." They had lost their furniture and clothing as well as their homes. "Add to this, that these poor women were most of them mourning for their dead husbands, or for husbands and sons lying in prison at Regina waiting for trial, and you can conceive how much these unfortunate people deserve our compassion." Similarly, a small item in the Ottawa *Free Press* of 27 July 1885 made it clear that there was much distress among Métis families, that two women had recently died of exposure and several were so sick that they were not expected to live.

Reports of this nature had not been published during the weeks of conflict, when the impression had been given that Métis women and children were humanely cared for, in contrast to the treatment of Gowanlock and Delaney. An illustration in the *Montreal Daily Star*

"After the Battle." This sketch left the impression that Métis women
and children were humanely cared for by government and military
authorities following the battle of Batoche, in contrast to the alarming
reports about the treatment of Mrs Delaney and Mrs Gowanlock.
In fact, there was much distress and suffering in the Métis settlement.
(*Montreal Daily Star*, 30 May 1885)

of 30 May was designed to leave the impression that General
Middleton had compassion for the families of "dead rebels" after
the battle of Batoche. The caption read, "He contemplating their
wretchedness reassures them, they are in no danger of injury."
Other news reports complimented the troops for the "respect, courtesy, and kindness with which the men, flush with victory, treated the
women" and stated, "Had they been their own mothers, sisters or
wives, they could not have shown them greater consideration."[56] Yet
recent research suggests that these reports were very exaggerated.[57]

Indian women also suffered during the months of conflict, and
many experienced a worse fate than that of Mesdames Delaney and
Gowanlock. On 23 April a detachment of the field force found a
dead woman with a bullet through her head in a house on a reserve
near Battleford;[58] two Cree women were killed by the gunfire of
Steele's scouts at Loon Lake; and a woman in Big Bear's camp committed suicide by hanging near Loon Lake. Kitty McLean in later
years described this woman, who was crippled at the knees so that
she could neither stand nor walk. She was:

Dakota Chief Whitecap and his daughter, detained for questioning
after the fall of Batoche (Saskatchewan Archives Board R-A6494)

such a refined, placid looking woman, who always made me think of a nice
lady. She dressed so nicely and had such a well groomed appearance. Her
hair was always done smoothly and she always had some bright remark to
make to those who passed by. She had had a cart to ride in until it had to
be given up as there was no road; then she rode in a travois until that had
to be abandoned on account of the density of the bush; then she was
helped on her pony and rode on horse-back, but now someone had stolen
the pony. Here we found her three weeks later on our return. She had
hanged herself by reaching up to a big limb just over her head, and had
used her belt to hang herself by! And so we found her with her little dog
dead by her side.[59]

The deaths of Aboriginal women received little coverage. Instead,
the image of "squaws" projected during the months of conflict was
of their horrible brutality. The press reports portrayed them as even
more treacherous and bloodthirsty than the "braves," whom they
were said to instigate to the worst atrocities.[60] It was widely reported
early in June that "Stoney squaws" had exhumed and horribly mutilated the body of Private Osgoode of the Ottawa Sharpshooters, who
had been killed at the battle of Cut Knife Hill. This news "created
the utmost indignation in camp [of the field force], and threats
loud and deep are uttered on all side [sic] against the Indians."[61] In
settlements such as Prince Albert, rumours flourished that "squaws"
had bargained with Riel for the privilege of killing the women of the

town if it was captured.[62] None of these stories proved to have any basis in reality, but they served to inflame public opinion among a terrified, exhausted populace. In Prince Albert, in response to the periodic rumours of imminent attack, the residents barricaded themselves behind a high wall of cordwood thrown up around the Presbyterian church and manse.

In a letter from his mission at Morley, published in the *Missionary Outlook* of June and July 1885, the Methodist missionary John McDougall added to these perceptions of violent Aboriginal women. After describing them as "full of sorrow and vice!" and saying, "No wonder their offspring grew up cruel and savage," he stated that an old warrior had told him that although the babies of enemies melted his own "savage heart," the women would brutally murder them: "'I tell you, praying man, our women are hardhearted and bad, very bad.' Alas! too true, I thought," commented McDougall.[63] It would be impossible to believe that after hearing or reading about the brutality of these women, people would feel any sympathy for them. It was much the same response as that in India during the "mutiny," when stereotypical images of Indian women as passive had been replaced by representations of them as inciting the mutineers to torture and other brutalities.[64] Similarly, during the Jamaican "revolt," in order to justify his actions, Governor Eyre's reports to the Colonial Office had stressed that the black women were even more brutal and barbarous than the men.[65] These images were harshly at odds with configurations of the proper nature of womanhood, exemplified in the endangered white women. A ballad written in 1894 by Dr T.A. Patrick of Yorkton, which described the dangers faced by the Yorkton Home Guard in 1885, typifies this fabricated misconception of the brutality of Aboriginal women:

> But the squaws were the worst, of these demons accurst,
> With the spirit of war and of woe
> For they would have shot those two men on the spot
> And they aimed with the arrow and bow.[66]

INDIGNITIES TO WHITE WOMEN

As anxiety over the fate of Mrs Gowanlock and Mrs Delaney increased during the months of April and May, rumours abounded about their treatment. In the Edmonton *Bulletin* of 25 April it was reported that an Indian had told a resident of that town that Big Bear now had a white wife and that many others would soon have white wives. By mid-May it was widely reported that Mrs Delaney had been bartered several times, that she had repeatedly suffered "a fate worse than death" and would soon die, and that she was ill treated more than Mrs Gowanlock because John Delaney had been so disliked.[67] Some papers refused to publish these rumours, generally those that supported the government, but others were willing to seize on any grim detail in order to criticize the actions of the government. Thus, the *Toronto Daily Mail*, a Conservative paper, insisted that there was little fear that the women would be ill treated, since "outrages of this sort has never been, and is not now, an Indian habit," but other papers emphasized the horrors of the "fate worse than death."[68]

Until the turning-point of the campaign at Batoche on 9–12 May, when the North-West Field Force under General Middleton successfully assaulted the Métis settlement, the Métis (and to some extent the Cree) had succeeded in dealing the Canadian authorities a series of devastating blows – at Duck Lake, Fish Creek, and Cut Knife Hill. There were also the events at Frog Lake and the "fall" of Fort Pitt. Terrified settlers at Battleford, believing themselves to be under siege, had deserted their homes and taken refuge in the police barracks. There were rumours of an "Indian rising"; the Native people were said to be gathering in large numbers and planning other massacres. One of the women barricaded at Battleford wrote to her mother in Prince Edward Island, "I hope the Indians won't kill any white women; but they take them prisoners, which is worse."[69]

After the police's disastrous encounter with the Métis at Duck Lake, the Canadian government mobilized more than 5,000 men for the North-West Campaign. Over 3,400 of them came from the East, from as far away as Halifax.[70] An image of the brutal treatment of the hapless brides, now widows, from the East was clearly used to galvanize the troops, to inspire their determination, and also to motivate their mothers, wives, and daughters, whose contribution to the war effort was considerable. By the end of May, with Riel and Poundmaker in custody, the last task of the field force, the column under General Strange, was to bring in Big Bear and secure the safety of the hostages. There was criticism, in some quarters, of Strange's delay and hints at his incompetence. The *Toronto Morning News* claimed that it was "scandalous apathy" and a

MAJOR CROZIER,
Of the North-West Mounted Police.

COLONEL SCOTT,
91st Battalion of Winnipeg.

MRS. GOWANLOCK,
Captured by Indians at the Fort Pitt Massacre.

Crow Foot, Blackfoot Indian Chief.   Three Bulls, Indian Chief.

In early May 1885 rumours abounded about the diabolical treatment of the two widows. Here Theresa Gowanlock is portrayed at the centre of the contest between the warriors from East and West. Reports and illustrations were not always accurate. Crowfoot and Three Bulls were not in fact involved in these events. (*Montreal Daily Star,* 2 May 1885)

discredit to humanity that so little was being done to release the captives from their "inhuman custodians."[71] This would surely encourage similar atrocities on defenceless women, stated the *News.* The field force must "impress upon Indians that the honour of a white woman is sacred, and that outrage and murder will be promptly avenged, no matter at what cost." Strange's reputation did not improve after he fought an inconclusive battle with the Cree at Frenchman Butte on 27 May while the hostages were securely protected in earthworks they had hastily built in the woods. The *Macleod Gazette* declared early in June that it was rather strange that no greater effort had been made to rescue those "unfortunate women."[72] Their prompt rescue, it said, should have been one of the first objects of the troops, and "one cannot help feeling indignant at the thought of the terrible sufferings of those who might have been our own wives or sisters or mothers."

Stories of "Indian atrocities" abounded during these weeks. Horrifying tales of humiliation and torture took hold of the colonial imagination and inflamed public opinion. Riel's diary, found after the fall of Batoche, was said to reveal plans that "the Sioux squaws were to receive the white women of Prince Albert as their own private prisoners, and the dusky ladies were to torture them according to their own pleasing fancies."[73] One rumour (which bears a striking resemblance to the Indian Rebellion fabrications of white women having to parade naked) was that an English missionary and his wife "were stripped naked and marched twelve miles to Pitt before the Indians."[74] On 20 May it was widely reported that Mrs Delaney had been killed, that she had been the "victim of foul outrages on the part of Indians, and torture on the part of squaws."[75] A headline in the Ottawa *Free Press* that day proclaimed that she had been "hacked to pieces by squaws." This report was attributed to Adjutant La Touche Tupper, who was with Colonel Smith's battalion. Some days later it was reported that Mrs Gowanlock's mutilated body had been found dumped in a well, another story that may have been inspired by tales of the rebellion in India. Although Lieutenant-Governor Edgar Dewdney dismissed these as sensational stories and stated on 29 May in Regina that not one reliable word had yet been received regarding Mrs Delaney or Mrs Gowanlock, such rumours flourished.[76] They served to galvanize the troops still in the field. After hearing them, there was "fearful excitement" among the volunteers under Strange: "Threats are freely made that if the abuse of the women is confirmed a war of extermination will be waged against the Indians under Big Bear."[77] The tales of atrocities may also have served to deflect criticism, diverting attention from Strange's increasingly ineffective pursuit of the Cree and their captives.

The account of Charles R. Daoust, who was with the 65th Montreal Battalion, gives some insight into how these rumours flourished among French-speaking as well as English-speaking soldiers, and the function the rumours served among men who had marched five hundred miles and literally "tramped the soles off their boots."[78]

There had been some concern that the 65th felt sympathy for the Métis and Indians and might not be willing to fight them.[79] Perhaps for this reason, rumours about the mistreatment of white women were assiduously circulated among the battalion. According to Daoust, while they were encamped at Fort Pitt late in May, the reports of the scouts did much to "excite the impatience of the soldiers to again engage the enemy. Here is what was reported to the soldiers concerning Madame Delaney: 'after cruelly maltreating her the Indians stripped off her clothes, bound her feet, dislocated her hip joints, and then in turn outraged her until she was dead. They continued as long as her body was warm.' "[80] The scouts also informed the soldiers that two of the McLean girls were slaves of the lesser chiefs. Daoust wrote, "Hearing these stories the spirits of the soldiers were very high. They found a shirt in a meadow bearing the initials of one of the McLean girls. It was torn to the shoulders and the sleeve was spotted with blood. There was no doubt that the young girls had suffered the final outrage."

Dr John P. Pennefather, a surgeon with the Alberta Field Force, wrote in his book *Thirteen Years on the Prairies* (1892) that the "revolting" stories of the fate of the women wound the "whole force up to a pitch of fury." He added, "Had Big Bear and his band fallen into our hands while these reports were credited, I do not think man, woman, or child would have been spared." When the rumours (which Pennefather described as having been "industriously circulated") proved false, "the interest of the campaign died away."[81] Editors of the Toronto *News* wrote on 21 May that once the captives had been delivered safely into the hands of their friends, "our troops may find no other course open than the exaction of a blood atonement from Big Bear and his gang." After describing how Mrs Delaney purportedly met her end, the editor of the *Macleod Gazette* asked, "Will you blame us if we kill, men women and children of such an outfit?" and replied, "No but we will never forgive you if you don't."[82]

These reports not only helped steel military resolve in the campaign against the Cree; they also served the purposes of those who wished to condemn the government's administration of the North-West. It was suggested in the *Moosomin Courier*, for example, that the government should get an "illuminated copy of the account of Mrs. Delaney and Mrs. Gowanlock's treatment at the hands of Big Bear's band, nicely framed and hung conspicuously in the Legislative Hall in memoriam of the hellish effects of their 'Dishwater Administration' in the North-West Territories."[83] Presented as an "unbiased view" in the *Macleod Gazette* was the following observation from a reader: "One's heart bleeds for Mrs. Delaney and the other unfortunate women, and it makes one all the madder against Dewdney *et hoc genus omne* [government officials]." This reader said that there was too much "general corruptness" and rottenness in political matters, and he used the fate of Mrs Delaney to argue that the North-West ought to separate from the rest of the country, "say at the east boundary of Manitoba."[84]

The young Nellie McClung (who in later life was prominent in the campaign for woman suffrage) was on her family's farm in Manitoba in 1885, and she later recalled the great agitation that arose in the district: "Up to that time the 'trouble' was a vague and abstract state, far away and impersonal, but now the menace had come out into the open, and the evil had assumed shape and image; painted savages, brandishing tomahawks and uttering blood-curdling cries had swarmed around the lonely and defenceless farm houses, and overpowered these two women and carried them away to the Indian teepees somewhere in the wood, holding them as hostages."[85] McClung wrote that while the fate of Mrs Delaney and Mrs Gowanlock "was a shivery subject for conversation," her mother stood firmly by her belief that the Indians would not hurt the women: " 'Women are safer with Indians than they would be with some white men,' she said, but she was talked down by the others, who had terrible tales of atrocities in Minnesota and it seems that most of them had relatives who survived that terrible time. At that stage in the conversation I was always sent to bed."[86]

THE CAPTIVES AND THE ELECTORAL
FRANCHISE ACT

Mrs Delaney and Mrs Gowanlock were also dragged into the debate about the Macdonald government's 1885 Electoral Franchise Act. As initially introduced on 19 March 1885, the act provided that persons occupying real property of a value of $250 or more in rural areas would be eligible to vote. Indians as well as widows and unmarried women who met the necessary property qualifications would be granted the franchise.[87] The bill was the subject of heated debate in both the House of Commons and the press throughout the course of the resistance in the North-West. Indeed, it was suggested that the franchise bill was a diversionary tactic to draw the attention of the House away from the events in the North-West and to help the prime minister appear enlightened on Native issues at a time when his policy was under attack.[88] While the extension of the franchise to widows and unmarried women was soon dropped from the bill, the question of the "Indian vote" remained before the House during the weeks of military engagement in the North-West. The Liberal opposition objected to the bill on the grounds that most Native people were pagan, illiterate, and did not have sufficient intelligence to use the vote wisely. One member of Parliament declared, "To give the franchise to women would interfere with their proper position ... it would be a burden instead of a benefit to them. This, I believe, to be exactly the case as regards the Indians ... it will be doing him an injury rather than a benefit to give him a power which neither by training, education nor instinct he is able to appreciate and to wisely exercise.[89]

Opponents of the Electoral Franchise Act seized on the events in the North-West to argue that Macdonald was prepared to give the vote to a horde of "bloody vindictive barbarians" who were ready, "on the slightest pretext, to return to their ancient habits of rapine, pillage and murder."[90] Throughout the month of May especially, newspapers showered scorn on what was described as "one of the most monstrous propositions ever submitted to a free legislature," since it would mean that "Piapot, Poundmaker, White Cap and their horde of savages who have been butchering women and children, and devastating their homes with fire, will be entitled to the elective franchises."[91] Often it was pointed out how unfair it was that those "massacring white people" would be qualified voters, while white women and younger white men – many of whom had been sent out west to restore law and order – were not so entitled. As declared in the Ottawa *Free Press* on 1 May, "The Tory majority in the House of Commons have refused to bestow the power of voting upon the intelligent white women of Canada; but they decided to enfranchise Poundmaker and the other reserve Indians of the territories whose hands are red with the blood of white men and white women." Outrage at the prospect of Indians voting was also exhibited in papers south of the border. The *Boston Journal* of 19 May expressed dismay at the idea that Poundmaker, Big Bear, and their "murderous warriors, after they get through robbing the settlers, maltreating women, and spreading ruin through the North-West, have only to go back to their homes to be qualified for the rights of citizenship, while some of the plucky young fellows who are fighting them, being unable to meet the new property qualifications, will be disenfranchised."[92]

The sensational fabrications about the fate of Mrs Delaney circulating during the last part of May were used as ammunition against the franchise bill. Readers of the Ottawa *Free Press* were warned that the bill "would confer the ballot upon the wretches who dishonored Mrs. Delaney, till her death mercifully relieved her of the sense of the ignominy to which she had been compulsorily and brutally subjected."[93] The issues of woman suffrage and the Indian franchise were often linked. This same editorial was critical of a bill that would give the vote to the "savage" who had "violated the unfortunate woman until she died, but refuse it to the intelligent women of Canada, who might use their ballots to avenge their sister's wrongs." This volley of fire met its mark, and on 26 May Prime Minister Macdonald introduced an amendment disqualifying the Indians in Manitoba, Keewatin, and the North-West Territories (as well as those anywhere who had failed to improve their distinct tracts of land by the value of $150). The opposition demanded that the disqualification be extended to British Columbia. The prime minister agreed and two days later introduced an amendment to his own amendment adding the province to the list of exempted regions.[94] Criticisms of the Aboriginal people of British Columbia also centred on their treatment of women – that they were "notoriously among the most degraded and lowest type of Indians in the world ... Lust and licentiousness are their ruling passions. Chastity and morality are unknown to them."[95] The act that was eventually passed gave the federal vote only to all adult male Indians in eastern Canada who met the necessary property qualifications.

FREEDOM AND FIRST PUBLIC DECLARATIONS OF THE FROG LAKE WIDOWS

It was with profound relief as well as shamefacedness in some quarters that the world learned on 8 June that Mrs Gowanlock and Mrs Delaney were safe. The women arrived at Fort Pitt on 5 June, along with forty-three Métis men, women, and children (a preponderance of children), including the Pritchards, who had escaped

Theresa Gowanlock after her two months in Big Bear's camp. (Glenbow Archives, NA-4796-1, photo by Malcolm T. Miller apparently taken at Fort Pitt)

with them.[96] A correspondent with the *Minneapolis Pioneer Press* was on hand at Fort Pitt to describe the scene: "A long line wound down the hill to the remains of the old fort, to be surrounded instanter by eager soldiers, and questioning correspondents. There were half-breed carts drawn by ponies of spare habit, buck-boards with calico cayuses in the shafts, and wagons at whose poles huge oxen, who long ago gave up the lusts of fleshly appetite, lumbered heavily along." He then described the two women who were the centre of attention:

Mrs. Gowanlock is not more than twenty, rather good-looking, with large, dark eyes, long black hair, exceptionally good teeth and well-developed figure. Mrs. Delaney is rather spare, and her features, though not regular, are pleasant to look upon, while her conversation betrayeth an active mind. She is more than thirty and less than forty, and this is as close a guess as to age as I care to venture. Both women were comfortably dressed, Mrs. Gowanlock in black delaine, her companion in blue print, and both had evidently taken advantage of their rescue to indulge in ablutions which they feelingly averred had been denied them, except at rare intervals, since the fatal 2nd of April, when they were made captive.[97]

Although it was widely proclaimed that they had been "rescued," this large group had in fact taken the initiative in leaving Big Bear's camp.[98] Under the cover of heavy fog one morning, they had fallen to the rear of the main group and then struck off eastward. For three days they had travelled in many directions through the bush to avoid being discovered, until a party of ten scouts led by William McKay and Peter Ballendine found them. McKay and Ballendine were Métis, and both had been recruited to work as scouts for the troops. Neither received any public recognition for their role in the "rescue," although Mrs Gowanlock specifically named them in *Two Months*.

In their initial statements, the women announced that they had been treated well, had had plenty to eat, and had been subjected to no cruelties or "indignities."[99] There were occasions when the menacing behaviour of certain individuals had made them fear for their lives and their virtue, and both had suffered mental anxiety, but they had been well protected and had met with little suffering. They had cooked and laundered but had not been forced to do these tasks; they had done them of their own accord because it had given them some occupation. Their principal problem had been loneliness, since neither spoke Cree or French. Unlike most of the others in the constantly moving camp, including the McLeans, the two women did not have to walk; they had ridden in the Pritchards' wagon. Once or twice they had walked off together when their cart was not ready, but they had never been compelled to walk on foot. In fact, John Pritchard had often made his children walk so that the two might ride.[100] Mrs Gowanlock even retained her jewellery. One of their greatest concerns was for the safety of the females still being held hostage by the Cree, because two Aboriginal women from Big Bear's camp had been killed by Steele's scouts during the Loon Lake encounter. According to the two widows, "Big Bear had pointed out to his young men that the whites never killed women, and thus kept the female prisoners safe; now he cannot use that argument, which heretofore has been so successful."[101]

The Quinneys had escaped some days earlier, together with W.B. Cameron, Henry Halpin, and the Dufresnes. Their Woods Cree custodian, Longfellow, knew of their plan and had informed Mrs Quinney that all the Indians were willing for them to escape.[102] On the first day they had gone about twelve miles from the fugitive Cree when a party of men was dispatched to find the soldiers of

Two versions of the "rescue" of Mrs Delaney and Mrs Gowanlock. In fact, the women were not dramatically rescued. They were among a group of about forty who parted company with the moving Cree camp under cover of fog one morning. They travelled for three days until discovered by a party of scouts under the command of William McKay and Peter Ballendine. Both these men were of part-Aboriginal ancestry, and they received no public recognition for their work. (*Canadian Pictorial and Illustrated War News*, souvenir edn., 20 June 1885, Glenbow Archives, NA-1480-3; Gowanlock and Delaney, *Two Months*, 124)

Strange's column, which they succeeded in doing by the next morning. A group of twenty-four, including the McLeans and Manns, were allowed to leave the Cree camp on 17 June because food supplies were low. They were provided with horses and flour and set adrift, arriving at Fort Pitt on 22 June. In W.J. McLean's first statement, given to a reporter from the *Globe*, he too testified that they had not been badly treated: "Of course we underwent a great deal of hardship, the nature of our wanderings made that unavoidable, but otherwise we were treated with the greatest respect. Nothing in the nature of an insult was ever offered us. The only reason the Indians kept us was to protect themselves in case they were cornered. I was never as much as asked to do any work."[103] McLean stated that he had placed himself and his family in the hands of Big Bear because he had felt at the time that he would not have been able to reach Battleford alive in a country that was possibly swarming with hostiles.[104] He further stated, "Never for a moment were the lives of myself or family endangered" – except when his youngest daughter narrowly escaped being shot by Steele's men when she was crossing a creek.[105]

Correspondents commented at length on the "plucky" McLean girls.[106] They were all reported to be strong and healthy, particularly Amelia, the eldest, who was described as "plucky enough for life guardsmen." She was praised for her courage, especially for having shouldered a Winchester, taking her turn at sentry duty. Amelia said that she "would not have believed the endurance they all manifested possible, but now looks back at most of it with enjoyment."[107] One of the McLean girls told a correspondent that although she was glad to have her life among the Indians at an end, she had "rather enjoyed the trip as a whole. She appeared inclined to look upon their experience as a joke."[108]

Mrs Gowanlock and Mrs Delaney reserved the highest praise for their Métis benefactors, John Pritchard, Adolphus Nolin, and Pierre Blondin. Both credited them, especially Pritchard, with having saved them from hardship and suffering as well as from the menacing behaviour of some of the Plains Cree men. According to the women, Pritchard and Nolin had each given the Cree a horse for Mrs Delaney, and Pierre Blondin had given two horses for Mrs Gowanlock; through this bargain, they had been allowed to remain with the women.[109] From time to time, Nolin and the Pritchards had given up other possessions, such as blankets and

John Pritchard is presented here in a heroic stance, keeping a steady
eye on the Indian camp in the background. His image was
increasingly tarnished by a non-Aboriginal public that was not willing
to view a person of part-Aboriginal ancestry in a heroic light.
(*Canadian Pictorial and Illustrated War News*, souvenir edn., 4 July 1885,
Glenbow Archives, NA-1480-42)

dishes, to ensure the safety of the women. In answer to a question
from the Toronto *Globe* correspondent aboard the steamer *North-
west* on 6 June, both women declared that before the "massacre,"
they had not been acquainted with any of the "halfbreeds" who had
befriended them except the Pritchards. Mrs Delaney was distressed
to learn that Nolin – who had left the Cree camp at Frog Lake in
mid-May on the pretence of acting as a scout for the Cree and had
gone to Prince Albert for assistance – was a manacled prisoner. In
Prince Albert, he had been immediately arrested, no one believing
his story of how he had helped the two women.[110] In custody Nolin
had stated that the women were safe and that although he had
offered them the chance to escape with him, they had chosen to
remain with Pritchard.[111] This had been regarded as the weakest
part of his story. Mrs Delaney pleaded for his immediate release.
Nolin had been charged with treason felony but was released on
22 July 1885 because of his efforts in securing the safety of
Mrs Gowanlock and Mrs Delaney.[112]

Mrs Delaney had some critical words to say about the administration of Indian affairs. According to one correspondent, she laid at Edgar Dewdney's door "the greater portion of the blame for the Indians' antipathy to the instructors, and to his door, a share in the causes that led to the massacre."[113] She said that on his visits he had made many promises and had raised expectations, which were not forgotten by the Indians:

It would be no use for the agent to remind Mr. Dewdney of his unfulfilled pledges, the reply would simply come that the rations already granted were more than ample. The Indians, intensely suspicious, when once deceived, between two conclusions would take that one that the promises of Mr. Dewdney had been fulfilled so far as he was concerned, but their performance frustrated and prevented by the agent and so the wrath of the Indian, that has brought so much sadness and sorrow to many a once happy home, was turned against an innocent and unoffending person.

Criticism of the government was also expressed by James Delaney of Gloucester County, near Ottawa, a brother of the deceased. He believed that his brother had likely been killed while defending the supplies that were in his trust, as he had had to do on other occasions. His brother should have been given assistance, Delaney told the Ottawa *Free Press* on 13 April 1885. He added, "I consider the government as criminally negligent in the matter."

In the weeks and months to come, the widows' initial statements about their relatively good treatment, their ability to cope reasonably well, the kindness and assistance of certain people during their ordeal, and the mistakes of government administration were obscured and revised. The story that emerged in *Two Months in Big Bear's Camp* represented their captivity as a tale of barbaric savages and helpless white women.

CHAPTER THREE

"Untold Suffering and Privation": Changing and Conflicting Stories of Captivity

The story the women told of their experiences, especially the murder of their husbands, was indeed harrowing, but their relatively good treatment in the Cree camp and the consideration and assistance they had received from from the Métis men and their families did not answer the needs of the hour. The widows had not, after all, been "reserved to suffer the nameless horrors of Indian indignity and savage lust."[1] Nor had they been butchered. In fact, they had not suffered very much during their two months in the custody of the Cree. This would not do. They must have endured hardships and indignities of some kind, for they had been in the hands of the enemy. The heroes of the hour could not be Métis like Pritchard; they had to be the "conquering heroes" from the East. Similarly, criticism of the administration of Indian affairs was not welcomed in many quarters. The original statements of the two widows were thus eroded and altered. The military and police authorities, as well as the correspondents at Fort Pitt, were not sure how to regard Pritchard and the other Métis, since all were viewed as enemies. To say the least, the honesty of their intentions was questioned. Pritchard's heroism, for example, was celebrated only to a most modest extent. Even though a *Globe* editorial praised the noble and chivalrous conduct of the "French Halfbreeds" who had incurred grave personal danger in order to shield the two English-speaking women from the "nameless horrors which threatened them," it nonetheless portrayed the men as "our foes" whose arms were "turned against us."[2]

In the weeks that followed, Pritchard's image was increasingly sullied by a public that seemed unable to regard a "halfbreed" in a chivalrous light. By the time the widows reached Winnipeg early in July, the press was already stating that Pritchard had only *represented* himself as a prisoner and, moreover, that he was a thief. A story in the *Daily Manitoban* of 7 July, which was reprinted in newspapers across Canada, stated that the two women "were not compelled to walk in traveling but they rode in a stolen wagon which had belonged to Gowanlock & Laurie, and were drawn by oxen also stolen from them"; as well, they had been fed stolen provisions. According to this reporter, the Métis had only pretended to exchange horses for them: "The ladies heard the half-breeds say that they had got their horses back again from the Indians." Pritchard, it was stated, had been paid for keeping the women, and although they had not been treated with violence, they had been annoyed in many ways. Pritchard had been "kind enough in his way," but Mrs Pritchard had not; and the two women had performed duties such as carrying wood and water "because the work was neglected by others." This article concluded that the two widows "do not give the half-breeds any credit which would entitle them to recompense at the hands of the whites."

A Reverend Dr Hooper of Kingston, who had served in the field force, was in the forefront of the movement to discredit Pritchard. He claimed that the Métis men had purchased the captive women for their own vile purposes and "were only defeated in their intentions by the resolute conduct of their victims. Foiled in their base plans they made literal slaves of them during their captivity."[3] In a letter published in the *Toronto Daily Mail* on 8 August 1885, Pritchard defended himself against the charges. It was not true, he wrote, that the horses given to purchase the women had been taken back by him. "As for the stolen oxen and wagon, the oxen were the property of one of the ladies [Mrs Gowanlock] as also the provisions. We had to use something to move about, and we had to have something to eat." Regarding the accusation that the women had been purchased for his "own vile use," he replied, "Far from it, I would not commit such a crime as that. I had my wife and children." Pritchard stated that within a few hours of their capture the women had been under his protection: "It was for the love of God that I tried hard to get them from the hands of the Indians, remembering that they were white women, and decent." At one point early in their captivity, some Indians had broken into their tent and threatened to take the women unless Pritchard paid them whatever they had. They had nothing, not even a gun, and the Pritchard family had given away their bedding in order to satisfy the intruders and save the women. Pritchard's final statement in the letter was, "The two ladies can corroborate that themselves."

A major purpose of Dr Hooper's campaign was to terminate all efforts to reward Pritchard and the other Métis who had assisted the widows. When news of the women's safety first became public, there had been some talk of a reward for Pritchard and Blondin.[4] The *Week* of Toronto on 18 June had stated: "A woman proposes that every one of her sex who is able to do so should contribute twenty-five cents with which to form a fund to reward the men by whom the liberty of the captives was purchased. Should the sisterhood act upon the suggestion, John Pritchard and Pierre Blondin will not go unrewarded." Hooper wanted the ladies of Toronto to know that they were "working upon a mistaken idea of the real facts."[5] Partly as a result of his efforts, the sisterhood did not act on the *Week*'s proposal, and the Métis benefactors of Mrs Delaney and Mrs Gowanlock were never rewarded in any way.

W.B. Cameron, who became a journalist, actively campaigned for a reward, a pension, or some recognition for Pritchard even after Pritchard's death in Battleford at the age of eighty-five in 1925. Pritchard's story after 1885 is a sad one. His wife Rose contracted tuberculosis around 1895, and hearing about a marvellous cure available in Medicine Hat, Pritchard sold his Bresaylor farm and stock and moved his entire family there.[6] Rose died in 1897. Pritchard raised horses for a time in the Prongua area but lost his sizable herd through an outbreak of disease. From then on he supported his large family on a meagre income from a series of odd jobs in the Battleford district, where he was known as "gentleman Johnny." The year he died, Cameron wrote an article called "The Passing of John Pritchard" in which he stated that Mrs Gowanlock and Mrs Delaney had justly been given government pensions, but if it had not been for Pritchard they would not have lived to require them.[7] It was not too late to put up a monument to Pritchard, Cameron argued: "Pritchard was a true Canadian. His skin was dark, but his heart and his life were white." (Pritchard's son Sam appeared uncomfortably on the television show "Front Page Challenge" in 1959 at the age of ninety-eight, but the panel showed little interest in the story of Frog Lake, so many miles and years away.)[8]

Others in the Battleford district continued to be suspicious of Pritchard's activities in 1885. In her unpublished and undated memoir of the events, Effie Storer, daughter of *Saskatchewan Herald* editor P.G. Laurie, wrote that the two widows were "ostensibly" under the protection of Pritchard.[9] She claimed that Pritchard had been aware of the unrest among the Indians but "did not breath a word of it to his employers until the night before the massacre and even then the information given did not prove true." To many, according to Storer, Pritchard's actions "savored of disloyalty" because he was in the employ of the government. She believed that he had pretended to protect the women in the hope of getting compensation, and she believed that he had received a government allowance for the rest of his life in recognition of his "care" of the women. To illustrate just how callous Pritchard had been, Storer stated (though this was not mentioned in any other account) that Mrs Gowanlock had fallen off the cart while crossing a slough and hurt her back. "The fact that she could scarcely walk for several days caused Pritchard no concern," commented Storer. "When crossing mud-hoes [*sic*] or going down steep side-hills the women were left to hand [*sic*] on to the contents of the wagon as best they could to keep from falling off."[10]

In their original (early June) statements, as recorded in the press, the two women also credited Pierre Blondin for their safety during their two months of captivity. By early July this had changed. Although it was acknowledged that Blondin had given his horse and thirty dollars for Mrs Gowanlock, this was described as "no act of generosity, but of a selfish and bad man who was trying to secure his own vile ends."[11] As will be discussed later, Blondin appears in a treacherous light in the narrative of Mrs Gowanlock and is said to have been implicated in the deaths of the men. Louis Goulet, his fellow Métis captive and a witness to the events at Frog Lake, defended his friend even after Blondin's death in St Boniface in 1906. Goulet maintained that Blondin had had nothing to do with the deaths at Frog Lake and he stressed that, like the two women, Blondin had been a prisoner of the Cree.[12]

In the western press, keen resentment was expressed about the sympathetic treatment of any Métis. An editorial in the *Saskatchewan Herald* of 11 January 1886 criticized the women of the Montreal Protestant churches who had united for the purpose of sending help to impoverished Métis. They should instead be assisting the "loyal" settlers, stated the *Herald*: "The ladies are no doubt actuated by what they think are motives of charity. True charity is not bounded by the narrow limits of race or religion, and we would suggest to these ladies that they extend their kindness to their white brethren and their families whose ruin was brought about by the men who seem to be the first object of their solicitude. The sufferings of many loyal settlers thrown on the world without a change of clothing – reduced in a moment from comfort to penury – are none the less acute because they have not been paraded before the world."

The issue of who should be rewarded for heroic deeds, who should receive scrip and medals, and who should be compensated for rebellion losses was widely debated as the conflict concluded and for many years after. Some wondered why General Middleton should be awarded a gratuity of $20,000.[13] He had made no financial sacrifice in his move west, unlike most of his officers and men, who had sustained heavy financial losses by leaving home. Many of the volunteers were unemployed as a result of answering the call to duty. Settlers in the North-West had also suffered, in some cases as a result of looting by the field force. P.G. Laurie's stove and sets of furniture had been purloined by the Queen's Own Rifles for use in the officer's mess.[14] Many people felt aggrieved and short-changed. Which widows were entitled to a pension was also a bone of contention. The widow of NWMP bugler Paddy Burke, killed at Cut Knife Hill, was initially denied any pension and was allowed rations only while she remained at Battleford. This was described in the *Macleod Gazette* as disgraceful, considering that pensions were "given right and left to the wives of deceased volunteers."[15] The NWMP, it was argued, had rendered better service to Canada than the volunteers ever had, yet they had been "treated to snub after snub, and insult after insult, not only by such snobs as Middleton, but even by the government." (Mrs Burke, a Métisse, was granted modest provision by an order-in-council of October 1887 which allowed her one year's pay for her husband, about $275, and four months' pay for each of her six children, in addition to a compassionate allowance of 37.5 cents a day while she remained unmarried.)[16]

The experiences of Mrs Gowanlock and Mrs Delaney continued to be a battleground long after the widows recovered their freedom. The glad tidings of their safety was used as a pretext for both congratulating and condemning the government. An editorial in the Regina *Leader* of 23 June 1885 said that the fact that all the prisoners had been restored without having been ill-treated "shows that the past policy of kindness to the Indians has not been in vain." "The way Big Bear's band treated Mrs. Gowanlock and Mrs. Delaney shows the civilizing influence of kindness," noted the *Leader,* and the "white scoundrels" who invented the stories of abominable atrocities "should never be allowed to put their foot in decent society again." The *Prince Albert Times and Saskatchewan Review* of 19 June took a similar approach, stating that the idea of "wholesale shooting, or presenting cast-off clothing of small-pox patients to the red man" could now be dismissed. The paper hoped that those who had suggested such measures would have modified their views "since learning that their countrywomen have not, as was believed, been subjected to outrage worse than death." It pointed out that the Cree had not treated the prisoners "in what they themselves would consider a harsh way," whether this was because of contact with civilization, missionary influence, or a sharpened faculty of looking ahead to possible disaster to themselves.

A more representative opinion was that of P.G. Laurie, editor of the *Saskatchewan Herald* of Battleford, who had ceased publishing for several weeks while he had been barricaded with the other citizens in the police barracks. Laurie took great exception to such complimentary statements about the treatment of the hostages. "Big Bear," he wrote, "had sold the unfortunate women just as he would horses, regardless of what fate might be in store for them," and it was heartless to "say that two months imprisonment of these ladies in the camp of savages is neither injury nor ill treatment."[17] Others were quick to blame the government for having allowed the hideous reports about the women's fate. The *Toronto News,* which had not hesitated to print any and all rumours, declared that it had been natural to conclude that the captives had suffered an even worse fate than the Frog Lake victims, and it blamed the government for the lack of reliable information and for not having made greater efforts to rescue the women.[18]

Quite a number of people felt that there was ample evidence to conclude that the Hudson's Bay Company – the other outside authority in the North-West beside the government, and one of much longer standing – had clearly retained the trust of the Aboriginal residents, while the police and Indian affairs officials were loathed.[19] A further use that the experience of the women was put to was to add fuel to Louis Riel's funeral pyre. In addition to his "murder" of Thomas Scott in Manitoba in 1869–70, here was a further reason for Sir John A. Macdonald to see him hanged: "Now that he [Macdonald] has got him [Riel] it is to be hoped that he will be forced to avenge, not only the murder of Scott but the lives of those who have been sacrificed for their country, and make him atone in some small degree for the terrible outrages perpetrated on defenceless women by his Indian allies."[20]

As the original story of the two women was altered and eroded, the dominant image that began to solidify was one of the great suffering and insult they had endured, despite the fact that they had retained "all that a woman holds dear."[21] In an 1885 history of the North-West "troubles" entitled *From Savagery to Civilization*, the women captives were said to have been "in hourly fear for their lives. Dragged to and fro over a wild and desolate region, they for a time lived a living death."[22] Weak and helpless without their husbands, they had been "dragged from the lifeless bodies of their loved protectors, and for two months were the terror-stricken captives of the Indian murderers."[23]

Even though there was no evidence of any white women meeting "the fate worse than death" during these months of conflict, it was often stated in the press and by prominent spokesmen that the "savages" of the West had embarked on a campaign of rapine, rape, and murder. This was the dominant impression that remained with the public. Late in May 1885, Edward Blake said in the House of Commons that many people in Canada thanked God that there were so few "ladies" in the North-West: "Savage Indians had started out on a career of slaughter, rape, pillage. Age, nor sex, nor sacred office, nor faithful friendship, availed to prevent the outrages, which the savage called war. Against these also the volunteers had done their duty like men and soldiers."[24]

RETURN TO THE "SACRED PRECINCTS OF THE PATERNAL HEARTH"

Mrs Gowanlock and Mrs Delaney spent two weeks with the Laurie family of Battleford, sharing their accommodation at the police barracks (for the Laurie home was in ruins) while arrangements were made for their transportation to their former homes. The widows were not asked to give evidence in court. When they arrived in

Regina, Judge Charles-Borromée Rouleau was anxious that they should remain to give evidence, especially when it was learned that Big Bear had given himself up;[25] but Brigade-Surgeon Frederick William Strange considered it necessary for Mrs Gowanlock's health that she return east, and Lieutenant-Governor Dewdney arranged for the two women to leave, on the understanding that they would return if their presence was required. They were accompanied on their journey by Mrs Laurie and her daughter Effie. Crowds of well-wishers greeted them at many of the stops on their route. Effie (Laurie) Storer remembered that when the engines were changed at Moose Jaw, Mrs Delaney and Mrs Gowanlock were not told that hundreds of people were on the station platform hoping to see them; according to her, their nerves would not have stood the strain. The blinds of their coach were lowered (though this was partly to keep out the warm afternoon sun), but the mayor of Moose Jaw stepped into the coach and expressed the townspeople's sympathy for the widows and their gratitude that they had been rescued.[26]

The journey was described in the press at every stopover. When the party arrived in Winnipeg on 6 July, a *Daily Manitoban* reporter had the opportunity to observe the two widows closely as they rode the streetcar from the station to their hotel:

They were both attired in sombre black, and their faces bore the evidence of the extreme suffering and heartrending they have been called upon to endure. They both had a forlorn, hopeless look in their faces, and it seemed as if they could never smile again. Mrs. Delaney is a rather hale woman, of comparatively slight build, rather prominent features and black eyes. Mrs. Gowanlock, on the other hand, is rather low of stature, and inclined to be stout, although the severe experiences she has just passed through has deprived her of any surplus flesh. She has an oval face with jet black eyes, and black hair, and sun-burned as black as she is, a cursory glance would give the impression that the blood of the Indian coursed through her veins. She is retiring and bashful in her disposition.[27]

In Winnipeg the women stayed at the home of Mrs C.F. Bennett, who had been moved to write them a letter on 8 June just after her husband had informed her of their safety. When issuing the invitation, Mrs Bennett had told them that their sufferings had "given you a sister's place in every heart" and "*every one* in Winnipeg would be deeply disappointed if you did not give them an opportunity of expressing their deep sympathy and regards."[28] The "lady friends" of that city presented the two widows with a purse of $167, along with "many articles of apparel and other comforts" because they were in "straitened circumstances through having lost everything."[29] A large number of sympathizers were on hand at the Winnipeg railway station to see the women off to Port Arthur, and they were described as "weary and worn looking, dressed in black" when at last they walked down the gangway of the steamer *Alberta* onto the wharf at Owen Sound.

RETURN OF THE CONQUERING HEROES

Mrs Delaney and Mrs Gowanlock were the nation's heroines, but their sombre return in widows' weeds was very different from the festive atmosphere that marked the massive celebrations for the return of the nation's heroes. On 24 July a "royal and right national" reception was held for the return of the Ottawa Sharpshooters. Seldom had the authors of editorials waxed more eloquent: "Everyone seemed to look upon them not only as true and tried soldiers of the Dominion, but as something nearer and dearer; as if their toils, hardships, dangers, and triumphs had opened up an artery, a channel through which a vivifying breath of national hope and national aspiration had received new prompting and new life, and the laurels won on the prairie by the Capital's contingent in the struggle for a nation's integrity and honor were of homage and loyalty."[30]

The troops disembarked at the railway station, where they were greeted by the mayor and council and by wives, sisters, and mothers, while cheer after cheer went up from the multitude, such cheering as Ottawa had rarely heard. As they marched in procession to Parliament Hill, their entire route was packed with spectators. From every window, women waved handkerchiefs and cheered. In many addresses and presentations, the "boys" were congratulated for upholding the honour of the country and for helping to increase the self-confidence and self-respect of the Canadian people. They had worked to make Canada a nation that was admired and respected abroad. Two Sharpshooters, Privates Osgoode and Rogers, had been killed in action, and they were remembered as martyred heroes who had died a glorious death. They had made the greatest sacrifice, not only to uphold law and order and the integrity of confederation, but to "rescue the women and children whose safety was jeopardized by the Indian uprising."[31]

Reception of the 12th Battalion York Rangers at Parkdale, Ontario
(University of Saskatchewan Archives, Special Collections,
Canadian Pictorial and Illustrated War News, souvenir edn, 25 July 1885)

In towns and villages large and small the citizens enthusiastically welcomed home their gallant sons. Martial music, fire and church bells, and rousing cheers rent the air during the procession from the depot to the drill shed in Bowmanville, Ontario, late in July.[32] King Street, a living sea of surging people, was decorated with welcoming arches of drapery, brooms, cut knives and bayonets, guns and flags. Here too the theme emphasized in the press was that the fearless and hardy troops, who had thrown down the implements of their various callings at the call of the country, had "shown that the Dominion is a *nation*; able to take care of itself, able to vindicate its authority in its own territory." They had saved the honour of the country, shown that the honour of a white woman was sacred, shown the Indians and Métis that they had to respect the laws of the country, and created a place that was safer for white women to live.

Much poetry on patriotic themes was produced during and after the events of 1885. The following are typical of the prevailing attitude:

Conquering Heroes

Conquering heroes! Yes; what is it they have not conquered?
Wearisome miles on miles up to the far North-West;
Limitless breadths of prairie, like to the limitless ocean;
Endless stretches of distance, like to eternity.
Farther still, – to their seeming far as the starless spaces
That loom in the measureless void above some desolate heart.
How the unnumbered miles threatened them like an army, –
Then perished in silence beneath the tread of resolute feet.

Not alone did they march, our brave Canadian soldiers.
Grim Privation and Peril followed them hand in hand;
Sodden Fatigue lay down with them in the evening,
And Weariness rose with them and went with them all the day
Inexpressible Sadness at thought of the homes they were leaving
Hung like a cloud above them, and shadowed in the path before.
These, all these, were slain by our brave, our conquering heroes.
Ah! but the battle was long, – long and bitterly hard.

Crueller enemies still; – treacherous, scarcely human.
Hard and fierce in look, but harder and fiercer in heart;
Verged in animal cunning, warily waiting in ambush;
Merciless in the purely animal power to smite.
Swift in their veins runs the hot, vindictive blood of their fathers;
Deep in their hearts lies a hatred, strong and cruel as death.
The heart of our country is beating against the knife of the savage;
But the knife has dropped to the ground, the heart is conqueror still.

Ah! but the brave boys wounded and dead on the field of battle,
Giving their brave young lives for a cause that was dearer than life.
Say you they who have yielded their all have conquered nothing, –
Nothing remains to them but the sad deep silence of death!
No, a thousand times, no! For them are the tears of a nation –
Tears that would fain wash out the pitiful stain of blood.
These are their victories; The love that knows no forgetting,
Measureless gratitude, and the fame that forever endures.

Agnes E. Wetherald of St Catharines,
in the *Week,* 23 July 1885

Forward

Who sneers she's but a colony;
No national spirit there;
Race differences, action's feuds
Her flag to tatters tear?

What rises o'er those snowy plains?
What floats the western sky?
Whence on the virgin white those stains?
Whose is that crimson dye?

Rebellion's ensign blots the blue,
And mars its fretwork gold,
And near those stains of crimson hue,
Canadian hearts lie cold.

Another ensign! Trumpets ring!
A youth this flag upholds
And lo! from every side men spring
And range beneath its folds.

Nor race, nor creed the patriot's sword
Nor faction blunts today
"Forward for Canada" is the word
And eager for the fray.

Our youth press on and carpers shame.
Their bearing bold and high,
For this young nations peace and fame
Ready to do or die.

They come from hamlet and from town
From hill and wood and glade,
From where great palaces look down
On streets that roar with trade.

From where by floe and rocky bar
The Atlantic held in check

From where Wolfe's glory, like a star
Shines down on old Quebec.

From where Mount Royal rises proud
O'er Cartier's city fair
From where Chaudiere with thunder loud
Flings high its smoke in air.

From pleasant cities rich and old
That gem, Ontario's shore;
From where Niagara's awful plunge
Makes its eternal roar.

From each new town just spring to life
Mid flowery prairies wide;
From where first Riel kindled strife
To Calgary's rapid tide.

Upon the field all rancour healed
There's no discordant hue
The Orange marches with the Green
The Rouge beside the blue.

One purpose now fires every eye
Rebellion foul to slay
"Forward for Canada's" the cry
And all are one today.

> Written by a recruit during
> the Riel Rebellion, Regina
> *Leader*, 12 May 1885

The Rose of a Nation's Thanks

A welcome? Oh, yes, 'tis a kindly word, but why will they plan and prate
Of feasting and speeches and such small things, while the wives and
    mothers wait?
Plan as ye will, and do as ye will, but think of the hunger and thirst

In the hearts that wait; and do as ye will, but lend us our laddies first!
Why, what would ye have? There is not a lad that treads in the gallant
    ranks
Who does not already bear on his breast the Rose of a Nation's Thanks!

A welcome? Why, what do you mean by that, when the very stones must
    sing
As our men march over them home again; the walls of the city ring
With the thunder of throats and the tramp and tread of feet that rush
    and run? –
I think in my heart that the very trees must shout for the bold work done!
Why, what would ye have? There is not a lad that treads in the gallant
    ranks
Who does not already bear on his breast the Rose of a Nation's Thanks!

A welcome? There is not a babe at the breast won't spring at the roll of
    the drum
That heralds them home – the keen, long cry in the air of "They come!
    They come!"
And what of it all if ye bade them wade knee-deep in a wave of wine,
And tossed tall torches, and arched the town in garlands of maple and
    pine?
All dust in the wind of a woman's cry as she snatches from the ranks
Her boy who bears on his bold young breast the Rose of a Nation's
    Thanks!

A welcome? There's a doubt if the lads would stand like stone in their
    steady line
When a babe held high on a dear wife's hand or the alarm that swim
    and shine
In a sweetheart's eyes, or a mother's smile, flashed far in the welded
    crowd,
Or a father's proud voice, half-sob and half-cheer, cried on a son aloud.
O the billows of waiting hearts that swelled would sweep from the mar-
    tial ranks
The gallant boys who bear on their breasts the Rose of a Nation's
    Thanks!

A welcome? O Joy, can they stay your feet, or measure the wine of your
    bliss?

O Joy, let them have you alone to-day – a day with a pulse like this!
A welcome? Yes, 'tis a tender thought, a green laurel that laps the sword –
But Joy has the wing of a wild white swan, and the song of a free wild
    bird!
She must beat the air with her wing at will, at will must her song be
    driven
From her heaving heart and tremulous throat through the awful arch of
    heaven.
And what would ye have? There isn't a lad will burst from the shouting
    ranks
But bears like a star on his faded coat the Rose of a Nation's Thanks!

Isabella Valancy Crawford

"The Rose of a Nation's Thanks" is perhaps the best known of these patriotic poems. It first appeared in the Toronto *Telegram* on 11 June 1885.[33] "To One of the Absent," written by "Cleomatis," carried a tribute to the heroic men who had defended and saved imprisoned women:

With your men you went cheerful and willing,
To defend and take peace to the poor
Helpless children and sad prisoned women
Who had homes on Saskatchewan's shore,
And now I'm so proud of you darling
I can worship a hero so brave,
While I pray for your safe home returning;
When the peace flag shall quietly wave.[34]

THE BOOK *TWO MONTHS IN THE CAMP OF BIG BEAR: THE LIFE AND ADVENTURES OF THERESA GOWANLOCK AND THERESA DELANEY*

When the two widows walked down the gangway of the steamer *Alberta* they were met by Andrew Gowanlock of Parkdale, Theresa's brother-in-law, who accompanied them to Toronto.[35] It was Gowanlock's newspaper company that published the book *Two Months* in short order. Almost from the time of their taking leave of the Cree, the two women had been approached by agents, bureaus, and even ministers "to take the lecture platform," and

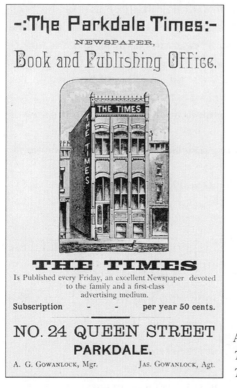

Advertisement for the Parkdale *Times* (Gowanlock and Delaney, *Two Months*, 139)

before leaving Moose Jaw on her way home, Mrs Gowanlock had received a letter from a Brantford clerical gentleman "asking for the 'first chance' of a lecture by her, he so strongly 'sympathized' with her afflictions."[36]

According to some descendants of Mrs Delaney's family, she was pressured into preparing her account by the Gowanlock family, and both women were reluctant to criticize government actions or policies for fear of jeopardizing their chance of receiving a government pension.[37] Having lost their husbands and their living, the women may have hoped to earn money from the book, but there is no evidence that either ever took to the lecture circuit. It seems that they continually refused, as one reporter wrote, "to parade themselves thus before the public to ostentatiously speculate on the death of their husbands and their own woes."[38] The women probably had a very personal reason for wishing to publish the account; the rumours that had circulated about their suffering "the fate

worse than death" would have made it difficult for them to function socially on their return to central Canada, since they would
have been viewed as "tainted." In the introduction to her section of
the book, Theresa Gowanlock states that she wrote it in order to
correct the false impressions of what had happened to her and also
as a debt of gratitude to the brave men who had sacrificed their
business and comfort, as well as to the women who had planned
their comfort and supplied the wants of the gallant men who "no-
bly responded to the call of duty and cry for help."[39] As a publisher,
Andrew Gowanlock may have urged the women to produce it
quickly, for he could expect to profit from a book that detailed the
experiences of the women who had captivated the nation that year.

As mentioned earlier, the story presented in *Two Months* differs in
significant respects from some of the statements the women made
immediately on their release from detention. In *Two Months*
Delaney and Gowanlock have become the classic victims of the classic captivity narrative. They are represented as reluctant narrators,
as not "aspiring to literary excellence" but promising a truthful and
accurate rendition. They move from a state of blissful contentment
to one of inconceivable horror at the hands of "savages" before
they are rescued, released from wild adventure, and returned to
calm security; the "savages" are stock characters, infernal and not
human beings; and there are continual reminders of the threat of
sexual violation.

The narrative of Eliza Fraser, written nearly fifty years earlier and
about another continent, exhibits remarkably similar conventions.
Fraser promises a "plain, unvarnished tale; exaggerating nothing,
but recording truly and faithfully the particulars."[40] Delaney
promises "the simple truth: nothing added hereto; nothing taken
therefrom" (128)[41] Eliza's melodramatic statement, "Alas, it is impossible to reflect on what I endured ... to imagine the shock of
horrors to come ... The reader cannot have any idea of the horrors I suffered,"[42] is echoed in Delaney's declaration, "But I could
never describe all the miseries I suffered during those few
weeks ... There is no possibility of giving an idea of our sufferings"
(118–19). Gowanlock's section of *Two Months* concludes with a
"panoramic view of the whole" from the security of the paternal
home. Readers are reminded of the beauty, peace, and contentment of the industrious little community of Frog Lake and of how
this little hamlet was entered and its domestic quietness destroyed.

Particular incidents of shameful and brutal treatment are singled out for final emphasis. Delaney's section concludes with patriotic words and the hope that future generations will not forget the troubles and sacrifices of 1885 and the people who helped build a great and solid nation.

Two Months is squarely within the "frail flower" mould in that it emphasizes the "untold suffering and privations" the women experienced at the hands of "savages" as they wandered amid the "snow and ice of that trackless prairie." (While there may have been some snow and ice at the outset, it could not have lasted the whole period; after all, this was April, May, and June.) The women do not cope; they are prostrated by their bereavement, by fatigue, exposure, and "the constant dread of outrage and death" (5). Mrs Delaney wrote: "There is no possibility of giving an idea of our sufferings. The physical pains, exposures, dangers, colds, heats, sleepless nights, long marches, scant food, poor raiment" (119). This impression of suffering, frailty, and incapacity was not the feeling they conveyed to the several correspondents on the scene at the time of their escape. Moreover, *Two Months* does not mention that the two women never had to walk and that they rode in a wagon; the impression given is one of difficult travel on foot through mud and water, with thin shoes, while "the Indians were riding beside us with our horses and buckboards, laughing at us with umbrellas over their heads and buffalo overcoats on" (33).

In *Two Months* John Pritchard is praised by both women, especially Mrs Delaney, for his role in saving her "from inhuman treatment, and even worse than a hundred deaths" (117). She does, however, suggest that on the morning of 2 April at Frog Lake, Pritchard was involved with Big Bear's son Ayimasis in the theft of horses from the Indian agency, a theft that had helped to incapacitate the white settlers at Frog Lake (110–11). There is more than a hint throughout that the Pritchards were not entirely trustworthy. The morning they were found by scouts, Mrs Pritchard is described as saying, "with unfeigned disgust, 'that the police were coming'" (52), clearly drawing into question the idea that the Pritchards were ever truly captives. Both Mrs Delaney and Mrs Gowanlock stressed that even with Pritchard's protection they were not safe and never knew what moment might be their last. The heroism of Pritchard was further diminished by other details. For instance, although he had built pits to protect them from gunfire at Frenchman Butte, Mrs Gowanlock wrote that she would have preferred to keep out in the open in the hope of being rescued (46). She also stated twice in the book that she had saved herself from a fate worse than death by persuading Pritchard's young daughter to find her father to come to her assistance. Similarly, although the women had initially told reporters that they had not been forced to do any work, the Pritchards are depicted in the book as wanting "to work us to death" (36). The women state that they had to bake, cut wood, carry water, and sew for the nine children with fabric and clothing which originally came from their own homes: "Not work enough, after walking or working all day, after dark we were required to bake bannock and do anything else they had a mind to give us" (36). Moreover, the food they were supposed to eat disgusted them. Mrs Gowanlock described seeing a rabbit boiling in a pot, complete with its head, eyes, and feet, a sight that robbed her of any appetite (35).

Gregory Donaire and Pierre Blondin are two Métis who are especially vilified in *Two Months*, despite that fact that the women had initially voiced their appreciation for Blondin in particular. Mrs Gowanlock included an elaborate story of Blondin's premeditated plan to acquire her as well as all the Gownanlock possessions. At the beginning of the massacre, she claimed, Blondin had gone to their house to gather up the furniture and other goods: "The wretch was there with evil intent in his heart ... Why did he go down to our house when that dreadful affair was going on? Why did he help himself to our goods? Oh! God I saw it all. He had everything arranged for me to live with him. All my husband's things; all my things; and a tent" (60). Despite the fact that Mrs Gowanlock told reporters that she had not been acquainted with any of the Métis except the Pritchards before her captivity, Blondin and Donaire are described as having been employees at the Gowanlock mill since mid-March 1885: "They were continually going too and fro among the Indians, and I cannot but believe, that they were cognizant of everything that was going on, if not responsible in a great degree for the murders which were afterwards committed" (19). Mrs Gowanlock also stated that she had a great aversion for André Nault, another Métis (50).

In each of the narratives, the description of the days before 2 April focus on the fertility and potential of the land, the women's domestic happiness, the sterling qualities of their husbands, the peaceful tranquillity of Frog Lake, and the placid contentment of the local Aboriginal population. In short, the settlement is presented as an industrious little community in which the people were "living in the bonds of friendship with all mankind" (58). A drawing of Frog Lake, clearly done by an artist unacquainted with the terrain, depicts an idyllic setting reminiscent of the English countryside. Captivity narratives typically begin with deliberately ornamental diction for the purpose of establishing a contrast to the horrors that follow. As an example of this, Richard Van Der Beets cites Fanny Kelly's descriptions of berries and flowers and of beautiful scenery that "filled our hearts with joy."[43] Such descriptions clearly suggest that this fertile territory should be in the possession of people who would transform it into cultivated fields dotted with houses. True to the tradition, Mrs Gowanlock described her home as follows: "There they nestle in a pretty valley, the simple house, the store, and beside the brook, the mill. The music of the workman's hammer alone breaks the stillness that pervades the scene, and the hills send back the echo without a discordant note. The hills were covered with trees, principally poplar and spruce, interspersed with berry-bearing shrubs. A most beautiful and enchanting location" (17). But Theresa Gowanlock had arrived at Frog Creek in December and had left forever in April, so she only ever saw her beautiful oasis when it was covered with snow or was looking drab and brown.

In her section of the book, Mrs Delaney emphasized that Aboriginal people were treated with generosity and kindness by the government (a marked contrast to her earlier statements). She wrote, "There is one thing I do know and most emphatically desire to express and have thoroughly understood and that is the fact, *the Indians have no grievances and no complaints to make*" (100). The government, according to her, had spared no effort to make the Aboriginal people adopt an agricultural way of life. She said that reserve farmers had many advantages over the English, Scottish, and Irish settlers who were striving to take up a farm for themselves; they never went hungry. Mrs Delaney also insisted that her husband had been respected and beloved by all. Evil-minded people, she said, had instilled into excitable heads the false idea that the Indians had been persecuted by the government (101). The true villain in Mrs Delaney's account was the Hudson's Bay Company, whose interests were completely at odds with those of the government. While the government wished to enlighten and civilize, the company wished to keep Aboriginal people in a state of "savagery." According the Mrs Delaney, the HBC did not wish to see Indians farming, because the company then acquired less fur. Nor did the HBC favour rationing, for it meant that the company could sell fewer goods. She said that even war paint and feathers could be acquired from the HBC posts. In short, she claimed that rebellion served the interests of the HBC (102).

Much of *Two Months* dwells on the description of Aboriginal people as "vicious, treacherous and superstitious" (37), "childlike and simple," and "murderers of defenceless settlers, the despoilers of happy homes, the polluters of poor women and children" (43). However, both women made distinctions between the Woods and Plains Cree, the former being described as quiet and industrious while the latter were idle, worthless, and cruel. Mrs Gowanlock's account contains many passages that rail against those who had a romantic idea of the noble savage: "It might sound musical in the ears of the poet to write of the virtues of that race, but I consider it a perversion of the real facts. During the time I was with them I could not see anything noble in them, unless it was that the were *noble* murderers, *noble* cowards, *noble* thieves" (43). In a chapter entitled "Indian Boys," she wrote that they were wild and untamed, full of mischief and cruelty, with nothing in their character that could be called love. Their behaviour was intolerable, their morality in a very low state. Similarly, in Mrs Delaney's account there are passages that describe the Indians as demons, "beings not human, but infernal" (120). Any union with such beings was depicted as an abomination. Her descriptions of the fearful appearance of Indians preparing for war served to enhance the bravery and courage of the conquering heroes. "When one sees, for the first time, these horrid creatures, wild, savage, mad, whether in that war-dance or to go on the war-path, it is sufficient to make the blood run cold, to chill the senses, to unnerve the stoutest arm and strike terror into the bravest heart" (115).

There is particular focus in *Two Months* on the mistreatment of Aboriginal women within their own society and on their poor skills as mothers, homemakers, and cooks. Readers were invited to share the distaste for a society in which women acted this way and were treated in this manner. The "tenderly reared" widows appear in sharp relief to these unfortunate creatures. Mrs Gowanlock's first pages are devoted to the theme of how Aboriginal women func-

"War Dance." *Two Months in the Camp of Big Bear* contained vivid
descriptions of the fearful appearance of Indians preparing for war,
though it is unlikely that either woman ever saw a "war dance."
(Gowanlock and Delaney, *Two Months*, 78, Glenbow Archives, NA-3988-4)

tioned as "beasts of burden" (which is the caption beneath a sketch
of a woman carrying wood on her back). They were said to do all
the work and to suffer beatings from their husbands. Many passages describe their deficient mothering skills. Although Theresa
Gowanlock described herself as weak and only half-conscious when
she was first taken captive and shoved into a teepee, she was able to
give a detailed description of a baby she saw and thought was dead
because it had been left alone in a corner and was wrapped up in a
moss bag (27). Similarly, the little Quinn girl is described as being
badly cared for, wearing nothing but a thin print dress and with
bare feet: "She would stay with us until her mother would come
and take her away … How I did feel for her, she was such a bright
little girl, her father when alive took care of her. It was very hard to
see her going around like any of the Indian children" (37). That
Jane Quinn also had been widowed by the events at Frog Lake and
was deserving of sympathy was overlooked. Once or twice there was
mention of "friendly squaws" who threw them a blanket or offered
to feed them some distasteful item, but the book leaves an overwhelmingly negative impression of the abilities and treatment of
Aboriginal women.

This drawing was entitled "On the Line of March – Illustrating the Noble Red Man's Idea of a Fair Division of Labour." The image of the degraded position of Indian women was a standard cliché and one that was industriously circulated in 1885. The dog was a common feature of these illustrations, which provided a startling contrast to the frail and rarified ideal of white womanhood. (*Canadian Pictorial and Illustrated War News*, souvenir edn, sketch by W.D. Blatchley, Glenbow Archives, NA-1353-26)

BEASTS OF BURDEN.

Two Months in the Camp of Big Bear paints a bleak picture of the life of the Indian woman. Readers were drawn to the conclusion that white women enjoyed a much more elevated status. (Gowanlock and Delaney, *Two Months*, 13)

There are various inconsistencies and improbabilities in *Two Months* which suggest that the story was altered for dramatic and other purposes. In the first place, it is unlikely that some of the events described were actually seen by the widows. For example, Mrs Gowanlock wrote that during the first two days after the murder, the bodies of the men were lying on the road exposed to the view of everyone: "It was dreadful to see the bodies of our *poor dear* husbands dragged back and forth by those demoniac savages" (30). She returned to the subject at the end of her narrative, adding greater detail about the desecration of their husbands' bodies: "Not content with murdering them in cold blood, they must needs perform diabolical deeds which causes me to shudder when I think of it. They danced around them with demoniac glee, kicking and pulling them in every direction, and we were the unwilling witnesses of such behaviour" (61). However, it is unlikely that either woman witnessed any such behaviour. Mrs Delaney specifically said in one of her first statements that after she was pulled away from the scene of the deaths she had no opportunity of returning to her dead husband and had "never seen him since."[44] The campsite to which the women were taken was some distance from the Frog Lake settlement, and they spent about three weeks there before moving on towards Frenchman Butte (30).[45] Another discrepancy is that although the women did not understand Cree, the words and conversations of the Cree are detailed in several passages in the book. Also, Mrs Gowanlock described seeing one of the McLean girls carrying her little sister over a large creek in water up to her waist; but according to McLean family accounts, this event took place towards Loon Lake after the two widows had parted company from the Cree.

It is not too far-fetched to suspect that at least parts of *Two Months* – Mrs Delaney's account in particular – received the attentions of a ghostwriter, though it is certainly possible that she may have written the whole section herself; her conversation was described by one of the correspondents as indicating an "active mind,"[46] and when her possessions at Frog Lake were itemized by her family after her death, books worth fifteen dollars were listed.[47] Nevertheless, the abundant literary references and rhetorical flourishes that characterize Mrs Delaney's section of the book, combined with her apparent reluctance to write at all, suggest that some assistance was given to augment an otherwise skeletal account. To add to the sparse details about her life before her marriage, for example, a lengthy passage expands on the loss through death of her father and brother, foreshadowing the loss of her protective husband: "Had it not been for these two events [the deaths of father and brother] I might drop a veil over all the past and consider merely that I had lived through such a number of years: – these years, like the great desert of the east, would stretch back, an unbroken tract, with no object to break the monotony of the scene. But, as the kirches, tombs or monuments of Arabia, rise up in solemn grandeur from out the loneliness of the plain, casting their shadows on the sandy waste, so these two monuments or tombs appear upon the level scene of my uneventful past" (85).

The literary passages are wide ranging. Referring to the use of smoke signals among the Cree, Mrs Delaney wrote: "Like the *phares* that flashed the alarm from hill-top to hill-top, or the tocsin that sang from belfry to belfry in the Basse Bretagne, in the days of the rising of the Vendée, so those beacons would communicate" (122). In describing the land around the Qu'Appelle River Valley, she remarked that the scenery would "demand the pencil of a Claude Lorraine, or the pen of a Washington Irving to do it justice" (92). Touching on the topic of the priests at Frog Lake, she wrote, "Even there in the far west ... we have what Sir Alexander Selkirk mourned for so much, when alone on Juan Fernandez – *Religion*" (98). Lengthy quotations from Milton, Father Abram J. Ryan, "the Poet Priest of the South," Thomas A. Kempis [*sic*], John Whittier, anonymous Canadian poets, and Philip Freneau flesh out the text. In her final reflections on the troubles, she remarked that they had "proven that our country possesses the means, the strength, the energy and stamina, to crush the hydra of disunion or rebellion, no matter where it may appear. For like the upas tree, if it is permitted to take root and grow, its proportions would soon become alarming, while its poisonous influence would pollute the atmosphere with misery, ruin, rapine and death" (129). A clue that Mrs Delaney may have received some assistance with her narrative may be found in the following declaration: "As I was never destined to be an authoress and my powers of composition were dealt out to me with a sparing hand, I can but express my regret that an abler writer does not hold my pen" (88).

Some American captivity narratives were known to have been written with the assistance of ghostwriters.[48] One of the more famous, *Narrative of the Life of Mrs. Mary Jemison*, was written by

James E. Seaver, who did a series of interviews with Mrs Jemison when she was eighty years of age. She was a woman of little formal education and at the time of her interviews could remember the name of only some of the letters of the alphabet, yet Seaver put some very flowery speeches into her mouth, as when describing why her parents had come to the United States: "The intestine divisions, civil wars, and ecclesiastical rigidity and domination that prevailed in those days, were the causes of [my parents] leaving their mother country."[49] Journalistic assistance with the writing of a book was part of the publishing scene in Canada as well. The author of another quickly produced book of 1885, Charles Pelham Mulvaney, noted on his title page that his *History of the North-West Rebellion of 1885* had been "assisted by a well-known journalist," though the journalist was not named.[50] Mrs Gowanlock and Mrs Delaney were certainly acquainted with several of the many journalists who were on the scene in 1885. The Toronto *Mail* correspondent George Ham participated in the rescue of the captives, and he was with the group that first encountered the McLean family when they parted company with the Cree.[51] Years later, Ham wrote that this experience reminded him of the Beadle's Dime Novels he had read as a boy, in which "a lovely heroine ... was captured by Indians and rescued by a gallant, brave and loving hero, after no end of miraculous escapes, in which he did many unheard-of feats." "The romantic days of fiction had passed," Ham wrote. "But one fine June morning at Fort Pitt, I found they hadn't."[52] On their return journey to eastern Canada, Mrs Gowanlock and Mrs Delaney were accompanied by William Baillie of the Toronto *Globe* and William W. Fox of the *Mail*,[53] and it is possible that one of these journalists assisted in the writing of *Two Months*.

CONSTRAINTS, PRESSURES, AND *TWO MONTHS*

A recent analysis by Sara Mills of women's travel writing from the period of high British imperialism in the late nineteenth century can help us understand why *Two Months* appeared in its particular form, with its content and emphasis varying so much from the authors' initial statements. According to Mills, there were numerous constraints that determined the way English women writers presented their experience of travel in foreign lands. What a woman author could say was governed by literary conventions, by the type of language she could use, and by the experiences she could describe. The texts were produced through the interaction of a variety of constraining factors and should not be understood as originating solely from the author or from "reality." These texts cannot therefore be read as straightforward accounts of journeys to other lands. Mills draws on the systems of discursive rules as seen by Michel Foucault in *The Archaeology of Knowledge*. In Foucault's terms, "rules of formation" allow certain things to be described, and "what happened," "what was seen to happen," and "what was written" are entirely dependent on these rules.[54] Mills argues that "writing is constrained by a variety of factors; that is texts are produced in situations where there are numerous textual, economic, social, political, historical and personal forces at work which impinge on the writing process."[55]

Travel writing of the nineteenth century had its own distinctive characteristics and conventions. The various works had similar textual features, narrative incidents, and descriptions. There were conventions, for instance, about the kind of information that could be included. Mills writes that "there are numerous incidents which are frequently included in travel narratives, and thus seem to form part of genre expectations."[56] One of these, as Mary Louise Pratt has pointed out, was the narrator imagining the scene peopled by the British, emptying the landscape of its indigenous inhabitants, and imposing British order.[57] Travel writing was also limited by colonial textual constraints. An authoritative body of texts, literary and non-literary, written by westerners about the people of "foreign lands" constituted a "colonial discourse" that posed as telling the truth about another country and its inhabitants. Although these texts did not always present a unified vision, in general they served to objectify the inhabitants of colonized countries and in the process affirmed Britain in its colonial position. There were conventional ways of describing the people of other nations, and there were conventional ways of describing English women in colonial settings – they were featured as objects of purity, symbols of domesticity. Women's travel writing was also constrained by discourses of femininity that set out for middle-class white women a limited range of roles; as weak and frail symbols of home and purity, they required male protectors, for they were unable to fend for themselves. Male narrators and travellers conventionally adopted a heroic, adventuring stance in which they appeared to be the master of all situations.

This heroic stance was not available to women writers. Women wrote as gendered individuals with clearly delineated roles in accordance with discursive rules and gender expectations. They were advised to exclude certain material, avoid certain subjects.

A wide variety of pressures and constraints helped determine the form and content of *Two Months*. In the first place, there were conventional ways of writing about Indian captivity. In the nineteenth century the experience of Indian captivity was to be understood as a savage and inexplicable brutality against innocent, virtuous people. Certain plot and narrative structures, incidents, and descriptions appeared with predictable frequency. Happy and contented settlers were ruthlessly torn from the sacred precincts of hearth and home, dragged through the wilderness, and made to suffer indignities, cruelty, and privation before returning to the sanctity of their own civilization. Certain features were included so regularly in captivity narratives that it appears that, as with travel writing, there were certain genre expectations. There were the conventional descriptions of the Indians, the men being depicted as wild, savage, villainous, and brutal, while the women were overworked drudges. Similarly, convention dictated that the white female protagonists be portrayed as delicate and domestic symbols of purity and home, defenceless and powerless without protective white males.

In writing their book – whether or not it was with the assistance of ghostwriters – Mrs Delaney and Mrs Gowanlock thus had to accord with literary conventions, a discourse of femininity, and a colonial discourse, all of which influenced the way their text was produced. There were also economic, political, and personal pressures, which are evident in the way their story was altered for and by them even before they set pen to paper. A Métis such as Pritchard could not receive unqualified praise as the heroic protector of the women. The role of heroic protectors had to be reserved for the soldiers, police, and other white males. Criticism of government administration had to be eliminated in favour of praise for the benevolence and altruism of the government's policy and agents. As widows in need of pensions and of compensation for "rebellion losses" from this same government, the two women were obliged to speak favourably while emphasizing how helpless they were without their providers and protectors.

It was perhaps not entirely fortuitous that the November 1885 release of *Two Months* coincided with the hanging of Riel in Regina

A carefully composed photograph by O.B. Buell, taken at the time of
the 1885 trials in Regina. The photograph conveyed the message of a
restoration of law and order, of the victors and the vanquished,
the past and the future. The hands of the priests are clearly posed to
rest on the shoulders of Big Bear and Poundmaker, though neither
was a convert to Christianity. The chiefs did not want the photograph
taken and were given pipes as an inducement to sit for it.
Back row, left to right: NWMP Constable Blache, Father Louis Cochin,
NWMP Superintendent Burton Deane, Father Alexis André,
prosecutor Christopher Robinson; *front row, left to right:* Horse Child
(son of Big Bear), Big Bear, Hamilton police chief Alex Stewart,
Poundmaker (Glenbow Archives, NA-3205-11)

(15 November) and of the eight males at Battleford (27 November),
among whom were those found guilty of the Frog Lake murders.
The perspective presented in the two women's accounts would have
helped steel resolve that this public spectacle of repression of indigenous people was the best and most obvious course. Public opinion
was divided on the hanging not only of Riel but also of the eight
Cree. In the editorials of several of the eastern newspapers, the
wholesale execution of eight people was condemned as a sight un-
worthy of a civilized nation and as carrying bloodthirstiness too far
when there had been enough blood shed already.[58] The *Montreal
Herald* called for the hangings to be postponed indefinitely in favour
of life imprisonment, stating that "the proposal to give the public an

exhibition of wholesale hanging is terribly repulsive to all humane persons and recalls the hanging matches which once disgraced Ireland and the deeds of Claverhouse in Scotland."[59] One paper noted that in the case of Wandering Spirit, there had been no "mention of an appeal to the privy council, or a suspension of execution pending an appeal. Wandering Spirit is a pure-bred Indian. He has not the talisman of a little French blood."[60] By being released just at this time and serialized in papers such as the *Huron Expositor, Two Months* kept the issue of Frog Lake and indignities to white women before the reading public.

THE PUBLICATIONS OF THE McLEAN SISTERS

In 1946 and 1947 Elizabeth (Eliza) McLean published in the *Beaver* three instalments of her memories of the events of 1885, as told to Constance James (though she did not live to see the last two instalments in print, for she died in April 1947).[61] Her account of the events of 1885, when she was sixteen, is remarkably different in tone, content, and form from that presented in *Two Months*. There are many reasons for this. In the first place, the events of those months were not as unusual, wrenching, or melancholy for the McLeans as they were for the "fair daughters of Ontario" who had been transplanted briefly to the West. The McLeans had been born in the West. Their childhood home was on the prairies at Fort Qu'Appelle and Fort Pitt. They enjoyed riding and shooting, they spoke Cree and Saulteaux, and were playmates of Indian children. Their mother also had been born in the West, and she was partly of Aboriginal ancestry. The oldest McLean girls were teenagers in 1885 and thus had a youthful resilience to the hardships of those months with the Cree, which several of them described as a grand adventure. During the affair, they displayed bravery, resourcefulness, stamina, independence, and shooting skills. Girls who had taken turns at sentry duty could not easily conform to expectations of women as weak, vulnerable, and passive. Moreover, their status as prisoners was ambiguous; their father had opted for the protection of this group of Cree, rather than travelling to Fort Battleford to take refuge within the stockade with the other white people of the district. Finally, the McLeans were representatives of the Hudson's Bay Company, and the government attributed responsibility for discontent to the influence of that company. Perhaps it was for all

Eliza McLean at the ruins of Fort Ellice
(Western Canada Pictorial Index, 0248-07921)

these reasons that the story of the McLean family and their months
with the Cree was not immediately seized on by a publisher or journalist. Their experience could not easily be conformed to meet the
needs of the hour. Although the story of the McLeans did receive
some attention in 1885, it was by no means the same sort of attention as that bestowed on the two widows. However, we can use it today to illustrate that in 1885 there were people who were more
sympathetic towards the Métis and Aboriginal people.

There is one further reason that may explain why Elizabeth
McLean's account is so different from that contained in *Two
Months*. She was recording the events more than sixty years after
they had occurred, so she may have forgotten some of the hardships and perils. Yet what is clearly evident in comparing *Two
Months* with her account, and what must in part explain the difference, is that they are products of different ages and of different
constraints, frameworks, and pressures. There were not the same
sort of pressures and expectations on the production and reception of Elizabeth McLean's memoirs in the late 1940s – probably
not even much interest. In reading them, you become aware of the

stultified, mannered, and manufactured nature of *Two Months*, produced by women who had to negotiate complex constraints. As
their initial statements to correspondents suggest, Mrs Gowanlock
and Mrs Delaney might well have given different opinions, a different account of events, and different descriptions of their experience if they had not had to contend with these pressures and
constraints.

Elizabeth McLean explained that there was unrest in the Frog
Lake district in the winter and spring of 1885 because of dissatisfac-
tion with the treatment given by Indian agent Quinn.[62] Captain
Francis Dickens of the NWMP is presented as ineffectual and indeci-
sive, a man who had little understanding of the Indians or their tac-
tics. His inexplicable decisions caused the death and injury of his
own men. Elizabeth McLean described the routine of the two
weeks at sentry duty, including how to "fix" the sight of a rifle, and
she noted that the Cree had great respect for her father and her
mother. Her mother had a reputation for assisting people with
home remedies. The Cree also admired the courage and "nerve" of
the McLean sisters who walked directly into the camp at Fort Pitt
uninvited to learn how their father was.

Elizabeth does not try to disguise the fact that there were moments when they felt they were in great danger, for there were a few
"hotheads" who were not easy for anyone to control. Yet she and
her sisters knew how to deal with such situations verbally, displaying
courage and defiance. Amelia, for example, demanded that Lone
Man return her hat, which she had caught sight of in his hands:
"'No one shall ever wear this hat! It belongs to me!' she declared
emphatically; and with that she tore it up and threw the pieces in
the fire."[63] Individuals such as Wandering Spirit appear not as stock
villains but as men racked by remorse over their actions. His hair
turned from jet black to grey and then white during these weeks,
and he was anxious to know how the Christian God would punish
him. He was so sad and dejected that Mrs McLean took pity on him
and he "was accepted as one of our camp."[64]

There were many trusted friends and protectors among the Cree
as well as the Saulteaux. Overall, McLean's descriptions of camp
life stressed the kindness of individuals, especially the Aboriginal
women, who did what they could to make them comfortable. A sort
of "protective society" was formed by the Indian women to "save us
girls from the chance of being carried away by any of the young

braves."[65] Various ruses, disguises, and movements to other tents were used to ensure that the McLean girls were not harmed. There were of course hardships, such as crossing a muskeg, when the older McLeans carried the younger on their shoulders and feared they would slip into the muddy quagmire. There is, however, not the same general description of trackless prairie covered by snow and ice as that found in *Two Months*. Eliza remembered that they often enjoyed walking in the lovely spring weather. The shots fired by Captain Steele at Loon Lake endangered them, as did the death of five Indians from this gunfire, for there was then talk of revenge against the white prisoners. During this time of apprehension, the McLeans were protected by the Wood Crees, as Eliza recalled: "I remember wondering if Manoomin were really standing guard at the back of the tent as arranged. As the moon rose, I saw the shadow of his head and shoulder gradually come into view. He was leaning on his rifle, perfectly still. I felt so relieved and grateful that we had such a faithful friend. Then I wondered if Louison were still standing at the front. When the moon was at its height it was as bright as day. Then, as it gradually went down, I saw the full silhouette of Louison, a silent sentinel and a trusted friend."[66]

When the McLeans were set free, some of the women gave them moccasins and four pounds of bacon: "These they handed to my mother with their best wishes."[67] They also provided the family with a guide who knew the country well. Back at Loon Lake, a "widow woman" told them where two canoes were hidden, as well as where a cache of flour and bacon could be found. It was shortly after this that they encountered a scout employed by Major S. Bedson, the children's uncle, and teams and ambulance were sent for to accompany them back to Fort Pitt. It is a curious feature of Elizabeth McLean's memoirs that Mrs Gowanlock and Mrs Delaney are not mentioned at all, nor is there any reference to their account of these same events.

Elizabeth was the only McLean sister to leave a detailed description of these weeks with the Cree camp, but in 1935 Kitty McLean Yuill gave a fifteen-minute talk to the North-West Field Force Association, which had gathered in Toronto on the fiftieth anniversary of 1885.[68] Kitty focused on the crossing of the big muskeg at Loon Lake, which was the most difficult part of their journey. The mile-wide muskeg had blocked the further passage of the field force, which had turned back there. The muskeg remained a sensitive

The 65th Mount Royal Rifles navigating the muskeg in pursuit of Big Bear
(Glenbow Archives, NA-1480-28)

and controversial subject. Middleton, with almost four hundred men – horse, foot, and artillery – had decided on 7 June 1885 that it was impassable; he had sunk in it up to his horse's girth. His decision seemed ridiculous to others, including NWMP Superintendent Sam Steele, who had been able to pursue Big Bear with only fifty mounted men. In his memoirs, Steele wrote that it was absurd to say that the muskeg was impassable "in the face of the fact that delicate women and children had been able to traverse it a few days previously."[69]

Nevertheless, crossing the swamp had been a four-hour ordeal for the McLeans, and Kitty described it in detail, wishing to assure her audience of veterans that the muskeg would indeed have been impassable for their heavy horses and gun carriages. Like her sister, Kitty recalled that some of their captors had behaved in a menacing or annoying manner, and she too had defied her tormentors. When five Indian men sneered at their exhaustion after crossing the muskeg, Kitty

just "saw red," and swinging the rogan from my back, I turned on them drawing my knife and saying "Oh you cowards, you cowards! You are such 'brave old women' that you had to take even the little pen-knives from the white men at Frog Lake before you stood them in a row and shot them down! Death is too good for you. If I could only have your bare hearts so that I could stab, and stab, and stab, and stab! – little short quick stabs!" – (and I gestured stabbing into the air), "so that you would feel what we are suffering, until you were dead! Dead!" There was a pause. Some said, "Kill her, shoot her," but one said, "Oh, but these people are brave!" And stepping forward he continued, "What have you in your rogan, Little Sister, food? Come, we will build a fire and you cook something for your sister and make tea, and feed her and she will revive."[70]

Like her sister, Kitty had kind words for the people in the Cree camp who had been of great assistance to them. A young man, for example, came to the aid of Helen McLean in the muskeg, jumping off his horse right into the muddy water, not giving a thought to his beautiful beaded moccasins, leggings, and fine coat: "He lifted mother on to his pony and he let her have it all the rest of the day, carefully leading it himself and often putting his hand up to support her."

The only other publications of Kitty McLean – excerpts from her journals and memoirs – focused on her childhood at Fort Qu'Appelle and their Saulteaux and Cree friends, and described how they came to learn about and respect Indian customs.[71] Her first "formal dance," for example, was a gift dance at the Saulteaux camp which she attended with Eloquent Voice, a daughter of Chief Pasquah. Her first dance partner was "a handsome hunter of the plains" who presented her with beads. Her father provided her with a large piece of Nigger Head Twist tobacco to offer in return as a gift. Kitty wrote, "In later years, I often thought of my first dance in the Qu'Appelle Valley, and my partner, that gentle hunter of the plains. How kind he was to ask me to dance. I sometimes wondered whether he remembered me as I remembered him on that wonderful day, or to paraphrase Kipling, did he say to himself, 'A white woman is only a woman but Nigger Head Twist is a smoke.'"[72]

Kitty's eldest sister, Amelia McLean Paget, published a book entitled *The People of the Plains* in 1909.[73] Amelia was living in Ottawa at the time and was married to an Indian Affairs bureaucrat, Frederick Paget. In 1906 she had received some government funding to travel west to the scenes of her childhood and the reserves of the Cree, Saulteaux, and Assiniboine to visit old friends and interview them concerning "their history, their wars, traditions, their early customs, folklore etc."[74] She required an interpreter only for her Assiniboine informants. Paget's manuscript was submitted to Duncan Campbell Scott, deputy superintendent of Indian Affairs (and poet). Paget was not further consulted about the publication. Scott edited the book and wrote the introduction, and it was he who corresponded with the publisher about the book's title, design, cover, and illustrations.[75] He also corrected the page proofs. Amelia Paget's original design for the cover was rejected, as was her title, which was in Cree or Saulteaux. (The publisher wrote, "I shy at that musical but formidable title. It looks like a deliberate attempt to provoke lockjaw.")[76]

The People of the Plains, despite Scott's editing, is a sympathetic portrait of plains life, in which Paget challenged conventional views. An example of this is her portrayal of the work of women, which she described as not particularly burdensome. Although they carried all the wood, this was not a great hardship, she explained; they used little fuel in summer, especially on the prairies where they used buffalo chips, and during the winter the fuel that women carried was of the lightest kind, and "they never overburdened themselves." Heavy logs were drawn by horses, and young men did all the chopping and cutting. Paget concluded this discussion with, "The popular idea of the poor Indian woman doing all the hard work has too often been overdrawn."[77]

Amelia Paget's portrait of plains life was so positive that, in his introduction to the book, Scott felt it necessary to provide a word of explanation. He gave some details of the author's background, which Paget had not mentioned in the text. He informed readers that the author and her family had been captured at Fort Pitt by Big Bear and his men and for a time had "shared all the hardships of his shifting camp." It was this experience, according to Scott, that accounted for her positive portrait of plains life: "During this experience Mrs. Paget's knowledge of the Cree language and her intimacy with all the ways of the Indians, even the very fashion of their thoughts, proved a constant defence for the whole party. The following pages must be read by the light of these facts; they account for the tone of championship for all Indians, and for the idealistic tendency which places everything in a high and favorable aspect. If there were hardship and squalor, starvation, inhumanity and superstition in this aboriginal life judged by European standards, here it is not evident."[78] Scott suggested that both the author and her informants had overlooked the "real felicities of the situation" and that their memory of the events had been "heightened by the glow which might be spread over the reminiscences of some ancient chief whose lines had been cast in pleasant places, and to whom everything in the old days had become transfigured." He described Amelia Paget as a "cordial advocate" rather than a "frigid critic" of the western tribes.

Although Scott felt it necessary to apologize to readers for the positive portrait of plains life, Amelia Paget was nonetheless allowed to publish as a cordial advocate and to do so under the auspices of the Department of Indian Affairs. By contrast, nearly a quarter of a century earlier, Theresa Delaney and Theresa Gowanlock had been required to be frigid critics. Of course, when Amelia and her sisters wrote, they were not under the same pressure to portray Native savagery and white female vulnerability. Views on the experience of Indian captivity had changed. Scott even ventured to suggest that the time spent with the Cree had provided Amelia with greater insight and sympathy, which might account for her idealistic championing of all Indians. Another reason why she was allowed to be a cordial advocate was that in 1909 the Aboriginal people of western Canada were no longer regarded as a threat. Indeed, they were viewed as a weak and waning race. The very inspiration for the book, according to Scott, was the idea that before long "the ancient manners and customs of the Crees and Saulteaux [will] have changed and become either a matter of conjecture or of vague recollection."[79]

As those in the dominant society looked back on the past, they regarded 1885 as the final triumph of civilization over savagery. An example of this can be found in a 1927 book by the Methodist missionary John Maclean, who described Poundmaker's surrender to General Middleton at Battleford.[80] Sixty or more Indians arrayed in paint, war costume, and "adorned with various garments worn by white ladies such as kid gloves and hats" faced the general and his assembled company of troops and civilians. "Civilization and savagery were in striking contrast," wrote Maclean, "a picturesque scene, never to be repeated on the Western plains, the last protest of the lords of the prairies, and the closing chapter of the history of the red man of the West as master."

When Mrs Delaney and Mrs Gowanlock produced their account, Canadians were not certain that such scenes would never be

repeated. It was therefore necessary to help "crush the hydra of disunion and rebellion," as Mrs Delaney apparently wrote. There was
certainly a great variety of pressures that influenced their text in
1885. Nor the least of these was the need to provide for their future
by securing a pension.

GOVERNMENT PENSIONS

Mrs Delaney and Mrs Gowanlock both received a government pension. By an order-in-council dated 14 November 1885, Mrs Delaney
was granted $400 per annum, which was paid until her death in
1913. She received the same as military widows whose husbands
had died on active service, half of the deceased's annual salary.[81] It
appears that Mrs Delaney lived in relative obscurity following her
ordeal. She moved to the Ottawa Valley and never married again.
One relative remembered her as a "broken woman" who supported
herself by various means, including teaching.[82] Another relative,
however, the father of editor and journalist Robert Fulford, gave a
very different picture and "spoke of her with affection, as the family's celebrity."[83] Anson A. Gard, author of *Pioneers of the Upper Ottawa*, encountered Mrs Delaney on his 1906 stroll along the Aylmer
Road, during which he stopped at all the historic farms.[84] He
found her sitting under the shade of the lawn trees, a pleasant-
spoken lady. It is difficult now to know how her story filtered
through to Gard – how much he understood and what he omitted
or simplified – but her story as he told it in his book did not contain a hint of bitterness or resentment. Mrs Delaney stated that she
and Mrs Gowanlock had suffered no indignity, and she described
the Cree as "friendly Indians."

Shortly after her death, members of Mrs Delaney's family, the
Fulford heirs to her estate, applied to the government for compensation for her loss of property during the rebellion, since they had
had to assist her "with money and in other ways."[85] This application
for compensation was denied, for the Commission on Rebellion
Losses had long since been dispersed. It is perhaps this denial that
a member of Mrs Delaney's family was recalling when she said that
the widow never received a pension.[86] The Delaney house at Frog
Lake, along with the other Indian agency buildings that were destroyed, were government property, and Mrs Delaney was not eligible for compensation from these losses.

Theresa Gowanlock back home in Ontario after 1885.
She is seated at centre. (Courtesy of Margaret Comfort,
from the collection of Ada Comfort)

Mrs Gowanlock, however, was allowed $907 from the Commission on Rebellion Losses, and she eventually also secured a pension of the same amount as Mrs Delaney, though this was not granted until May 1888.[87] Mr Gowanlock had not been employed by the government, and for this reason her eligibility for a pension was in greater doubt. She died at the home of her parents in Tintern, Ontario, in September 1899.[88] It is very likely that both the women and their families had in mind their need for a pension (and, for Mrs Gowanlock, a rebellion losses claim) when they were writing *Two Months*. Even Mrs Delaney was not granted her pension until after this published version of the events appeared.

It is interesting to compare these pensions with that granted the widowed Jane Quinn, whose husband had held a government position superior to that of John Delaney. The Quinns had a child, while the other women did not, yet Jane Quinn was granted a mere twelve dollars a month "upon the understanding that she would lead a moral life."[89] This amount was not paid her after she left the Blood Reserve (where she had been living since 1885) and moved to Montana. On her return in 1912 she applied for her pension, and inquiries were duly made about whether she was leading a "moral life." When the chief of police at Fort Macleod reported that she was a "hard working woman with a good reputation in the district," her pension was resumed. Cheque no. 4540 for twelve dollars arrived at Macleod on the day Mrs Quinn died in January 1913.[90]

SKEWING THE STORY

In the months following the events in the North-West, grand panoramic paintings of the major confrontations were reproduced in colour and widely distributed throughout Canada and Britain. Although they were loosely based on the sketches of soldiers who saw action, they skewed both the landscape and the position of the combatants.[91] The North-West Field Force was consistently shown as decisive and orderly, which was far from the case, and the enemy was depicted mainly as "savage Indians" rather than as Métis whose dress was more Euro-Canadian. These visual images were carefully altered to support the ideology, cultural values, and artistic style of the dominant society, just as the original stories of Mrs Gowanlock and Mrs Delaney were altered to fit the existing stereotypes of women, Métis, and Aboriginal people.

To sustain the myth of savagery, the fact that the Cree had treated the two widows fairly well had to be suppressed, and Métis such as Pierre Blondin, who had originally been thanked for his kindness and generosity, had to be recast as sinister. Keeping the image of the "enemy" clear and uncluttered helped to support the legitimacy of using force and coercive measures. Similarly, the two women who had coped with their ordeal reasonably well had to be recast as vulnerable and frail. Their defencelessness was necessary for many reasons; it justified, among other things, heroic white male rescue as well as the hanging of Riel, who had to be made to "atone in some small degree for the terrible outrages perpetrated on defenceless women by his Indian allies."[92] It is not surprising that excerpts from *Two Months* were published in papers such as the *Toronto Daily Mail* two days after the news coverage of the hanging of the eight Cree at Battleford.[93] These excerpts featured the women's bereavement and defencelessness, and the hardships of their ordeal. The vulnerability of white women was essential to those who sought new prescriptions for securing white control in the West. The story presented in *Two Months* served to sanction not only the hangings, a public spectacle of repression, but also to sanction the series of repressive measures that were adopted after 1885 and were aimed at monitoring, controlling, and limiting the activities of Aboriginal people in the West.

THERESA GOWANLOCK'S LAST NARRATIVE?

In an October 1955 issue of the *Family Herald and Weekly Star,* a Montreal magazine for rural Canadians, an article appeared by the late Theresa Johnson Gowanlock entitled "Memories of Frog Lake."[94] In the editor's note, readers were informed that this "dramatic eye witness account of the Battle of Frog Lake in 1885" was written by Mrs Gowanlock and was left to her nephew, Arthur Johnson of Aldershot, Ontario. In the final paragraph the author wrote, "It is now thirteen years since that sunny April morning was suddenly engulfed by catastrophe," so it seems that the piece was written just one year before the death of Mrs Gowanlock in 1899. This article includes many new details, as well as some alterations to the version presented in *Two Months.* One detail missing from other accounts is that the Delaneys had a daughter, Nora, who became ill and died suddenly in March 1885. The article also states that there was "muttering of an outbreak" throughout that entire winter, whereas *Two Months* clearly conveyed the idea that there had been no discontent. As well, the article condemns John Pritchard unequivocally: "In his conniving way he was working for a bigger prize. If the Indians won the rebellion he could command a higher price for we two comely white women; while if the whites put down the rising they would pay him much more than the value of three Indian ponies and $30.00 for having 'protected' the widows of the two men. Another thought now presented, if the women killed themselves, he would not be oversafe."

Perhaps the most startling departure from the version presented in *Two Months* (as well as from military and other accounts) is the story of the two widows' rescue. According to the 1955 publication, at four o'clock in the morning after the mirage, a cannon was sounded, and by noon the camp was surrounded by troops. "Under a flag of truce the officers and warriors met to make terms of peace. The rebellion was over. The white man had won." At this point an officer called out, "Does anyone know the prisoners?" and "a young lieutenant stepped forward. It was Dick Laurie." It was he who recognized that one of the women was indeed Theresa Gowanlock.

The 1955 publication, purportedly written by Theresa Gowanlock
shortly before her death (*Family Herald and Weekly Star*
[Montreal], 20 October 1955)

A curious feature of the entire article is the prominence given to
Dick Laurie. A member of the 90th Rifles Battalion, he was the son
of *Saskatchewan Herald* editor P.G. Laurie and had been John Gowanlock's partner in the milling business. Readers were told that
the young Laurie was a graduate of the Royal Military College at
Kingston and that he had hurried to Winnipeg in March 1885 to
take a commission. "He had then walked and fought his way back
from Qu'Appelle with the rescue party, reaching Big Bear's camp
as part of Middleton's column. Their bravery enroute had earned
them the name 'Little Black Devils,' from the Indians." The
Lauries were featured prominently in the article. Mrs Gowanlock
was said to have stayed with the Laurie family in Battleford for several weeks in 1884 before moving on to Frog Lake that December,
a detail not included in *Two Months*. Dick was given a more central
role in the life of the Frog Lake community; it was said that when
he left for Toronto around the middle of March to get machinery
for the mill, "our little colony seemed considerably lonelier."
Finally, as well as mentioning Dick's role in the rescue, the article

noted that the widows had stayed with the Lauries in Battleford until they left for the East.

A still more curious feature of the 1955 article is that except for minor alterations and omissions, it is almost precisely the same as a story written by Effie (Laurie) Storer in 1925 entitled "Theresa."[95] This story tied for second prize in an essay competition sponsored by the Regina Women's Canadian Club on the topic of pioneer days. Focusing on Mrs Gowanlock, "Theresa" stylized and romanticized the tale of the widowed captives, and it altered some events and invented others in order to create clear heroes and villains. It begins with an idyllic scene of Tintern, Ontario, where a young Theresa Johnson is helping with the honey harvest on the evening of Johnny Gowanlock's proposal to her. But readers are soon informed that this happiness will be short-lived: "How could they guess that the inexorable sisters who spin the thread of human life were measuring but a short length for the lover, and for the lass a thread of such color as was to be known only to one other white woman of Canada?" Theresa's mother has a severe sense of foreboding about the marriage and the move to the North-West after the family see the young couple off at the station: "The golden-rod along the road and by the stone fences mocked the gloom that had fallen on their spirits. The sunset gleams could not dispel the forebodings felt by the mother." But the young couple's boundless love and their faith in the future make the trip enchanting. The log shanty at Frog Lake "could have no greater allure had it been a palace. Song and laughter were ever on the bride's lips and she never wearied the winter through of the scene of lake and wood on the one hand and of the swell and fall of the prairie horizon on the other. There were incredible flaming sunsets and northern lights of heavenly colors, forms and movements."

John Pritchard, "the shifty-eyed half-breed interpreter," is the first note of discord featured in the happy Frog Lake scene until the death of the child Nora. Clearly, Nora was invented by Storer to allow Mrs Delaney the following thoughts during her first hours of captivity: "Through the tent opening Mrs Delaney had been able to see during the day the little mound marking the spot where Nora had been laid to rest three weeks before and a forlorn content was in her mind that Death and not the savages had claimed the golden-haired maid of three. She pictured Nora and her father in the spirit-land and wished a bullet had been spent on herself."

Another item invented for dramatic purposes was the behaviour of a young "stalwart" and his two attempts to rape Theresa. "The second time, the young chief stooped and caught Theresa's shawl to take her by force. The blood froze in her veins. To be ravished by her husband's slayer! It should never be! Electrically the warrior sensed her will to murder the Indian who touched her. She must be an avenging spirit. A change of expression flashed across his face. He jerked his blanket over his eyes and stalked from the teepee."

Pritchard is portrayed as a villain in almost the same words as those later appearing in the 1955 article: "In his mind was working the thought that if the redskins won the rebellion he could command a higher price for the two comely white women; while if the whites put down the rising they would pay him much more than the value of the three Indian ponies and $30 for having 'protected' the women. The new idea was penetrating too that if the women killed themselves his own skin might not be over safe." Similarly, "Theresa" features Dick Laurie most prominently in the rescue of the widows. The story ends with the words, "For thirteen years Theresa tried to shut out memories of that sun-drenched April morning and the leaden weeks which followed, but in the end they crushed her. Only in death did her features regain a look of peace and girlish loveliness."

The main difference between Effie Storer's "Theresa" of 1925 and the "Memories of Frog Lake" published in 1955 is that the latter has been altered to make it appear that Theresa Gowanlock was its author. In some places this required considerable cutting and pasting. For instance, Storer's passage on "the inexorable sisters who spin the thread of human life" has become: "How strangely spun were the threads of fate that bound our lives together that happy summer of 1884. For Johnny Gowanlock a short length measured against all time, and for me, Theresa Johnson, a strand of such a color as was known to only one other white woman in Canada."[96] The sense of foreboding felt by Mrs Johnson when the newly-weds are seen off at the station has become a curious passage in which Theresa feels both foreboding and joy at the same time: "A strange sense of sadness and foreboding had fallen on our spirits, and the golden rod along the road and by the stone fences seemed to mock the gloom about us. But for Johnny and me it was the beginning of a joyous honeymoon." Only slight alterations have been made to passages such as the description of the "palace" at Frog Lake: "The winter scene of lake and wood on one side and the swell and fall of prairie horizon on the other was a never ending source of beauty. The incredible flaming sunsets and the fantastic color movements of the Northern lights all added to the sense of unreality." On the other hand, the threat of rape from the "young stalwart brave" has been slightly embellished. In the 1955 version there are two such men who attempt it twice. But when Theresa's shawl is grabbed, the wording is very similar: "For a moment the blood seemed to freeze in my veins, but the thought flashed through my mind that I would murder my husband's slayer before submitting to him. Evidently the brave sensed this fierce impulse and thought me an avenging spirit for a change of expression crossed his face and he drew his blanket over his eyes and stalked away."

Some parts of Storer's story have been excised in the 1955 version. For instance, although readers are informed of Nora's death, they do not learn Mrs Delaney's innermost thoughts about it during her early hours of captivity. Similarly, since Theresa Gowanlock cannot comment on the appearance of her own face after her death, the final lines of the story have been changed to read: "It is now thirteen years since that sunny April morning was suddenly engulfed by catastrophe and life became a dreary existence of endless memories which only death can erase."

Effie (Laurie) Storer's unpublished reminscences, which were probably written in the 1940s, contain many of the same passages that appear in "Theresa,"[97] but they include no mention of the character Nora or the central role of Dick Laurie in the rescue. These items were clearly added to her short story for dramatic effect. Effie Storer's memoirs were never published, though she dearly wished them to be. To help prepare her manuscript for publication in the 1940s, she sought the assistance of Dr W. Menzies Whitelaw, a member of the Department of History at the University of Saskatchewan from 1941 to 1946.[98] She felt, she said, "the blunt of having had so little schooling – the price I paid for pioneering," and wanted assistance with editing and completing the story.[99] When Dr Whitelaw moved to Springfield, Massachusetts, in 1946, he took with him Storer's manuscript and her collection of research material, including correspondence, diaries, photographs, newspapers, notes, and articles. In 1949 Storer wrote to Whitelaw asking him to return her manuscript, but it seems that this was never done. In her last letter to him, she indignantly remarked that he seemed to be more interested in her research materials, such as her copies of the *Saskatchewan Herald*, than in her manuscripts.[100] Effie Storer died in Saskatoon in 1951 at the age of eighty-four. Her manuscripts and other personal papers were donated to the Saskatchewan Archives Board in 1975 by a member of the White-law family. The mystery of just how the story "Theresa" became "Memories of Frog Lake" remains to be solved.

FICTIONAL REPRESENTATIONS

Like Australia's Eliza Fraser, Theresa Delaney and Theresa Gowanlock continued to excite the popular imagination for many years afterwards. The earliest fictional representations of their story employed the saintly white female victim to reinforce the race and gender hierarchies in the West. In the novels of Edmund Collins entitled *Annette, the Metis Spy* and *The Story of Louis Riel*, a happy and innocent young Mrs Gowanlock, recently married and buoyant with hopes for the future, is murdered by fiendish and treacherous Indians. She is shot while attempting to seize "the savage's arms from behind" in order to save another.[101]

The experiences of the two Theresas may well have inspired other works of fiction about saintly white female victims. In John Mackie's novel, *The Rising of the Red Man: A Romance of the Riel Rebellion*, the central character is eighteen-year-old Dorothy Douglas, a healthy and wholesome daughter of the prairie who has recently returned from Ontario, where she was sent for her schooling.[102] Dorothy is cast as more courageous than Mrs Gowanlock and Mrs Delaney – she is more like the McLean sisters – but the brutality of the Indians and Métis is just as evident. When her father, a rancher in the Battle-ford district, hears rumours of the uprising, he warns Dorothy that they may have to turn their kitchen into a "shooting gallery," but this does not disturb her, since she is accustomed to rifles.[103] Her father lectures her: "You don't seem to realize what a rising means amongst savages ... you must never let yourself fall into their hands; you understand me?" The Douglases take refuge in the barracks at Battleford, but plucky Dorothy ventures out, going in disguise among the Métis and Indian looters in the deserted town, where she is detected by the "half-savage" Katie. Dorothy, the "white witch," is taken prisoner and brought before Riel, who taunts her with descriptions of the brutality of the "squaws," dredging up the images that were so industriously circulated during the conflict of 1885. Riel informs Dorothy that Crowfoot, chief of the Blackfoot, is to be punished for declaring his "loyalty" and that "his squaws would one day stone him to death as judgment." Riel also tells Dorothy that "Fort Pitt, Battleford and Prince Albert must shortly capitulate to them, and then the squaws would receive the white women of those places as their private prisoners to do with as their sweet wills suggested."[104]

More recent novels such as Rudy Wiebe's *Temptations of Big Bear* and Mel Dagg's *Women on the Bridge* cast the widowed captives in a different light, showing greater sympathy for their Aboriginal hosts.[105] In Wiebe's novel, it is the Aboriginal people who are held captive in their native land, and Big Bear, the symbol of wisdom and faith, is cast as an "Old Testament prophet or patriarch who must try to lead his captive people through a wilderness of violence, loss and temptation."[106] The Terry Gowanlock and Theresa Delaney of this novel are not particularly good or evil, but are themselves held captive by an ideology and logic which they share with the other whites and from which they cannot escape. The Theresa Gowanlock who is the central character in Dagg's novel is introspective and unhappily married. Having been transplanted to the West, she is overwhelmed by loneliness, and through her experience she comes to realize (as well as to represent) the arrogance of the first wave of Ontario settlers. Perspectives have changed, sympathies have shifted. The former editor of *Saturday Night*, Robert Fulford, observed in a 1976 review of a collection of documents about Frog Lake that Mrs Delaney and Mrs Gowanlock have come to function as proof of white indifference and ignorance. As mentioned above, Mrs Delaney was Fulford's Great-Aunt Theresa. He wrote, "I've often wished she had been more curious, more questioning, more foresighted – an exception to something evil rather than an example of it."[107] This is a startling departure from the view of Mrs Delaney one hundred years ago. The once defenceless victims of the evil, selfish, and corrupt have themselves become symbols of the evil, selfish, and corrupt. It is not clear if either view does the two women justice, bringing us close to an understanding of their experiences; but these differing interpretations do suggest that as Euro-Canadian ideals of behaviour and femininity change and as the need to establish dominance over a people and their resources has diminished, the depiction of white women captives – and also their captors – has altered.

Yet the version of events in *Two Months* has proved resilient and remains influential. On a June day in 1925, the Historic Sites and Monuments Board of Canada unveiled a stone monument that bears the inscription:

North West Rebellion
FROG LAKE MASSACRE
Here on 2nd April 1885
Rebel Indians Under
Big Bear Massacred
Rev. Father Leon Adelard Fafard OMI
Rev. Father Felix Marchand OMI
Indian Agent Thomas Quinn
Farm Instructor John Delaney
John Alexander Gowanlock
William Campbell Gilchrist
George Dill
Charles Gouin
John Williscraft

They Took Prisoners
Mrs. Theresa Delaney
Mrs. Theresa Gowanlock

William Cameron was asked to unveil the memorial because he was the "sole white survivor of the massacre."[108] Cameron may well have been dismayed to find that the focus was still on the two women, even though he and a great many other people had also been hostages of the Cree. In the forty years that had passed, the murdered men and the widows had remained the centre of attention; the broader context and the experiences of the many others involved was not featured.

A sign "Frog Lake Massacre" on the Yellowhead Highway south of the site also perpetuates the image of the unprovoked and barbaric slaughter of innocent white people. Frog Lake band councillor Derrick Quinney recently stated, "That's history that has been misinterpreted for the last 100 years."[109] Because only one side of the story is given, emphasizing this negative view of Aboriginal people, many elders of the Frog Lake First Nation have expressed the opinion that it would be better if the site were not marked at all.

Others would like to see the Aboriginal perspective presented at a large Frog Lake complex that would encompass far more than just the area where the deaths took place.[110] Oral tradition and recent archaeological work have located what in all probability is the site of the camps of Big Bear and Oo-nee-pow-o-hay-oos. The remains include many cellar impressions, two cemeteries, and a Cree "image" which played a role in ceremonies. As the archaeologists who undertook this work wrote in 1991, the discovery of these camps presents an opportunity to place the 1885 event at Frog Lake in perspective, as one incident in a complex set of historical circumstances. This remains to be done, however, and the version of events that Delaney and Gowanlock were obliged to create remains dominant.

CHAPTER FOUR

Captivity Hoaxes and Their Uses

After 1885 there were no further captivities of white women in the Canadian West, but two sensationalized captivity hoaxes in the last decade of the nineteenth century kept alive the perceived threat to the infringement of white female honour as well as the need to pursue strategies of exclusion and control. The habitual image of white women as pale, frail, vulnerable, and in need of protection from the "fate worse than death" was promoted through these incidents, which served as reminders that there was still a menace, still work to be done. In both cases the supposed captives were young girls, which fed widespread fears that Aboriginal people were lying in wait to pounce on white children and spirit them away. At the same time, the hoaxes kept alive the image of predatory Aboriginal males who were a threat to the sanctity and purity of white women. They also reinforced ideas of the drudgery that was said to be endured by Aboriginal women. Overall, they reinforced the need for a racially stratified and divided society.

THE "WAIF OF THE PLAINS"

In 1889 the story of a white girl held captive by the Blackfoot of the Canadian West first appeared in the London (England) *Graphic*.[1] The purveyor of the story was Frederick Villiers, the special artist of the *Graphic*, who had accompanied Governor General Lord Stanley and the viceregal party on a trip across the continent in 1889. Villiers said that at a grand reception which the Blackfoot had held at Gleichen on 18 October to honour the visitors, a "captive" white girl

Governor General Lord Stanley and the viceregal party touring western
Canada, 1889 (*Graphic* [London], 25 January 1890, 112,
Provincial Archives of Manitoba)

Frederick Villiers's sketch of
the "Waif of the Plains," who
was said to be a white captive
of the Blackfoot (*Graphic*,
30 November 1889, 667,
Provincial Archives of
Manitoba)

of about nine had been led into the camp on a pony; she was dressed in "rich beadwork vestments which ill became her fair hair and little white face."[2] Villiers hoped that publicity would result in the child being "handed over to people of her own color," though he admitted that she appeared to be treated with great care and affection by her captors. It was the fate that awaited her when she was a few years older that Villiers found "sad to contemplate." He claimed to have been told on good authority that the child had been captured during a raid in the United States, during which her officer father had been killed.

While he was in New York early in 1890, Villiers embellished the story of the "waif of the plains" for the New York *World*.[3] This time, the captive maiden was described as "almost regal"; "her little white face, with small, regular features, and bright gray eyes stood out of a wealth of golden hair," though this glorious mane was besprinkled with dust and grit. Villiers declared that he had never seen a whiter complexion in his life and that he believed there "was no Indian blood in her veins." He said that the old man on the reserve who claimed to be her father simply wanted to draw her daily rations and annuity. In his elaborate description of the child, Villiers said that as she "gradually disappeared through the surging crowd of braves it was as if a ray of sunshine was playing about the dusky warriors and their squaws."

Many more details had been added to the story by the time it was reported in the *Macleod Gazette* on 30 January 1890. According to this paper, an interpreter by the name of Winnipeg Jack claimed that the child, captured in a raid across the border, belonged to him. It also said that Lord Stanley had tried to induce the Blackfoot to part with the child, but they had refused, though they had agreed to sell her buckskin dress to Lady Stanley. Readers of the *Gazette* were informed that the matter had attracted the attention of the American government and it had been confirmed that the little girl was indeed the daughter of an American officer. Moreover, at that very time, under instructions from the American government, an American officer was in the North-West intent upon rescuing the child at any cost. The editor of the *Gazette* expressed the hope that the North-West Mounted Police (NWMP) would aid in the search so that the girl could be "saved from the wretched fate which awaits her, should she remain with the Indians."

The matter did in fact receive attention at the War Department in Washington. According to the New York *World,* Adjutant General Kelton had telegraphed General Ruger at St Paul to send an officer to investigate the matter.[4] The adjutant general was reported as saying, "It is not a matter in which international formalities or complications are involved. I do not anticipate that our officer will have any trouble. The Canadian authorities I expect, will co-operate with him, and give him, as far as they can, all the assistance he may need."[5] A Lieutenant Ahern of Fort Shaw went as far as the St Mary's River to investigate the matter but turned back after communicating with the NWMP.[6]

Early in February, it was boldly affirmed in the *Gazette* that there was not the slightest doubt that the story was true.[7] The Canadian government was called on to take immediate action to rescue the girl from "the horrible fate that is surely in store for her ... even if it brings every Indian in the North-West Territories about their ears." Assistance would not be lacking, noted the paper, as "common humanity would prompt every able-bodied man in Alberta to join in so righteous a crusade." If no government action was taken, it warned, the fathers and brothers of Alberta would together see to it that the child was rescued, with their wives and sisters wishing them Godspeed. An anonymous letter to the *Gazette* expressed similar outrage, saying that the news of a white girl in the Blackfoot camp, if true, "makes ones blood boil": "England has gone to war before now, and sacrificed many lives to rescue a white man from savage tribes, and here is a white girl in the hands of a savage tribe, under England's own rule, liable to the most degrading life, and nothing has been done to save her!" This letter writer said it was an everlasting disgrace to Canada that this had been allowed even for a day, and that it took an Englishman, an artist traveler, to call attention to it, and the Americans to inquire into it. To redeem herself in the eyes of the civilized world, Canada must take immediate action.

It was a distant American newspaper, however, that sponsored the expeditionary force into the heart of Blackfoot country. It was not unusual for some papers to patronize this type of activity. In 1869 the New York *World* had sponsored the expeditionary force into the heart of Africa led by Henry M. Stanley, a newspaper correspondent, to find Dr Livingstone. The *World* prided itself on sending agents to all corners of the globe to right the wrongs of the "weak and oppressed."[8] Its readers showed great interest in the story of the captive girl and apparently sent scores of letters protesting the "outrage" and demanding that the little unfortunate be rescued. There were offers to adopt the girl, and one old gentleman wanted to organize a band of cowboys to march on the Blackfoot and seize the child by force.

A Mr C.R. Saffery of New York City, who was late of the NWMP in Blackfoot country, suggested a *World* expedition to investigate the matter and rescue the girl. For this suggestion, "a labor of humanity and a public service," the Committee of Ideas awarded Saffery the second prize of $500 in the Idea Contest. (It is not clear what idea received the first prize.) As a result, a *World* reporter was commissioned to take guides and ransom money to the "remote" regions of Canada's North-West. Saffery volunteered to assist in the rescue, and he and the *World* reporter met in Montreal to plan the expedition.[9] Saffery knew Jerry Potts, a scout employed by the NWMP at Fort Macleod, and believed he would be the best person to help engineer the scheme. Saffery was certain that the child could be bought and that Indians ordinarily sold their children for between ten and twenty-five dollars. The rescuers expected to be asked fifty dollars for a white child but were prepared to pay ten times that amount if necessary. In case the Canadian authorities objected to the child being taken away, a quick escape was planned. From Fort Macleod they could head directly south, instead of east on the transcontinental. Along this southern escape route there were no railways or telegraphs to overhaul them, and in three days they could be in Great Falls, Montana.

The *World* reporter and Saffery left Montreal on 13 January 1890, travelling in the luxury of a palace car on the Canadian Pacific Railway. Four days later they disembarked at Dunmore Junction, about 2,500 miles from the *World* office. A temperature of thirty-five degrees below zero greeted them. From there, a freight train took them to Lethbridge, and a stagecoach "of the Deadwood variety" brought them on to Fort Macleod. There they were disappointed to learn that the NWMP surgeon had ordered Potts not to leave his house since he was suffering from the "grip." A scout by the name of Ben Deroshe was hired in his stead. Meanwhile, the rescuers learned from Potts, through a meeting in secret, that Dog Child, the "captor" of the girl, had been in Montana at about the same time that the child was born. A man from California believed his infant daughter had been stolen by Indians in Montana around that time.

The *World* rescuers were soon to be disillusioned, however. Their long trip across the cold continent, the secrecy, the escape route, and the ransom money all proved to be unnecessary. The captive girl turned out not to be a captive at all. Many local people, including the Blackfoot and officials of the Department of Indian Affairs, had been aware of this all along.[10] A year before the viceregal visit, the Toronto *Empire* had included an item on a Blackfoot sun dance in which mention was made of two white children in the possession of an Indian woman. The Indian agent Magnus Begg had been asked to investigate the matter, and he had determined that the children were the offspring of Pretty Gun, who was married to a man named Dog Child, who had no doubt that these were his own children. In November 1889, when public attention was focused on the Blackfoot "captive," Begg had amassed the testimony of many witnesses who had been present on the reserve when Pretty Gun gave birth, and copies of affidavits establishing the girl's parentage had been sent to the department headquarters in Ottawa. The NWMP had also investigated the matter. Superintendent J. McIllree was instructed to make careful inquiries about the parentage of the girl. His investigation confirmed that she was the daughter of Pretty Gun. Furthermore, Dog Child told him that he had invented the story of the child being white and being given to him at Fort Benton "because he was always being bothered by people about her, and he used to tell them the first story that occurred to him."[11]

The *World* expedition thus returned empty-handed. The headlines read "Pappoose After All," "The Supposed Captive White Girl Turns Out to Be a Half-Breed," and "Her Mother a Squaw."[12] The story of the expedition was nonetheless full of "thrilling adventures in the wilderness of Upper Canada." The rescuers lost their way in a blizzard at one point on the Blackfoot Reserve. They talked to the supposed captive, named Spotted Girl, who indeed had golden hair, as did her sister Morning Star. The father, interviewed on the question of Spotted Girl's future, stated that he hoped she could get an education before she got married. She had been sent to Father Lacombe's school near Calgary, but she had cried for nine days and wanted only to go home. She was to return when the weather was warmer. Crowfoot, the aged chief of the Blackfoot, was also interviewed by the New York reporter. Crowfoot was apparently "very much surprised to think that the *World* should send so far to look after the interests of one solitary little papoose." It was

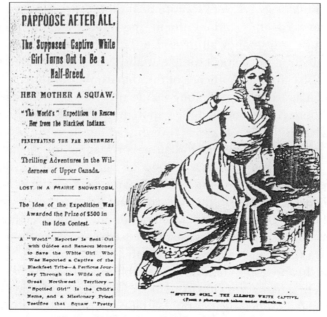

"Spotted Girl, the alleged white captive."
This drawing, which accompanied an article on
the expedition sent to "save the white girl," was
"from a photograph taken under difficulties."
(*World* [New York], 11 February 1890)

explained to him that agents of the paper were sent to every quarter of the globe to help the weak and oppressed. The reporter added that although the expedition had failed to rescue a captive, it was hoped that the result would "relieve the hearts of many anxious mothers."

"FLAXEN HAIR" IN ABORIGINAL COMMUNITIES

The frenzy of interest in "rescuing the captive" is somewhat surprising. Most people at all familiar with the Canadian West at this time knew that children with light hair and complexions were not uncommon in the camps and on the reserves, and had not been since the early days of the European fur trade. There were well-known examples, such as the Cree Sutherland boys, sons of a Highland Scot named Hugh Sutherland of the Hudson's Bay Company.[13]

D.W. Davis, a whisky trader who in 1887 was elected the first member of Parliament for the District of Alberta (Glenbow Archives, NA-659-58)

One of the boys was called in Cree Oo-sa-us-tik-wan, or Yellow Hair, and the other Tip-oo-es-tik-wan, or Curly Hair. They had a great reputation as Cree warriors, "without an atom of fear in their composition," and they died in the last great battle between the Blackfoot and Cree near the present-day town of Lethbridge in the winter of 1869.

Stories were legion of prominent men who had children in the Indian communities. There was the subconstable in the NWMP who later became a peer of the British realm, Arthur John Trepol, who, while stationed at Qu'Appelle, fell in love with a mixed-blood woman on Pasquah's reserve and whose eldest son grew up there as a farmer. (This son did not succeed to the title when Trepol died in his sixty-third year.)[14] By the 1880s, some men who had risen to prominence in the West were divesting themselves of their Aboriginal wives and children, and marrying non-Aboriginal women. For instance, D.J. Grier of the NWMP, who later became mayor of Fort Macleod, had originally married Molly Tailfeathers, a Peigan woman, with whom he had three children, but by 1887 he was remarried to a white woman.[15] For a short time the children from his first marriage lived with their mother on the Peigan Reserve, but the two eldest were taken from her and placed in the care of Grier's parents, who had settled in Fort Macleod. Then there was D.W. Davis, who began his career in the West as a whisky trader at the infamous Fort Whoop-Up but by 1887 he had been elected the first member of Parliament for the District of Alberta.[16] He had a family of four children with a Blood woman by the name of Revenge Walker, who was Chief Red Crow's sister.[17] In 1887 he married a recently arrived schoolteacher from Ontario, Lillie Grier (sister of D.J. Grier), with whom he had a second family. Davis did, however, acknowledge the children from his first marriage and provided for their education.

In a letter that was widely published in the western papers, Father Albert Lacombe, who had been a missionary in the area since 1852, replied to the sensational reports of white girls stolen by Indians and "exposed to a fate worse than death."[18] Lacombe said that he was astonished at the naiveté of some tourists, who would easily believe anything during their flying visits from the platform of a Pullman or the verandah of a hotel. There were no grounds for reports about white girls captive in the camps or reserves, he insisted, and he invited the philanthropic reporters to spend some time among the people of Treaty 7: "They would see and recognize many white boys and girls 'with flaxen hair and pre-possessing features'; who have not at all been brought from white settlements, but who are really the children of Indian women, and the offspring of white men." Instead of accusing the Indians of such outrageous robbery, he said, reporters who genuinely wanted to practise their zeal for humanity could reproach "those white people who demoralize the ignorant savage and neutralize the missionary world. Now you have the secret of these so-called captives among the Indians." The Indians did not want to steal white children; they had plenty of their own. Instead of making foolish inquiries to recover captive girls, stated Lacombe, "I would rather suggest to the proper authorities to compel the white fathers of these flaxen hairs to provide for their offspring and not have the Government bear this burden."

Notes of scepticism were expressed by others too. A Mr A.A. Vice of Lethbridge wrote to the *Manitoba Daily Free Press* in February 1890 saying, "If the Canadian government intend laying claim to all the children living in Indian camps who have light hair, blue or grey eyes and fair skins in the Northwest Territories, it will have its hands full."[19] He objected to having the police march in and forcibly seize the child from the people who had raised her. For any such action, an order from a court of proper jurisdiction had first to be obtained. Vice also objected to the New York papers embellishing the story, which he believed was "the greatest hoax of the season."

Similarly, the Oblate missionary Father Léon Doucet was indignant at the absurdity of the rumour "flying around the whole country" that a "white captive" had been abducted from her own people.[20] He noted in his diary, "Slowly the white people calmed down and the excitement passed by. It was mostly the people of Fort Macleod who had clamored the most." It is surprising that it was the residents of Fort Macleod who had become so exercised, since they must have been well acquainted with the situation that had led to the many "flaxen-haired children" in the Aboriginal communities. Indeed, some of the fathers of their own community had children on the Treaty 7 reserves.

THE CAMPAIGN AGAINST "INDIAN DEPREDATIONS"

For some years, the *Macleod Gazette* had been waging a campaign aimed at removing the Indians of southern Alberta to a remote northern location.[21] Member of Parliament D.W. Davis was pledged to support any scheme aimed at separating them from the whites.[22] (One western paper had noted, "There are few men in the country who more thoroughly understand the Indian character than he.")[23] It was said to be inconvenient, even menacing, to have "Indian reserves scattered about in the midst of white settlements, and of having the Indians wander about the country at their own sweet will, stealing settler's [*sic*] horses and killing their cattle."[24] Many rationales were produced to support the "Indian territory scheme." One was that association with white people had demoralized Indian people: "The more they are brought under civilizing influences, the worse they get … The Indian who has associated among whites long enough to be able to talk English is a far bigger villain than the one who never leaves his reserve." This scheme would thus ultimately be in the best interests of the Indians.

The *Calgary Herald* agreed to the idea of one large reserve, or Indian territory. It suggested, however, that instead of being sent to the remote north, the local Indian people should all be placed on a reserve along the Red Deer River, the north side being assigned to the Cree and the south side to the Blackfoot.[25] It argued that Indians were not prepared for "a complete change from their nomadic habits and their uncouth notions, to the full comprehension and practical adoption of a complete civilization," since they did not have "sufficient brain power, sufficient will, perseverance or physical strength, to undergo successfully the sudden change." Nevertheless, the *Herald* agreed that reserves were an obstacle to settlement, stating that there was scarcely any place in the country where an immigrant could take up land without being "exposed to the unwelcome visits of these people."

In the late 1880s the *Macleod Gazette* and other western papers featured numerous articles on "Indian depredations" – horses stolen and cattle killed by "thieving and murdering redskins."[26] There were threats to put an end to these outrages through law-and-order vigilante committees. Another charge laid at the door of the Aboriginal residents of the West was that they were responsible for the destruction of wild game, fowl, and fish in the territory. This was given as a further reason for establishing an Indian territory, where the residents would be "prevented by the strictest possible laws against leaving it."[27] If such a territory could not be established, the Indians should at least be kept on their reserves. Even if freedom of movement was a treaty right, the government should "endeavor to secure such a rearrangement of the treaties as will prevent this go-as-you-please business from continuing."[28]

During the turbulent events of 1885, a pass system had been inaugurated in western Canada. It was designed as a temporary measure to control and monitor the movements of the Indians and keep them from joining the "rebels."[29] The possibility of implementing a pass system had been raised on occasion before then but had been rejected because it ran directly counter to promises made in the treaties. However, the system continued to be maintained after 1885. All those who wished to leave their reserves had to carry a pass signed by the Indian agent or farm instructor, declaring the purpose for being off the reserve and the length of time permitted. Non-Aboriginal residents of southern Alberta felt that the pass system was too lenient and allowed too much movement off the reserve, and during the late 1880s the local papers were urging that the pass system be abolished and that the residents be strictly confined to their reserves without any permission to leave.[30] In June 1890, Superintendent Sam Steele's report for Fort Macleod described a "universal desire on the part of all the ranchers to have the Indians confined to their reserve, and prevented from roaming at will over the prairie." Steele's report was brought to the attention of Sir John A. Macdonald, who agreed that measures ought to be taken to restrict Indians to their reserves and that they not be issued passes at all.[31]

It is curious that part of the rationale for the Indian removal scheme was that "lazy" Indians would learn to be self-supporting farmers or industrious tradespeople, for the possibility of "Indian competition" was a matter of grave concern to many non-Aboriginal residents of the West at this time. There were loud objections to Indians selling their hay, wood, potatoes, or other produce to non-Aboriginal settlers. Their competition was seen as "unfair" because it was widely believed that the government lavishly supplied them with equipment, stock, and seed, so that they did not have to worry about the price at which their products were sold. This perception was unfair and did not reflect the difficult conditions faced by Aboriginal farmers, who had to contend with the restrictive policies of the Indian Act and the Department of Indian Affairs. Nevertheless, it was a widely held view. According to one reader of the *Macleod Gazette*, it was an outrage to allow the Bloods to bring hay into town in large quantities and to enter into competition "with white men who, even with hard work, find it difficult to make both ends meet and provide for their families."[32] Clearly, a policy of removal to a more remote part of the territory would satisfy the demands of those who believed that Indian competition was injuring the livelihood of the non-Aboriginal settlers.

The alarm that was raised about a white girl captive among the Blackfoot was useful to those promoting schemes of Indian removal or, barring that, of strict confinement to reserves. Here was a depredation of the most serious nature imaginable. As in 1885, the potential violation of a white woman and the threat to the safety of white women on isolated homesteads and ranches was a useful means of rallying the non-Aboriginal community in a racist consensus against Aboriginal people. By promoting the image of a young white girl – the most symbolically vulnerable section of society – all "alone" on an Indian reserve, the makers of this propaganda were able to conflate powerful messages of the ever-present danger of violence to white women. The protection of white women demanded that relations between the peoples be highly regulated.

It is interesting to note that there was so much concern for the safety and honour of one "flaxen-haired" girl on the Blackfoot Reserve when this was a time of very great suffering, especially on the reserves, because of a severe influenza epidemic. In January 1890 the epidemic took many victims, especially children and older people, yet this was not mentioned at all in the many articles that focused on the Blackfoot "captive." Father L. Doucet's diary describes the deadly results of the epidemic, the first major sickness of that kind ever seen in this country.[33] The influential leaders North Axe and Crow Eagle died that January from influenza.

FABRICATED FEARS OF "KIDNAPPED" CHILDREN

The frenzy of interest in the "captive" girl may also have been stimulated by the fact that there were many missing children in Canada and the United States, and people hoped that theirs had been discovered. A Mr A. Wimperis of Winnipeg, for example, wrote to the *Free Press* in February 1890 explaining that he employed a boy of sixteen named Johnnie Rowell who had a missing sister, Louise, aged fourteen.[34] Their father had left the country, and their stepmother had given the children away. Louise had gone with a couple to Fort Macleod, but this marriage had broken up, and it was believed that the girl had been left to shift for herself. Johnnie was most anxious to find his sister and thought it was not improbable that the girl with the Blackfoot was Louise.

Some of the early non-Aboriginal settlers lived in constant fear that their children would be stolen. In the local histories there are many outlandish tales of attempted abductions, along with other folktales of "Indian visits." May Oakden, who lived on a ranch at Slide Out near the Blood Reserve, was home alone when two wagons of Indian visitors stopped at her ranch. She heard a noise and discovered that her baby was missing from the carriage. "May chased the Indian woman around the table until she got the baby. The Indian woman was trying to tell her she only wanted the baby to take to town to collect the five dollar treaty money they paid for each child, then she would return him. However, May had a small dog in the house which she 'sicced' onto the woman, who beat a hasty retreat. The dog bit her heel and from that day on no Indian dared to step foot on the grounds of the ranch unless someone was there to permit it."[35] On an earlier occasion, May had allegedly been obliged to hold an intoxicated Indian at bay on the step of her house for four hours in forty-below weather.

Missing children were often assumed to have been kidnapped by Indians, though not even one such case was ever verified in the Canadian West. The ten-year-old daughter of the Anglican clergyman John Payne Sargent went missing from her home in Rapid City, Manitoba, in the early 1880s, and although there was a massive search, she was never found.[36] It was reported in later years that she was with a band of Indians near Qu'Appelle and was married to a "high Indian chief and wanted nothing to do with her white parents." There were also rumours that Sargent (who was appointed archdeacon of Assiniboia in 1897) worked as a missionary on various reserves trying to win his daughter back. A Sargent granddaughter, Vera Peel of Regina, said that all these stories were fabrications and that although the family spent hundreds of dollars searching, they never heard anything about the missing daughter: "Her marrying an Indian and being a princess is just a fairy story."

These one-sided stories suggest more than a bit of embellishment. Not mentioned in the local histories are incidents that were probably far more common – of children being cared for in Aboriginal communities regardless of their ancestry. The Reverend Alfred Garrioch told a story about the child of an Englishman and a Blackfoot woman. In 1872 this infant girl was discovered on the Peace River floating in a small raft with a red flag fluttering from a stick. The girl was raised by Beaver Indians, and it was only determined many years later that she must have been the child of the couple who had set out in the winter of 1871 to trap south of the Peace River.[37] Another such case concerned a baby of Irish ancestry who was deserted by its parents at Qu'Appelle around 1890. Father J. Hugonard, principal of the Qu'Appelle Industrial School, found a home for the child with the Louis O'Soup family of the Cowessess Reserve.[38]

THE SENSATIONAL TURTON DRAMA

In January 1898 the story of another white girl found among Indians became sensational news in Canada and the United States. The Reverend O.H. Sproul, pastor of First Methodist Church, Pierre, South Dakota, was travelling through the Cheyenne River agency in South Dakota when he encountered a family whom he believed to be harbouring a white girl of about fourteen named Annie

Russell.[39] The family maintained that Annie was one of them, but Sproul remained suspicious; he felt that they were keeping her carefully guarded, apart from the other children and the prying eyes of visitors. He was convinced that the girl's general appearance indicated that she was of "refined extraction," and although one woman in the family, Otter Robe, claimed to be Annie's aunt, Sproul demanded an investigation into the matter. The Indian agent, along with Senator James W. Kyle, succeeded in obtaining an order from the secretary of the interior for the removal of the girl from the family, and she was placed in a children's home at Sioux Falls.

Sproul believed that the girl was from Canada. Determined to find her real family or friends, he gave the facts as he knew them to a Winnipeg acquaintance, hoping that these would be published widely.[40] Sproul's "facts" displayed an imperfect understanding of the recent history of the Lakota of the Cheyenne River agency. The girl had been with a Lakota family who had spent some years in Canada and then returned to the United States. Sproul believed that her true family had returned across the border to seek safety "after the Riel uprising in 1885 or some such depredation" and that all except she had been murdered. He reasoned that their murder and her kidnapping had occurred on the Canadian side of the line, because there were so few white families between the Cheyenne agency and the border, and in the United States such a crime would have been "looked up." The *Manitoba Free Press* ran Sproul's story, but it suggested that the reverend gentleman might have some of the circumstances skewed, since the murdering of whole families was unknown in Canada, and any cases of kidnapping were as "likely to be 'looked up' here as there."[41] There was an element of truth in Sproul's tale, however. The girl's people had originally been part of Sitting Bull's band who had arrived in Canadian territory seeking refuge in 1876. By 1880 most had returned across the border, but a small group, including the girl's family, had remained until 1894, camping at Moose Jaw.

American newspapers showed little concern for veracity and were quick to print and enlarge on the "Romantic Mystery of a Beautiful Girl." The New York *Journal* wove a few of the facts into an otherwise fictitious story, complete with illustrations of the "massacre" of her parents, her capture by a fiendish "savage," and her dreary Indian home.[42] In this paper, the girl was given the name Swift Fawn and was depicted as a beautiful young maiden both in her Indian

Annie Russell, whose story was embellished by
the press, was said to be a white girl from
Canada who was being harboured on the
Cheyenne River agency in South Dakota
(*Journal* [New York], 18 January 1898)

and in her "civilized" attire. By contrast, her Indian mother was
said to have a hideous countenance. The *Journal* described how
Swift Fawn had spent fifteen years wandering as a "nomad, a savage," pounding maize, gathering acorns, dressing hides, and drawing rations. Her face was streaked with paint, she wore buckskin,
and she was decorated with beads, strings of tin, and rabbit-skin tas-
sels. She was to marry Black Dog, and she "looked forward to doing
the drudgery of this stalwart lazy buck without any idea that such a
destiny was in the least out of the ordinary."

According to the *Journal*, Annie was the daughter of a settler
named Andrew Russell and had been plucked from her family's
peaceful ranch home in Manitoba. Sitting Bull had been "out on a
raid with his devils," and they had swooped down on the lonely
house, murdering all but the child, who became the chief's pet. (In
fact, although Sitting Bull may have briefly visited Manitoba during
his years of refuge in Canada, neither he nor any of the other
Lakota performed any such act.) In the *Journal* the girl was

described as having changed "from an American baby into an Indian child" in her dress as well as her actions: "She was one of them when they murdered and burned, and she saw the men of her tribe kill white men and women, and destroy peaceful farms, without shock or qualm, for from her Indian point of view it was all right, and at the time Swift Fawn's only interest in the murdering like that of the other girls of the band, was merely on the question of whether she would get any gimcracks from the looted ranch houses, with which to deck herself."

There were several responses to Sproul's appeal to find the relatives of the "prisoner." A Mr Ludwig Stelter of Medicine Hat, for example, believed that she might be his child.[43] In 1894 his daughter Mathilde, aged six, had been lost. She had wandered away from Dunmore Junction heading south on the prairie towards Montana and had not been heard of since. A band of Cheyenne were rumoured to have been in the vicinity at the time (an unlikely occurrence), and Stelter thought they might have found the girl. Mathilde's description, however, did not match that of Annie Russell.

On the other hand, John and Adelaide Turton of Cannington Manor in the Moose Mountains of the North-West Territories became absolutely convinced, on reading about Annie Russell, that she was one of their nine children. They had long suspected that their missing daughter had been stolen by Indians. In August 1893, Mrs Turton had allowed three-year-old Gertrude Ellen (or Gertie) to call her father, who was working in the field across the road, to come for dinner.[44] The child was never seen again. Even though a massive search was undertaken, no trace of her was ever found. The Turton house was within a few yards of a thick wood, which extended many miles to the west and was filled with ponds and lakes, and on the other side was more open country, though it too was dotted with thick bluffs of poplar and willow.

From the beginning, the Turtons maintained that the child had been stolen by Indians. They were particularly suspicious of a woman who did laundry in their home, because about ten days after the child went missing this woman told the Turtons that Gertie was not dead but had "marched on."[45] As well, it was rumoured that there had been some "strange Indians" in the neighbourhood at that time, and one group was said to have had a crying child concealed in a covered cart.

In view of these rumours, Indian agent T.J. Campbell of the Moose Mountain agency thoroughly investigated the matter so that the reputation of the Indians would not suffer unfairly.[46] He had no difficulty in getting sixteen Assiniboine from White Bear's reserve to join in the search for the child without promise of reward. The woman who did laundry for the Turtons also joined the search. She had lived on the reserve since the incident under no suspicious circumstances. When questioned about her words to the Turtons, she said she had simply given her opinion that the child had not died but had wandered off. As for the "strange Indians" with the covered cart, Campbell determined that they had been Métis picking berries. They had travelled openly and conversed with many people, and it had been one of their children who was sick and crying. Moreover, Campbell established that they had not been within twenty miles of the Turton place. In his opinion, it was unnecessary to seek far afield for an explanation of the child's disappearance because of the thickly wooded terrain close to the Turton home.

Nevertheless, the Turtons remained convinced that Gertie had been abducted by Indians. They corresponded with the Reverend Mr Sproul, and when they received a photograph of the girl they were certain that she bore a family resemblance.[47] Neighbours also recognized family features, and they wrote to inform the American authorities who were in possession of the child. A lock of her hair that was sent to the Turtons was jet black, but Mrs Turton washed it and announced that it had been dyed. Its true colour, she said, was brown, the colour of Gertie's hair.

In February 1898 the Turtons went to Sioux Falls South Dakota, to see the girl – who was sick with measles at the time – and both immediately recognized her as their daughter. She was satisfactorily identified by a birthmark on her left shoulder.[48] There were several incongruities, but explanations for these were found. The Turtons were looking for an eight year old, and it was believed that Annie Russell was at least thirteen, but the Turtons were able to explain this away by recalling that their children were tall for their age and were early developers. Gertie's sisters had been much the same size as this when they were eight years old. The Turtons could also explain why Annie's complexion was not fair. Mr Turton's "knowledge of Indian practices led him to suspect that the girl's body had probably been dyed from head to foot with vegetable dye, which can only be removed very slowly and with great difficulty."

Mrs Turton believed that the colour was gradually coming out. The matron of the children's home apparently applied some acid to a small spot on the neck and proved that the colour was removable.

The Turtons and their newly found daughter were treated as celebrities during their ten days in Sioux Falls.[49] They were "shown every attention by the leading citizens, were received into the best of families and shown all the sights of the place." Mr Turton received two offers of marriage for his daughter, one from a young army officer. On their arrival in Winnipeg in March 1898, they were visited by a *Free Press* reporter who was rather more sceptical. He found the child remarkably large for eight years, and he commented that she showed "the effects of the dyeing process to such an extent that a stranger might be inclined to say that she had Indian blood."[50] Nevertheless, readers were asked to rejoice with the Turtons that "their little girl Gertie has been rescued from a life of degradation, and that the family circle has been made complete again."

A PALPABLE WRONG

The sensational Turton drama faded from the headlines, but this was not the end of the story. Indian agent Thomas W. Aspdin, who was in charge of the Assiniboine reserve Carry-the-Kettle in the District of Assiniboia, was well acquainted with the history of the girl and her family, and by April 1898 he was being urged to do what he could to have the child returned.[51] An official of the American Bureau of Indian Affairs, D.F. Carlin, informed Aspdin that the woman who identified herself as the child's aunt was very sad and was anxious to have the girl back. Carlin wanted affidavits and other evidence of the child's identity. Aspdin could not ignore this appeal, allowing a "palpable wrong to be done right under my eyes."[52] He was convinced the child would have to be given up, for the circumstances of her birth and parentage were well know. Indeed, he himself had been acquainted with the girl since she was a baby. A former member of the NWMP, Aspdin had been stationed at Wood Mountain during the years when Sitting Bull and his people sought refuge over the border. Moreover, Aspdin was married to a Lakota woman, and for several years he had been the government agent in charge of the Lakota camp at Moose Jaw. In this role, he had been instructed by the Canadian authorities to urge the group to return to the United States, and he had assured them that they would find kind and fair treatment there. He now felt it was the duty of the Canadian government to do everything possible to have the Turtons give up this child whom they wrongfully claimed as theirs. Aspdin was surprised that no effort had been made to corroborate the statements made by the girl's Indian family, who insisted she was theirs. He considered that the matter had been handled in "a hurried, unseemly manner, by a few people who were probably actuated more in trying to make a sensation than any other feeling, and the whole affair seems to have been carried out in a contrary manner to that which should characterize such a serious step as taking a girl of this age (15) from her natural people and sending her hundreds of miles with strangers."[53]

According to Aspdin, the girl had been born at Wood Mountain in the summer of 1883, which made her fifteen. Her father, a white man named Fred Cadd, had managed a trading store. Her mother, Susie Her Road, had lived with Cadd in the winter of 1882–83. The girl had been brought up in the Lakota camp, and after her mother died at Moose Jaw in 1891 she had been looked after by her aunt, Otter Robe Woman, and by her grandmother. In 1894 the Lakota, numbering about fifty, had moved south to the Cheyenne River agency. Aspdin was certain that the Turtons had not the shadow of a right to the child, and he provided the names of various ranchers, missionaries, and policemen who knew the girl's history.

The Turtons were informed of this history, but they remained confident that the child was their Gertie, and they refused to give her up. Aspdin believed that the law should be put in force and a heavy claim for damages brought against the Turtons, but he was willing first to travel to their farm to see if he could persuade them to give up the child quietly. He sympathized with the Turtons in the loss of their daughter but felt that "a woman's desire to find a long lost one appears to destroy their cooler judgment."[54] In his correspondence, Aspdin likened the Turton story to the Tichborne Case, the most celebrated impersonation case in English law. In 1854 Sir James and Lady Tichborne lost their eldest son Roger when his ship, bound for Jamaica, went down, and nothing more was seen or heard of this heir to an ancient Hampshire baronetcy. Then, in 1865, a certain R.C. Tichborne turned up in Wagga Wagga, Australia, and one year later, on Christmas Day, he landed in England as claimant to the Tichborne baronetcy, asserting that he was the lost Roger. In her grief, Lady Tichborne insisted he was her son, though the rest of the family did not agree, and it was eventually proved in court that he was an impostor, a Mr Arthur Orton, son of a Wapping butcher. Orton was sentenced to fourteen years' penal servitude.

The Turtons professed to be "positive" that the found girl was their child, and they threatened to prosecute those who made contrary statements.[55] However, even their neighbours and friends believed that the child's appearance, age, and size were all decidedly against her being a true member of the family. A "happy solution" to the Turton case was proposed by U.S. Senator James W. Kyle, chairman of the Senate Committee on Education and Labour.[56] In May 1898 he informed Canada's Department of Indian Affairs that an inspector in the U.S. Indian Department who was acquainted with Otter Robe Woman could "easily" get papers of release and consent to have the girl adopted by the Turtons. Kyle, who was still inclined to believe that she was "really a white child," said that as she was now approaching womanhood, she would be "a thousandfold better off in a good American home than among her former associates." (It appears to have slipped the senator's mind that the Turtons were offering a good *Canadian* home.)

In July 1898 Inspector James McLaughlin visited the people of the Cheyenne River reservation.[57] His report established beyond doubt that the girl was not the Turton's daughter, but he did obtain "written consent" to the adoption from Otter Robe Woman and her husband Dog Eagle. This was, however, only a conditional consent. The woman agreed that her niece Anatanwin (or Charging Female, or Annie Russell), aged fifteen, might be adopted by the Turtons provided she was properly cared for and educated. She was to write to her aunt at least once every three months until she reached the age of eighteen, at which time she was to "decide for herself, without any undue influence, and determine of her own free will, whether she elects to remain with the said Turtons or return to her relatives at Cheyenne River Agency." Her name was to be retained on the rolls of the agency until she reached the age of majority and determined whether she wished to return to her relatives or to remain with the Turtons.

It is a curious irony that in this last captivity hoax of the nineteenth century, the only person who could be described as having been made captive was Anatanwin, who spoke only Lakota and, renamed Gertie, was taken to Rosemont, the large stone house on the Turton homestead which stands to this day.[58] She became one of their eleven surviving children. (Adelaide Turton gave birth to seventeen children, including three sets of twins.) It appears, however, that Gertie elected to remain in her new life when she reached the age of eighteen, and she later moved to Creelman, Saskatchewan.[59]

There were no more captivity hoaxes on the scale of the sensational Turton drama in the Canadian West. Times had changed as the twentieth century dawned. The Aboriginal people of the West no longer appeared menacing to the new order, which was becoming firmly established as prosperity finally rewarded many of the new arrivals. Physical, social, and cultural boundaries had been clarified between the indigenous people and the newcomers. It was no longer necessary to exaggerate or embellish stories of defenceless victims of evil or to promote hysteria over the issue of the safety of white women at the hands of Aboriginal abductors.

These captivity hoaxes had also served to draw attention to the prevailing ideas about the "life of degradation" endured by all women in Aboriginal communities. The horrors were more fully amplified as readers contemplated the possibility of a white woman living this life. Assumptions about the "wretched fate" that awaited these girls once they grew up both promoted and confirmed the negative images of Aboriginal women that were firmly embedded in the colonial imagination.

CHAPTER FIVE

In Sharp Relief: Representations of Aboriginal Women in the Colonial Imagination

In 1884 Mary E. Inderwick wrote to her Ontario family from the ranch near Pincher Creek, Alberta, where she had lived with her new husband for six months.[1] Her letter provides a perspective on the stratifications of race, gender, and class that were forming as the Euro-Canadian enclave grew in the District of Alberta. Mary Inderwick lamented that it was a lonely life, for she was twenty-two miles from any other women, and she had even offered to help some of her male neighbours "get their shacks done up if only they will go east and marry some really nice girls." The companionship of women such as "the squaw who is the nominal wife of a white man near us" was not considered. Inderwick had recently attended and largely disapproved of her first ball at the North-West Mounted Police (NWMP) barracks at Fort Macleod, for although it was "the first Ball to which the squaws were not allowed to go ... there were several half breeds." Inderwick was dismayed that her maid Lizzie, who had travelled with her from Ontario, had been invited to the same event, and she had since dismissed her, for Lizzie was discontented with her position as a servant. Commenting on the Aboriginal population, which still greatly outnumbered the new arrivals, Inderwick wrote that they should have been "isolated in the mountains" rather than settled on nearby reserves, and that the sooner they became extinct the better for themselves and the country.

At the time of Mary Inderwick's arrival in the West, the consolidation of Canada's rule was beginning but was not yet secure. Tensions were heightened in the 1880s not only because of the Métis resistance of 1885, which fed fears of a larger uprising, but

Mary Ella Inderwick,
North Fork Ranch, 1880s
(Glenbow Archives, NA-1365-2)

because of an uncertain economic climate, which threatened the promise of a prosperous West. There was a sharpening of racial boundaries and an intensification of discrimination. Women immigrants such as Mary Inderwick, who began to arrive in large numbers following the completion of the Canadian Pacific Railway through Alberta in 1883, did not introduce notions of spatial and social segregation, as has often been suggested in a variety of colonial settings.[2] But their arrival coincided with developments such as the treaties and the growth of ranching and farming, which served to consolidate the new order and to allow the recreation of Euro-Canadian institutions, and their presence helped to justify existing policies that were aimed at segregating the new community from indigenous contacts. The Canadian state at this time was increasingly adopting segregationist policies towards the Aboriginal people of the West, and central to these policies were images of Aboriginal women as dissolute, dangerous, and sinister, in comparison to their fragile and vulnerable pure-white counterparts.

While the position of women in the society of the white occupiers of the West indicated the level of civilization being established, the perception of the low status of women and their "depravity" under Aboriginal conditions was taken as confirming evidence of the inferiority of this society. Different types of femininity were compared directly with each other for the purpose of confirming the superiority of white femininity. This study has focused so far on the components of a white femininity as promoted through the issue of "captivities" in the Canadian West in the late nineteenth century, but as Vron Ware wrote in *Beyond the Pale*, discussions of white femininity make sense only in the context of ideas that were promoted at the same time about the relative status of women in the colonized community.[3] The contrasting representations of white and Aboriginal femininity articulated racist messages that confirmed cultural difference and the need for repressive policies. Powerfully negative images of Aboriginal women served to symbolize the shortcomings of that society.

DEVELOPMENT OF STEREOTYPES

From the earliest years of settlement on reserves in western Canada, Canadian government administrators and statesmen, as well as the national press, promoted a cluster of negative images of Aboriginal women, particularly Indian reserve women. These images served those in power, who used them to explain the conditions of poverty and ill health on the reserves. The failure of agriculture on the reserves was attributed to the incapacity of the men to become other than hunters, warriors, and nomads.[4] Responsibility for a host of other problems, including the deplorable state of housing, the lack of clothing and footwear, and the high mortality rate, was placed on the supposed cultural traits and temperament of Indian reserve women. As already noted, during the events of 1885, Indian women were popularly represented in the press as violent instigators of atrocities. They were also depicted as lewd and licentious, particularly after 1885, in order to deflect criticism from the behaviour of government officials and the NWMP, and to legitimize the constraints placed on the activities and movements of Indian women in the world off the reserve. These negative images became deeply embedded in the society of the most powerful socio-economic groups on the prairies and have proved stubborn to revision.

The images were neither new nor unique to the Canadian West. In "The Pocahontas Perplex," Rayna Green has explored the complex, many-faceted dimensions of the image of the Indian woman in American folklore and literature.[5] The beautiful "Indian princess" who saved or aided white men while remaining aloof and virtuous in a woodland paradise was the positive side of the image; but there was her opposite, the squalid and immoral "squaw" who lived in a shack at the edge of town and whose "physical removal or destruction can be understood as necessary to the progress of civilization." It was this latter stereotype that was pressed into service and predominated in the Canadian West in the late nineteenth century as boundaries were clarified and as social and geographic space was marked out. The either/or binary left newcomers little room to consider the diversity of the Aboriginal people of the West or the complex identities and roles of Aboriginal women.

It is important to note that not all shared these sentiments at all times. In 1895, for example, the Methodist missionary John McDougall upbraided a fellow missionary for using the term "squaw" in his recent book: "In the name of decency and civilization and Christianity, why call one person a woman and another a squaw?"[6] But even though it would be a mistake to assume a unified mentality among all Euro-Canadians or, for example, among all members of the NWMP, it is nonetheless clear that the negative stereotype not only prevailed but was deliberately propagated by officials of the state.

To explain why reserve land was not used to capacity and why reserves were pockets of rural poverty, Department of Indian Affairs officials invariably stated that it was because the men would not and could not farm, this being incompatible with their culture and temperament. Plains women were also held responsible; they were defined in the public pronouncements of the Canadian government as idle and gossipy. They did not want proper housing, it was claimed, because they preferred tents, which required less work to maintain and could be clustered in groups, which allowed visiting and gossip.[7] The government publications also said that because the women scrubbed and swept so infrequently, germs were preserved and disseminated, and this spread diseases such as tuberculosis; their love of dancing during the long winter evenings raised the dust that had not been attended to during their idle daylight hours.[8]

Indian reserve women were portrayed as slovenly and unclean in their personal habits as well as in their housekeeping. Administrators blamed the high infant mortality rate on the indifferent care of the mothers.[9] The neglected children of these mothers grew up "rebellious, sullen, disobedient and unthankful."[10] While the men were blamed for the failure of agriculture, the women were portrayed as resisting any progress towards modernization. An inspector of Indian agencies lamented in 1908, "The women, here, as on nearly every reserve, are a hindrance to the advancement of the men. No sooner do the men earn some money than the women want to go and visit their relations on some other reserve, or else give a feast or dance to their friends ... The majority of [the women] are discontented, dirty, lazy and slovenly."[11]

In the unofficial and unpublished reports of reserve life, however, it was widely recognized that problems with reserve housing and health had little to do with the preferences, temperament, or poor housekeeping abilities of the women. Because of their poverty, the people were confined in large numbers in winter to what were little better than one-room shacks, which were poorly ventilated and were impossible to keep clean because they had dirt floors and were plastered with mud and hay. One inspector of agencies noted in 1891 that the women did not have soap, towels, wash basins, or wash pails, nor did they have any means of acquiring them.[12] Similarly, it was frequently noted that the women were short of basic clothing and had no textiles or yarn to work with. Yet in official public statements, the tendency was to ascribe blame to the women rather than drawing attention to conditions that would injure the reputation of government administration.

Another common assumption, as already noted, was that plains women were victimized and subordinated within their own society. They were drudges who performed all the labour, chattels that were purchased and sold, and at the absolute mercy of their owners or husbands, who felt free to cast them aside when old or unwanted in order to make room for a new wife. In their many publications, the missionaries industriously circulated images of the degraded position of women in "pagan" society. The Methodist missionary Egerton Ryerson Young wrote, "In paganism she has not the life of a dog. She is kicked and cuffed and maltreated continually."[13] He also stated, "The men, and even boys, considered it a sign of courage and manliness to despise and shamefully treat their mothers, wives or sisters."[14] In an 1893 article, the missionary John McDougall referred to the "bartering and slaying of wives, and mothers, and daughters" that characterized "savage" life.[15] The central message the missionaries conveyed was that the lives of women were dramatically transformed for the better with the advent of "civilization" and Christianity. Women were being offered liberation from centuries of oppression.

ABORIGINAL MARRIAGE

Marriage in plains societies was widely depicted by non-Aboriginal people simply as a purchase, an exchange of property in which the father and would-be husband struck a bargain according to the market value. No ceremony took place; a commodity simply changed hands. Nor was any love or romance involved in these business transactions or any commitment by the men to cherish their brides, only for the brides to obey. Typically, George Ham, a correspondent with the *Toronto Mail*, reported in 1886 that the Peigan women were very poorly treated within their own society, since they were "sold like so many cattle to suitors, and whether willing or not, became the wives of those able to pay the price asked for them."[16] Similarly, the journalist Effie Laurie Storer wrote in her account of Indian life that women were merely slaves who had no choice of marriage partner. A woman's value amounted to one horse – or two if she was exceptionally popular. She was then her husband's property to do with as he pleased: "He might even kill her if she offended him without any remonstrance from her people. If she proved lazy he could gamble her away."[17]

Few non-Aboriginal observers appreciated the complexities of Aboriginal marriages, nor was there an understanding of the meaning of marriage within the broader social, political, and economic arrangements of a society. Among the societies of the Great Plains alone there were profoundly different systems of marriage. In *Marriage and Inequality in Classless Societies*, Jane Fishburne Collier proposed three models of marriage based on her analysis of Plains Indian societies: brideservice, equal bridewealth, and unequal bridewealth.[18] Even these models, she argues, fail to capture the complex realities of marriage within all Plains Indian societies. The equal bridewealth model may be most appropriate for analysing marriage among the Plains Indians of western Canada, though the model does not correspond in all respects, and there was variation among the several societies of the western plains. Collier stresses that men could not buy wives, nor were women sold: "Marriage was not a market transaction and women were not bought and sold as commodities and grooms did not buy their wives through providing valuables for his in-laws; he is assuming already-defined obligations of a husband and son-in-law."[19] Discussions were not about price and value, but about reciprocal obligations. Collier argues, however, that there was not complete equality between the sexes; men initiated marriage, and women were *given* as wives.[20]

The elders were central to the whole affair, since they most commonly initiated and then negotiated the marriage, validated it, and controlled the valuables that were exchanged in equal bridewealth societies. Few young men had the necessary valuables, so they required the help of senior kin; in this way young men established their dependence on senior kin. Women required the help of the senior women of their families to become successful in their roles, so it made sense for them to submit to marriage arrangements. In some cases, individuals chose their own mates, and the man or woman might ask that marriage arrangements be initiated. Elopement did occur, but the elders still had to validate the marriage.

Gift giving was central to marriage. Marriages were validated through an exchange of valuables between the relatives of the bride and groom. As the plains ethnologist Robert Lowie has explained, "There was generally rather an appearance of purchase than the reality. The girl's kin often gave back as much property as they received. The significant thing was an *exchange* of gifts between the two families. That exchange marked their sanctioning the new bond and cementing a relationship between two *groups* rather than two persons."[21] The man gave gifts and performed services for the kin of the woman he hoped to marry, and these served to validate the kinship bond. The gifts were seen as indicators of what the groom's elders thought of him and of the marriage. (They were not indicators of the "market value" of the bride, as outside observers concluded.) The family's willingness to provide gifts was seen as a sign of the man's worthiness and commitment. In some equal bridewealth societies, the son-in-law was expected to live with and work for his wife's parents; in others, he lived with and worked for his own parents; in still others, the newly-weds set up their own household but were expected to perform service for all their senior kin.

Marital disputes were handled by the elders. The woman's kin could keep a married woman from her husband if they did not approve of his behaviour, and they could allow a disunion or divorce if they were convinced that the grounds were serious enough. To obtain forgiveness and pardon, an abandoned husband had to rely on his senior kin, since negotiations concerning the return of the wife took place between the senior kin of a separated couple.

The popular view of Aboriginal marriage customs held by non-Aboriginal people was one of a cluster that symbolized the shortcomings of Aboriginal society, contributing to the overall impression that women were dreadfully mistreated. According to the ideal, which was often far from reality, white women achieved an elevation in status through marriage. Wives were loved, protected, and cherished by their husbands. The status of Aboriginal wives appeared as the exact opposite. These views about the superior position of white women and the inferior treatment of Aboriginal women were strongly held because they helped justify the displacement of Aboriginal people onto small reserves and the program of assimilation introduced in the late nineteenth century. They were also convenient misperceptions because they could be used to excuse the behaviour of those white males in the West who mistreated Aboriginal women.

Recent research has drawn into question many of these confident assumptions of an earlier age. Several studies suggest that plains women enjoyed greater autonomy, influence, and status before the advent of European influence and colonization.[22] In egalitarian hunting and foraging societies, women exercised control over their own lives and activities. Women and men occupied positions of equal value and prestige. Although their work was different, this did not imply inferiority for either gender. In plains societies, the gathering work of women was vital, and survival of the group sometimes depended on the efforts of the women. Women worked hard, and to non-Aboriginal observers their work appeared as drudgery, yet these observers failed to understand the social power which the labour helped the women attain. Plains women controlled the distribution of their family's food resources, and this gave them considerable power and influence. The growth of male-owned private property, with the advent of the fur trade and other European influences, transformed women in Aboriginal society. They became more dependent, and their status declined.

Studies of the reserve era suggest that government and missionary efforts to impose western patriarchal forms of family, labour,
property, and production resulted in the women's further economic dependence on men.[23] The legislation embodied in the
Indian Act left women who were defined as "Indian" with fewer
fundamental rights than other Canadian women or Indian men.
Only with the passage of this legislation did they legally become vir-
tually the property of their husbands, consistent with English common law.[24] The interpretation of this law in Canada allowed
husbands to beat their wives and denied women basic protection
against ruthless mistreatment. Under English common law, married women were legally denied any semblance of independence
and autonomy.[25] Nor did they have access to the jobs, professions,
or land that would allow them an independent income. In western
Canada, land and income were legally owned and controlled by
men. Unlike the situation in the western United States, Canadian
women were not, except in exceptional circumstances, allowed to
enter for homesteads, and in 1886 dower rights were abolished in
the Canadian West.[26] A white woman worker among the Omaha in
the late nineteenth century found that she was "more than once
interrupted by the remark that our laws showed that 'the white
man had neither love nor respect for his women.'"[27]

"LICENTIOUSNESS" AND GOVERNMENT OFFICIALS

Officials propagated an image of Aboriginal women as dissolute in
order to deflect criticism from government agents and policies.
This image was invoked with particular strength in the wake of an
1886 controversy over the alleged "brutal, heartless and ostentatious licentiousness" of government officials resident in western
Canada.[28] This controversy began with the remarks of Samuel
Trivett, a Church of England missionary who had been stationed
since 1880 on the Blood Reserve in present-day southern Alberta.
George Ham, the special corespondent for the *Mail* mentioned
above, was assigned in 1886 to look into the condition of the western Indians, and especially to determine whether there was any
basis to the rumours of an imminent uprising. Trivett, who was one
of Ham's informants, declared that there was no truth in the
rumours, but he did have suggestions for improvement. One was
that the Indian Department must pay more in order to get the best

men as officials. These jobs called for Christian, married men, he said: "Put a stop to white men living with Indian women unless they are lawfully married to them. Where are the young girls of 13 to 16 that have been partly taught in our schools and others before them? Sold to white men for from $10.00 to $20! Where are their children? Running about the reserves wearing rags! Where are the women themselves? They are prostitutes hanging around the towns. Stop the sale of Indian girls to white men and another great step is taken."[29] In his subsequent statements to the press, Trivett stuck by his words, though he made it clear that his quarrel was not with men involved in long-standing relationships in which both parents provided for the children; it was with the men who "rejected" the women after only a few months or years. Trivett claimed that these women either became the temporary wives of other white men or were "thrown upon the mercy of the camp," their children not provided for either by the fathers or by the government, since they were not considered wards.[30]

The Toronto *Globe* immediately picked up on Trivett's remarks and featured an article about the "brutal, heartless and ostentatious licentiousness" of government officials in the North-West.[31] The article referred to a scandalous situation in England that had been uncovered by the newspaperman W.T. Stead and suggested that similar things were going on in the North-West. In 1885 Stead, the editor of London's *Pall Mall Gazette*, had created a panic about "white slavery" when he attempted to prove that girls were being sold into prostitution. He claimed to have successfully purchased a thirteen-year-old London girl from her parents for a few pounds.[32] Stead's exposé of the vices of the city was printed in a series of articles in his paper and later reprinted as *The Maiden Tribute of Modern Babylon*. Samuel Trivett had been in England in 1885 (he was married to an English woman that year), and he may well have been influenced by the Stead revelations.[33]

Trivett's accusations, especially those suggesting the involvement of some government agents, were seized upon by critics of the administration of Indian affairs in western Canada. In the aftermath of the Métis resistance of 1885, opponents of John A. Macdonald's Conservatives had amassed evidence of neglect, injustice, and incompetence, and they were delighted to be able to add immorality to the list. In the House of Commons in April 1886 the Liberal MP Malcolm Cameron delivered a lengthy indictment of Indian

affairs in the West, focusing on the unscrupulous behaviour of officials of the Indian Department. Cameron quoted Trivett and
charged that agents of the government, sent to elevate and educate, had instead acted to "humiliate, to lower, to degrade and
debase the virgin daughters of the wards of the nation." He knew
of one young Indian agent from England, he said, who was unfit to
do anything there, who was living on a reserve in "open adultery
with two young squaws … revelling in the sensual enjoyments of a
western harem, plentifully supplied with select cullings from the
western prairie flowers."[34]

Cameron implicated members of the NWMP in this behaviour,
wondering why it was that more than 45 per cent of them were reported to have been under medical treatment for venereal disease. Cameron was not the first to raise the matter of police
impropriety. Concern about improper relations between the police and Aboriginal women had long predated the Trivett scandal.
It was part of a larger debate in the press and in Parliament over
charges of inefficiency, lack of discipline, the high rate of deser-
tion, and low morale in the force – a debate that had been going
on since the late 1870s, only a few years after the creation of the
force.[35] In 1878, Lieutenant-Governor of the North-West Territories David Laird had written to NWMP Commissioner James
Macleod: "I fear from what reports are brought me, that some of
your officers at Fort Walsh are making rather free with the women
around there. It is to be hoped that the good name of the Force
will not be hurt through too open indulgence of that kind. And I
sincerely hope that Indian women will not be treated in a way that
hereafter may give trouble."[36] Although Macleod and Assistant
Commissioner A.G. Irvine denied that there was "anything like 'a
regular brothel'" about the police posts, such reports persisted. In
1879 John F. Clark, who was part of an astronomical party sent by
the government to assist the work of surveyors, described the
police at Fort Macleod as being "a fraud of the worst description."
He wrote in his diary: "Their drill consists entirely of devising
means to swindle the Government, steal whiskey from civilians or
seduce squaws. The conduct of the officers and men has been
such that any honest man would blush to be called a Mounted
Policeman. The Force out here are properly called the Mounted
Inebriate Asylum."[37] In the House of Commons in 1880 Joseph
Royal, a Manitoba MP, stated that the NWMP was accused of

"disgraceful immorality" all over the West. Royal had evidence that at one of the police posts that winter there had been "an open quarrel between an officer and one of the constables for the possession of a squaw" and that one officer had slapped another "in the face on account of a squaw."[38] Royal had been informed that "many members of the force were living in concubinage with Indian women, whom they had purchased from their parents and friends." In 1886 public attention was once again drawn to police behaviour when the *Mail* informed its readers that between 1874 and 1881 the police had "lived openly with Indian girls purchased from their parents" and that it was only in more recent years, because of the arrival of settlers, that they had been compelled to abandon the practice or at least be "more discreet in the pursuit of their profligacy."[39]

There is little doubt that there was some foundation to the accusations of Trivett and the other critics. Evidence remains scanty, however. Since the missionaries, for example, depended to a large extent on the goodwill of government, they were rarely as outspoken as Trivett. Nevertheless, in 1885 John McLean, the Methodist missionary on the Blood Reserve near Fort Macleod, also characterized the type of person employed on many of the reserves as utterly incompetent, and he too urged the government to employ only married men "of sterling Christian character."[40] In 1886 Edgar Dewdney, who had succeeded Laird as lieutenant-governor of the North-West Territories, told the missionaries not to communicate with the newspapers "even if allegations against public officials were true," since this would do more harm than good, would affect their mission work, and could be used to stir up political strife.[41] Government officials generally investigated reports of government misconduct themselves, and this functioned to cover up or mitigate such allegations. Similarly, members of the NWMP themselves looked into complaints about police misbehaviour.

NWMP RELATIONS WITH ABORIGINAL WOMEN

The relations of police with Aboriginal women is a subject that is overlooked in analyses of police-Indian relations, nor is it generally mentioned in police reminiscences or the tributes to "red serge wives." Yet is is clear from some of the primary sources of the NWMP that there was a great deal of socializing and that some members of

Assiniboine girls at Fort Walsh, *c* 1878–79
(Glenbow Archives, NA-935-2)

Members of the NWMP at Fort Walsh in the Cypress Hills, 1880.
Left to right: Surgeon G.A. Kennedy, Sub-inspector L. Crozier, S.B. Steele,
F.J. Dickens, Inspector J. Cotton (National Archives of Canada, C-19018C)

Major James Morrow Walsh (RCMP Museum, Regina, 3.0-22)

Colonel James Farquhar-son Macleod (*standing*) and Captain Edmund Dalrymple Clark, 1879 (Glenbow Archives, NA-2206-1, photo by Topley, Ottawa, March 1879)

the force, especially the recruits of the 1870s and early 1880s, formed relationships with Indian and Métis women, as did a great many other of the predominantly male immigrants during these years.

Among the police, there were radically different points of view about what was suitable behaviour. Some of them married Aboriginal women in ceremonies sanctioned by customary law or Christian rites. Others clearly exploited the women. Some condemned all such relationships, while others believed that they were vital to the virile image of the force. An insight into these different points of view is provided in a letter that Colonel James Macleod of the NWMP wrote to his wife Mary from Fort Walsh in 1878. Macleod found himself having to sleep in the room and bed formerly occupied by Inspector James Morrow Walsh. "I cannot help thinking of the many companions who must have accompanied it with him," Macleod wrote. "Just fancy Walsh tried to make White [Comptroller F. White?] believe on the way up that it was the right thing to do when you stayed at Indian camps to take squaws to your bed when they were offered to you. That it gives the Indians a good notion of our *manliness* and that they think little of a man who refuses the embraces thus offered. Nothing could be further from the true state of the case. Indeed I think that Indians have a very much greater respect for the man who lives as a white man, and does not follow any of their practices."[42]

The first book published on the NWMP, Jean D'Artigue's *Six Years in the Canadian Northwest*, indicates that such relationships began as early as the 1874 Great March West.[43] According to D'Artigue, while they were camped at Fort Carlton one of the subconstables insisted that he was in love with an "Indian maiden" and intended to take her at any cost to Edmonton to marry her. Others were opposed to this plan, and the unhappy subconstable was dissuaded, his attentions soon diverted to other women. While at Edmonton, this troop of police attended a dance held at the camp of Plains Cree Chief Sweet Grass, and D'Artigue claimed that the chief wished him to marry his daughter, an offer he declined. In his memoirs of life in the force from 1879 to 1885, F.J.E. Fitzpatrick wrote that some of the policemen married Aboriginal women "Indian fashion," while others "retained them as their lawful wives." In other cases, noted Fitzpatrick, "just as in civilized parts of our country, they discarded them without much further thought."[44]

Simon J. Clarke at Fort Walsh, 1876
(Glenbow Archives, NA-644-1)

Sources from the district of what became southern Alberta show that in the earliest years of the force, the police regularly attended dances held in the Blackfoot camps. Dr Richard Nevitt, the police surgeon at Fort Macleod, frequently went to what he termed "squaw dances" along with many others, including Colonel James Macleod, who later became commissioner of the force, and Inspector Cecil Denny, who later became Sir Cecil Denny.[45] One February evening, Nevitt and Denny walked two miles to an encampment to attend a dance, bringing along gifts of coffee, molasses, and cornmeal, which were much enjoyed by all. The police danced until one in the morning, and Nevitt wrote that he "carried on a desperate flirtation with no less than four squaws; they made me get up and dance again and again ... I enjoyed myself very much."[46]

The police also held their own dances. One of the few candid police diaries from the early years of the force was that of Simon John Clarke, who served from 1876 until 1882 at Fort Macleod and Fort Walsh. Later, Clarke became one of the original members of the Calgary City Council. He was an alderman for many years and occupied such prominent positions as chairman of the Board of Public Works.[47] Although Clarke was educated in the public schools of Quebec and apparently was also well versed in law through his distinguished lawyer father, he had problems with basic spelling and grammar. In describing a dance at Fort Macleod given by C and E troops in October 1879, he wrote: "A good many of the Police got drunk with the citizens on Jamaica Ginger and there was nearly a rough house only the Citizens left in time, so there was no trouble. Half breed women and Indian women Where the Principly one at the dance."[48] On 4 December he described another dance: "Police Boys gave a dance in Corpl. Martins Hall. The Citizens tried to start one down at the other Hall but they could not get the Squaws. We got them at our dance." A New Year's ball held later that month in the barracks of C troop attracted about four hundred people from fifty miles around, according to Clarke: "Col. Macleod opened the ball with a Blackfoot squaw Mr. Davis women" (he was probably referring to Revenge Walker, the wife of D.W. Davis). Mrs Mary Macleod was also at this ball, having arrived at Fort Macleod earlier that year. She was one of six white women in that part of the country, according to Clarke's estimate. It was not unusual for white women to attend these dances in the early 1880s. In his diary, policeman William H. Metzler noted several dances held in June 1882, including one on the thirtieth: "Had another Ball last night sent a team up to Pincher Creek for some white Ladies, with the ladys from Pincher Creek and them around here made up about fifteen, there was about one hundred and fifty sat down to supper including Half Breeds and Squaws which made quite a crowd."[49]

Similar revelries took place at other police posts. Some of those held at Fort Walsh were lampooned in the *Fort Benton Record* by a correspondent who used "Cypress" as a pseudonym. In December 1876, Cypress described a "Grand Ball" held at Fort Walsh: "Among the ladies present I noticed the Misses McCoy, the Wells sisters, the Gopher, and other noted Belles, whose titles I am unable to master. The Gopher when requested to dance, said, Toke. She looked charming with a bandana handkerchief around her neck."[50] At Fort Saskatchewan, the police enjoyed attending Métis weddings and other celebrations at which the dancing often continued for several days. In February 1880, for instance, young Frederick Bagley, trumpeter for the force, noted in his diary: "For the past week a crowd of Scotch half breed girls from Victoria [60 miles North], and a couple of their male relatives, one of whom is a fiddler, have been 'camping' in the barrack room, and dancing has been there, and in the Colonel's [W.D. Jarvis, in command] quarters, night and day until the girls left for home yesterday."[51]

At Fort Macleod, the attendance of Indian women at police dances came to an abrupt end in 1884, though Métis women were still invited. The big social event of 1884, according to Mountie W.H. Cox, was the police ball on New Year's Eve. In his diary, Cox described what happened: "This year there were a lot of white ladies in the country who objected to dancing with the squaws, so a cut was made this year at the meeting. Sergeant Major Bradley asked me as an old hand what I was in favour of, black or white. I told him I was in favour of pinto. The old hands were outvoted. They made the cut. The first dress suits shown in Macleod were worn on this occasion."[52] Around this time, the *Macleod Gazette* was regularly mocking the appearance and behaviour of Aboriginal women in the town of Fort Macleod, drawing distinctions between their appearance and behaviour and that of "real" ladies. In 1885 the paper published an article, intended as humourous, in which it lamented that the "broncho," "fresh from the camp," had disappeared from the dance floors of the town. In dance-hall language the broncho was not a horse, the *Gazette* explained, but a "lady of the copper colored persuasion who is being initiated for the first time into the mysteries of a 'white' ball room, and to whom the many intricacies of the quadrille and waltz are as the labyrinthe of old, a mess which, the further she gets into it, the less hope she has of ever coming out of it alive." It does not seem to have occurred to the author of this article that the police had probably made spectacles of themselves when they danced at the Blackfoot events during the early years.

As noted above, some of the policemen married Aboriginal women in ceremonies sanctioned by Christian ceremony or customary law. The Lakota author-historian John O'kute-sica recorded that six "red coats" of the Wood Mountain detachment in the early 1880s married Lakota women from Sitting Bull's band and that most of these couples (including Mary Blackmoon and Thomas Aspdin, J.H. Thomson and Pretty Smile) lived together to old age and death.[53] One couple, Archie LeCaine and Emma Loves War separated because Emma did not wish to move with Archie to eastern Canada.

A story often told about the founding of Fort Walsh is that the site was chosen because the farm of the Métis family of Edward McKay,

The daughters of Edward and Caroline McKay,
early settlers of the Cypress Hills. In 1875 Fort Walsh
was built beside the McKay home.
Left to right: Emma (Mrs Peter O'Hare),
Maria (Mrs James F. Sanderson),
Rachel (Mrs Jules Quesnelle), Jemima (Mrs J.H.G. Bray)
(National Archives of Canada, NA-4541-1)

which included five daughters, was located there.[54] In 1876 Jemima
McKay married John Bray, who was an NWMP sergeant-major and
sheriff; Emma McKay married Constable Peter O'Hare, a tailor with
the force; a third McKay sister, Clara, was engaged to be married to
another policeman but tragically took her own life sometime between 1878 and 1880.[55] Sergeant F.W. Spicer, stationed at Fort
Walsh, Maple Creek, and Fort Macleod in the late 1870s and early
1880s, was legally married to a Blood woman, and on at least one occasion this family connection allowed him particular insight into a
case on the Blood Reserve.[56] D.J. Grier of the NWMP, who was mentioned in an earlier chapter, was legally married to a Peigan woman.
Both Spicer and Grier, however, eventually married white women.

Tahnoncoach, who was a member of Sitting Bull's band and wife of George Pembridge of the NWMP, Fort Walsh (Glenbow Archives, NA-935-1)

Three NWMP sergeants major, *c* 1880s. *Left to right:* Frank W. Spicer, R. Barker, J.H. Genereaux (Glenbow Archives, NA-1368-7)

Cree children at Maple Creek
(Glenbow Archives, NA-3811-12)

Of course, there were children. James Morrow Walsh, founder
of Fort Walsh in the Cypress Hills, who was renowned for the relationship of trust he established with Sitting Bull and the other
Sioux leaders who had sought refuge in Canada in 1876, apparently had a child with a Blackfoot woman and relationships with
several Sioux women.[57] Cecil Denny, while a sub-inspector at Fort
Macleod, had a daughter with Victoria McKay, a part-Peigan
woman who was the wife of another policeman, Constable Percy
Robinson.[58] Denny had to resign from the force for a time in
1881 because of the court case that Robinson brought against
him for "having induced his wife to desert him and also having
criminal connections with her."[59] According to the diary of a
policeman stationed at Fort Macleod at the time, Robinson sued
Denny for ten thousand dollars; but Denny got off because the
principal witness, the priest who had married Robinson and
McKay, was not able to appear.[60] Cecil Denny's daughter was
raised by her mother on the American Blackfoot reservation.[61]

Assistant Surgeon Henry Dodd of the NWMP had a daughter who lived on one of the Crooked Lake reserves in the Qu'Appelle Valley. There is a record of this in the police files only because Dodd was granted leave to attend to her when she was very ill in 1889.[62]

Other references to police relations with Aboriginal women include an entry in the diary of Constable R.N. Wilson, who noted in January 1883 that his commanding officer, N.F. Leif Crozier (then in command of Fort Macleod), had "tender feelings towards 'White Antelope's' daughter and cannot do too much to please the Old Gentleman." White Antelope was a prominent Blood. Wilson, who was removed from the charge of the Stand Off detachment, believed that Crozier had transferred him because he did not get along with White Antelope.[63]

Many of these relationships were of a casual and fleeting nature. One of the few histories of the force to refer to them is T. Morris Longstreth's *The Silent Force: Scenes from the Life of the Mounted Police of Canada* (1927).[64] Longstreth drew on the memories of some of the original members of the force. He quoted a policeman who described the quandary he was in as a young man stationed at Fort Walsh: "How can a buck policeman in barracks run his squaw on fifty cents a day and keep our wolf pack out of her teepee and not be caught by the authorities!"[65]

Constable Bob Patterson was partying with a woman in the shoe shop of Fort Macleod one night in December 1880 when the pipes were knocked off the stove and an entire row of buildings caught fire and were ruined. The true story behind the fire was recorded in the diary of Simon Clarke. To the public, however, Patterson was a hero, winning glory and a forty-dollar reward for responding quickly to the fire alarm.[66] Patterson became a prominent citizen of Fort Macleod, representing the Macleod constituency for two terms at Edmonton. It is certainly clear that the police engaged in a great deal of alcohol consumption, especially in the early years. Writing from Fort Macleod to his mother in Nova Scotia in the fall of 1875, James Stanford, who did not drink liquor, lamented, "One thing I do not like, we came out here to stop the whisky trade and instead of doing so most of the fellows are drunk half the time."[67] He then described the events of the previous evening, when the boys had nailed a blanket across the window after the bugle sounded "lights out," which enabled them to drink and party until the noise alerted the sergeant of the guard. A fight then broke out. Stanford instructed his mother not to repeat this, as it would get him into trouble.

There are regrettably few sources from this time that allow insight into the thoughts of Aboriginal women on relations with the NWMP. One Lakota woman, however, Mrs James Ogle of Wood Mountain, Saskatchewan, was interviewed at age eighty in the mid-1970s. Her mother had known Walsh and had a high opinion of the police. She recalled what her mother had told her about those times: "The police gave them hardtack biscuits and scraps ... There were no white ladies in those days. The policemen want wives so they go around and pick the ones they want. They give the starving families groceries to get the girls."[68]

John O'Kute-sica wrote at length about a customary marriage at Wood Mountain in which a policeman abused his wife. The marriage was between O'Kute-sica's aunt Iteskawin, or White Face Woman, and Superintendent William Dummer Jarvis, who was from a prominent Toronto family. Before arriving in the West, Jarvis had had a lengthy military career. He served with the Twelfth Regiment (later, York Rangers) at the Cape of Good Hope in the 1850s, and as Captain Jarvis he was put in command of the service company of the Queen's Own Rifles during the alarm over Fenian attacks in the mid-1860s. He retired from the military in 1872 and was permitted to retain his rank of lieutenant-colonel.[69] By this time, Jarvis had established a reputation as an undisciplined "libertine."[70] His personal life was in disarray, his wife having left him in 1870 with their two young sons, and his family faced the everlasting problem of "what to do about Willy." They were delighted when he secured a posting as superintendent with the NWMP as part of the original contingent.[71] (Missionary John McDougall singled out Jarvis to express his overall scorn for many of the specimens who joined the force. He called Jarvis's description of the Great March West a "gross blasphemy.")[72] Nevertheless, under Jarvis's command, Fort Saskatchewan was established, and in 1880 he was transferred briefly to Fort Macleod. He was then, it appears, stationed at Fort Walsh and Wood Mountain.

According to O'Kute-sica, his aunt had consented to marry Jarvis at the height of the starvation of the Lakota on condition that if she married him, he would ensure that her brothers and sisters would have something to eat twice a day.[73] O'Kute-sica explained that for

Iteskawin and her family the marriage to a white man was a terrible sacrifice, but "to look at the lean faces of the two brothers and little sister and to see her father return home late, empty handed, demanded something from her."[74] After only a few weeks of marriage, Jarvis publicly assaulted Iteskawin at a Lakota night dance, an incident that strained relations between the two communities, and she immediately left him. According to O'Kute-sica, Jarvis did not understand the intricacies of the customs involved in a night dance. When it was announced that it was the man's choice of partners, a young Lakota man asked Iteswakin to dance. According to custom, the lady had to kiss her partner at the end of the dance. If she refused, fruit sauce would be poured over her head. Iteskawin followed the custom, for she was anxious to spare her dress of white antelope skin, with its intricate quillwork designs. O'Kute-sica explained, "It is the practice of the Sioux to try the heart of a man – even so far as to court the wife." Jarvis, who was watching only his wife, did not see the other partners demanding and receiving the customary kiss. He moved quick as a cat, seized his wife, and "half-dragged" her out of the dance enclosure. Before they were out of sight, Jarvis, "crazed by jealousy, thrust his wife to the ground twice." After she was thrown down the second time, Iteskawin thrust a knife against his side. The next morning it was discovered that she had disappeared. Jarvis was hastily dismissed from the force in 1881.

Women such as Iteskawin, it seems, had little protection from the law when they suffered abuse. In the few cases where a record exists of Aboriginal women attempting to lay charges against policemen for assault or rape, the claims seem to have been dismissed as efforts to discredit or blackmail.[75] The broader question of the extent to which the police assisted Aboriginal women in laying charges of assault and rape is worthy of further investigation. A *Manitoba Free Press* report of 29 September 1876 indicates that they did not provide such assistance. A Mr Skeffington Thompson, a former member of the NWMP reported among other "interesting information" from the West: "A gross case of rape was perpetrated in the village of Fort Macleod by a trader, who is a member of an influential firm. Though the Mounted Police were brought to the house by the cries of the Indian woman subjected to the outrage, the non-commissioned officer with them hesitated to break in the door to seize the offender; the result is that he has so far evaded arrest."

GOVERNMENT OFFICIALS AND
ABORIGINAL WOMEN

Quite a number of the early employees on reserves in the West were married to Aboriginal women, and many of these marriages were as stable as any other. Robert Jefferson, for example, who taught school on Red Pheasant's reserve and was later appointed farm instructor on Poundmaker's reserve, married a sister of Chief Poundmaker.[76] But some government employees on the reserves clearly abused their positions of authority. In 1882, for example, Chief Crowfoot of the Blackfoot and his wife complained that the farm instructor on their reserve had demanded sexual favours from a young girl in return for rations, and when an investigation proved this to be the case, the man was dismissed.[77] Both the documentary and oral record suggest that several of the government employees who were among the men killed at Frog Lake and Battleford by Cree in the spring of 1885 were disliked intensely because of their callous and at times brutal treatment of Aboriginal women. The farm instructor on the Mosquito Reserve near Battleford, James Payne, was known for his violent temper. On one occasion, he beat a young woman and threw her out of his house because he found her visiting his young Cree wife.[78] The terrified and shaken woman, who was found by her father, died soon afterwards, and her grieving father blamed Payne, whom he killed in 1885. As a Touchwood Hills farm instructor told a visiting newspaper correspondent in 1885, the charges of immorality among farm instructors on the reserves were in many instances all too true: "The greatest facilities are afforded the Indian instructor for the seduction of Indian girls. The instructor holds the grub. The agent gives him the supplies and he issues them to the Indians. Now you have a good idea of what semi-starvation is."[79] In 1893 Chief Thunderchild complained that the farm instructor on his reserve was exchanging extra rations in return for sexual services. That year, too, there was a major Indian Affairs investigation into allegations made by the chief and councillors of the Hobbema agency that the Indian agent had indecently assaulted a number of women. The agent successfully argued that there was a widespread "conspiracy" to discredit him, and he remained agent at Hobbema for a time.[80]

BLAMING ABORIGINAL WOMEN:
"THE CHARACTER OF THE MEN OF
THIS COUNTRY HAS BEEN ASSAILED"

The most vocal response to the accusations of Trivett and other critics was not to deny that there had been immorality in the West, but to stress that it had nothing to do with the men. Rather, it was due to the character of Aboriginal women, who behaved in an abandoned and wanton manner and, in their own society, were accustomed to being treated with contempt and to being bought and sold as commodities. Like the Spanish soldiers among the Pueblo, whose conduct was investigated in 1601, these men "recounted no exploits, admitted no faults. Rather they spoke of the licentious Pueblo women," whom they described as having no shame and being unfaithful to their husbands.[81] In defending the NWMP in 1880, the Toronto *Globe* emphasized that Aboriginal women had "loose morals" that were "notorious the world over," and that "no men in the world are so good as to teach them better, or to try to reform them in this respect."[82]

These sentiments were echoed again and again in the wake of the 1886 controversy that had been sparked by Samuel Trivett's criticisms. For instance, the editor of the *Macleod Gazette*, a former member of the NWMP, argued: "Nothing is said about the fact that many of these women were prostitutes before they went to live with the white man, and that in the majority of cases the overtures for this so-called immorality come from the woman or Indians themselves."[83] The white men, he said, were simply "taking advantage of an Indian's offer."[84] Readers of the *Toronto Daily Mail* were told that Aboriginal men had sold their wives and children in the thousands to soldiers and settlers ever since the time of the French fur trade in order to be able to obtain alcohol, and that with the arrival of the police a great deal had been done to end this situation.[85] What was objected to more than anything was that "the character of the men of this country has been assailed." As the Macleod *Gazette* declared, "We deem it our duty to lift our voices in their defence."[86]

The *Gazette* insisted that there was no marriage in Plains Indian societies. All that was involved was a little lively bartering with the father, and a woman could be purchased for a horse or two. The argument that Indian women were virtual slaves, first to their fathers and then to their husbands, was called upon by all who wished to deflect criticism from government officials and the NWMP. The attitude of Sir Hector Langevin was typical, when in April 1886 he rose in the House of Commons to defend the government's record. Langevin's response to the charges of immorality was that, to Indians, marriage was simply a bargain and a sale, and that immorality among them had long predated the arrival of government agents in the North-West.[87]

The government's official response to the criticisms was contained in an 1886 pamphlet entitled *The Facts Respecting Indian Administration in the North-West.* As usual, the government had sent its own official to inquire into accusations about the misconduct of employees of the Indian Department and, predictably, no evidence of misconduct had been found. The man sent to investigate, Hayter Reed, the assistant commissioner of Indian affairs, was one of the unmarried officials who had been accused of having an Indian mistress as well as a child from this relationship.[88] Father Doucet, an Oblate missionary, noted that Reed was sympathetic to the agent and the other employees, and he described Reed's investigation as "so superficial that nothing was proven and nobody found guilty."[89] The government pamphlet stated that Trivett had been unable to come up with a shred of actual evidence (though the missionary vehemently denied this).[90] It also stated that although some men had acquired their wives by "purchase," this was the Indian custom: "No father ever dreams of letting his daughter leave his wigwam till he has received a valuable consideration for her." If the government stopped this custom, stated the pamphlet, there would be loud protests, over and above the Indians' "chronic habit of grumbling."[91] Furthermore, it was not fair to criticize the behaviour of the dead, such as Delaney and Payne, who had "passed from the bar of human judgment."[92] Moreover, such criticism might encourage Indians in their exaggerated, misled notions, and consequently white women might again be dragged into horrible captivity. The government publication thus played up the perils of white women in the West and of others who might move there.

Also evident in the later 1880s was the increasing use of the term "squaw man" to denote men of the lowest social class. There was disdain for those within the community who did not conform to the new demands to clarify boundaries. The police reports blamed "squaw men" for many of the crimes committed, such as liquor offences or the killing of cattle. Samuel B. Steele of the NWMP wrote from the Fort Macleod district in 1890 that the wives of these men "readily act as agents, and speaking the language, and being closely connected with the various tribes, their houses soon become a rendezvous for idle and dissolute Indians and half breeds, and being themselves in that debatable land between savagery and civilization possibly do not realize the heinousness and danger to the community."[93] The *Moosomin Courier* of March 1890 blamed the "squaw-men" for stirring up trouble with the Indians in 1885 and prejudicing them against policies that were for their own good.[94]

LIVES OF ABORIGINAL WOMEN

The overwhelming image that emerged from the 1886 "immorality" controversy was that Aboriginal women themselves were to blame for the situation. They and the traditions of the society from which they came were identified as the cause of vice and corruption in the new settlements of the Prairie West. This image was not accepted by all Euro-Canadians in the West. Nor, of course, did it reflect the lives of the vast majority of Aboriginal women. Just as few white women actually lived up to the virtues they were said to exemplify, few Aboriginal women actually behaved in the way fixed in the colonial imagination. Aboriginal oral and documentary sources suggest that in the early reserve years, particularly in the aftermath of the events of 1885, women provided essential security and stability in their communities, which had experienced so much upheaval. In these years of low resources and shattered morale, the work of women in their own new settlements was vital, materially as well as spiritually. Cree author Joe Dion wrote that when spirits and resources were low on his reserve in the late 1880s, "much of the inspiration for the Crees came from the old ladies, for they set to work with a will that impressed everybody."[95]

Moreover, far from being a danger to the well-being of the new communities, Aboriginal women played a positive role in maintaining the health of many of the new arrivals. As well as being important as midwives to some of the early women immigrants, they helped instruct them on what was edible or otherwise useful in the prairie environment and on how these products might be preserved. There are many examples of such assistance in the memoirs of the early settlers. For instance, a woman settler in the Qu'Appelle district recalled, "Whenever the stork visited us, a nice old Cree lady, Mrs. Fisher, from across the lake, acted as both doctor and nurse for the neighborhood. She couldn't speak a word of English and often told us long yarns in Cree, then laughed heartily because we couldn't understand her."[96] There was the same situation in the Battleford settlement where, in the early years, the community drew on the remarkable knowledge of Aboriginal women for assistance at childbirth and to cure ailments. In particular, a Mrs Longmore "knew all the places within three hundred miles where she could gather the leaves, the berries, the barks and the roots which formed her materia medica, and to her knowledge of their efficacy, and skill in their use, many a woman in those early days attributed her safe return from the Valley of the Shadow."[97] Just as the stereotype of the Aboriginal woman as a menace to the newly forming communities was not matched by reality, neither was the image circulated during the months of conflict in 1885, when Aboriginal women were said to have incited the men to violence and participated in violent behaviour. As noted in chapter 2, Cree women formed a "protective society" around the women and children hostages in Big Bear's camp, keeping them out of harm's way. Typically, this aspect of the drama was absent from the headlines of the day.[98]

CONSTRAINTS ON ABORIGINAL WOMEN

The characterization of Aboriginal women as an immoral and corrupting influence played an important role in how these women were defined and treated by the Canadian authorities. It meant increasingly narrow options and opportunities. Both informal and formal constraints served to keep Aboriginal people from the towns and settled areas of the prairies, and consequently their presence there became more and more marginal. While they may not have wished to live in the towns, their land use patterns for a time intersected with the new order, and they were interested in taking advantage of markets and other economic opportunities. But there was a widely shared belief among townspeople that Aboriginal people did not belong within the new settlements that were replacing and expelling "savagery."[99] Their presence was seen as incongruous, corrupting, and demoralizing. An English woman travelling in the West in 1912 derisively described the sight of an Aboriginal woman in the urban centres: "The big cities and towns, with their up-to-date civilization, know her not as a citizen; but at times she is still to be seen with her dirty blanket and mocassins, coarse black hair, high cheekbones, a clay pipe in her mouth, taking her place humbly at the back of her lord and master."[100] Classified as prostitutes, Aboriginal women were regarded as particularly threatening to morality and health. An 1886 pamphlet of advice for immigrants, entitled *What Women Say of the Canadian North-West*, was quick to reassure its readers that Aboriginal people were hardly ever seen.[101] The 320 women who responded to the question "Do you experience any dread of the Indians?" overwhelmingly replied that they rarely saw any. Mrs S. Lumsden, for example, thought they were "hundreds of miles away with sufficient force to keep them quiet."[102]

Following the events of 1885, government officials as well as the NWMP made strenuous efforts to keep people on their reserves. Because of the pass system that had been introduced, no one could leave a reserve without a pass from the farm instructor or agent. A central rationale for the pass system was that it would spare the towns and villages from visits by Aboriginal women "of abandoned character who were there for the worst purposes."[103] There is evidence that some Aboriginal women did work as prostitutes.[104] In 1883 the Cree chiefs of the Edmonton area complained in a letter to the prime minister that their young women were reduced by starvation to prostitution, something unheard of among their people before.[105] Predictably, the officials did not attribute prostitution to economic conditions; they maintained that it was based either on personal disposition or on the inherent immorality of Aboriginal women.[106] Classified as prostitutes, Aboriginal women could be subjected to a new disciplinary regime. Separate legislation under the Indian Act (and after 1892 under the Criminal Code) governed Aboriginal prostitution, and it had the effect of making it easier to convict Aboriginal women.[107] As legal historian Constance Backhouse has observed, this separate criminal legislation, "with its attendant emphasis on the activities of Indians rather than whites, revealed that racial discrimination ran deep through the veins of nineteenth-century Canadian society."[108]

The presence of Indian reserve women in the towns (for what were invariably seen as "immoral purposes") was also assailed through the pass system. Women who were found by the NWMP to be without a pass and without any means of support were arrested and ordered back to their reserves.[109] In March 1886 the police at

Battleford dealt with a woman who refused to leave town by taking her to the barracks and cutting off locks of her hair.[110] In March two years later it was reported, "During the early part of the week the Mounted Police ordered out of town a number of squaws who had come in from time to time and settled here. The promise to take them to the barracks and cut off their hair had a wonderful effect in hastening their movements."[111] Aboriginal women were accustomed to a high degree of mobility, and the pass system placed great restrictions on their movements, hampering not only their traditional strategies for survival but also their search for new jobs and resources. Employment and marketing opportunities were limited and were often further restricted by government officials. In 1885 one Indian agent urged the citizens of Calgary not to purchase anything from Aboriginal people or hire them, since this would help keep them out of the town.[112] The periodic sale of various produce, as well as art and craftwork, in urban or tourist areas could have been an important source of income for Aboriginal women and their families, as it was in eastern Canada. Studies of rural white women in western Canada suggest that in the boom-and-bust cycle that characterized the economy, it was the numerous strategies of the women, including the marketing of country provisions and farm products, that provided the necessary buffer against farm failure.[113] Aboriginal women were denied the same opportunity to draw on and market these resources.

The mechanisms that kept Aboriginal women out of the new settlements also hampered their access to some of the services the settlements offered. Jane Livingston, the Métis wife of one of the earliest farmers in the Calgary area, found that whenever there was a new policeman in Calgary, she and her children were asked for passes and trouble was made because of their appearance.[114] On one occasion when a child was sick and she needed medicine from downtown Calgary, she rubbed flour into her face, hoping this would make her look "like a white Calgary housewife" so that the new police constable would not bother her about a pass.[115]

MURDERS OF ABORIGINAL WOMEN

The case of the poisoning of a Blood woman and the murder of a Cree woman in the late 1880s in southern Alberta reflect the racial prejudice shared by many of the recent immigrants. In July 1888

Constable Alfred Symonds of the NWMP detachment at Stand Off was accused of feloniously killing a Blood woman, Mrs Only Kill, by giving her a fatal dose of iodine.[116] The woman had swallowed the contents of a bottle of iodene given her by Symonds, and she died the next morning. The same day, she had also eaten a quantity of beans that had turned sour in the heat. Although Only Kill died on a Wednesday morning, the matter was not reported to the coroner until late Friday night, and by then the body was too decomposed for post mortem examination. The coroner's jury decided that the deceased had come to her death either by eating the sour beans or by drinking the fluid given her by Symonds, who was committed to trial and charged with having administered the poison.[117] Constable Symonds was a popular cricketer and boxer, the son of a professor from Galt, Ontario.[118] In his report on the case, Superintendent P.R. Neale of the NWMP informed his superior, "I do not think any Western jury will convict him."[119] Symonds appeared before Judge James F. Macleod, the former commissioner of the NWMP, in August 1888, but the crown prosecutor made application for *nolle prosequi*, which was granted, and the prisoner was released.

During the 1889 trials of the murderer of a Cree woman (identified in legal documents and in the press only as Rosalie), who had been working as a prostitute, it became clear that there were many in Calgary who held that "Rosalie was only a squaw and that her death did not matter much."[120] By contrast, the murderer had the sympathy and support of much of the town. The murder was a particularly brutal one, and the accused, William "Jumbo" Fisk, had confessed and had given himself up to the authorities. Yet it was hard to find any citizen willing to serve on a jury that might have to convict a white man for such a crime. The crown prosecutor stated that he regretted having to conduct the case, for he had known the accused for several years as a "genial accommodating and upright young man."[121] Fisk was from a well-established eastern-Canadian family. Both he and his brother Thomas had served in 1885 with Steele's Scouts in pursuit of Big Bear and his captives.[122] He had been wounded and, as noted in the *Calgary Herald* during his trial, he was "now minus two fingers," which he had "patriotically contributed to the service of his country."[123] At the end of the first of the Rosalie trials, the jury found Fisk not guilty. Judge Charles Rouleau refused to accept this verdict, and he ordered a retrial, at the end of which Rouleau told the jury to "forget the woman's race and to

consider only the evidence at hand." He stated, "It made no difference whether Rosalie was white or black, an Indian or a negro. In
the eyes of the law, every British subject is equal."[124] At this second
trial, Fisk was convicted of manslaughter without premeditated intent and was sent to prison for fourteen years at hard labour. The
judge had intended to sentence him for life, but letters written by
members of Parliament and other influential persons who had
made representations to the court about his good character, combined with a petition from the most respectable people of Calgary,
persuaded Rouleau to go for the lesser sentence.[125] The people of
Calgary tried to show that they were not callous and indifferent
towards Rosalie by giving her "as respectable a burial as if she had
been a white woman," though several months later the town council
squabbled with the Indian Department over the costs incurred; the
department did not think it necessary to go beyond the costs of a
pauper's funeral.[126] As a final indignity, Rosalie was not allowed to
be buried in the mission graveyard, though she had been baptized
into the Roman Catholic Church, for the priests regarded her as a
prostitute who had died in sin.[127] The lesson to be learned from the
tragedy, according to a Calgary newspaper, was "Keep the Indians
out of town."[128]

ANGLO-CELTIC MORAL REFORMERS
AND ABORIGINAL WOMEN

The intensification of racial discrimination in western Canada in
the 1880s and the rigidifying of boundaries between the Aboriginal
people and the newcomers may be explained partly as a result of
the immigrants' exemplification of the increasingly racist assumptions of the British towards "primitive" peoples.[129] Like the "Jamaican Revolt" and the "Indian Mutiny," the events of 1885 had
sanctioned perceptions of Aboriginal people as dangerous and un-
grateful, and had justified increased control and segregation. The
conflict had apparently proved that there was a threat to the safety
of white women in the West and that Aboriginal women presented
particular perils and hazards. Since it was the Métis of the
Canadian West who had fomented the two "rebellions," there was
good reason to discourage such miscegenation, which could poten-
tially produce great numbers of "malcontents" who might demand
that their rights and interests be recognized.[130]

A fervour for moral reform in Protestant English Canada also began to take shape in the late 1880s. Sexual morality was a main target of the reformers, and racial purity their main goal.[131] There were fears that the Anglo-Celts might be overrun by more fertile, darker, and lower people, who were believed to be unable to control their sexual desires. The moral reformers' attitude towards the inhabitants of the cities' slums was similar to the categorization of Aboriginal people as "savages" who were improvident, filthy, and morally depraved. The NWMP's investigation of Cameron's charges of venereal disease among the police in 1886 proved that a number had the disease, although where and when they had contracted it was not determined.[132] Nevertheless, concern about Aboriginal "immorality" functioned to justify policies that served to segregate Aboriginal and newcomer communities.

THE INVALIDATION OF MIXED MARRIAGES

Also at issue in the West at this time was the question of who was to control whatever profits were to be made, who would be accorded privilege and respectability, and who would not. The possibility that the progeny of the numerous interracial marriages might be recognized as legitimate heirs to the sometimes considerable profits of the fathers may have acted as a powerful incentive to view Aboriginal women as immoral harlots who were accustomed to a great number of partners. As noted above, there is evidence to suggest that it became common in the 1880s for Aboriginal wives of Euro-Canadians to be left by their husbands for non-Aboriginal wives. Although many of the fathers continued to provide for their children to some extent, their former wives were excluded from positions of economic and social prestige in the non-Aboriginal community.

While the validity of mixed marriages according to "the custom of the country" had been upheld in Canadian courts earlier in the nineteenth century, all this changed with the influential 1886 ruling in *Jones v. Fraser*.[133] In this case, the judge ruled that the court would not accept that "the cohabitation of a civilized man and a savage woman, even for a long period of time, gives rise to the presumption that they consented to be married in our sense of marriage." [134] In 1899 the Supreme Court of the North-West Territories decided that the two sons of Awatoyakew (or White-Tailed Deer Woman, also known as Mary Brown), a Peigan woman, and Nicholas Sheran, a founder of a lucrative coalmine near present-day Lethbridge, were not entitled to a share of their father's estate. The judge reasoned that Sheran could have legally married Mary Brown but had not done so, though they had lived together from 1878 until Sheran's death in 1882.[135] Sheran had drowned at Kipp's Crossing on the Belly River when the water upset his buggy, and his body had never been found.[136] No one had attempted to notify Awatoyakew of the death; she learned of it a couple of days later when an NWMP patrol passed Coalbanks, the Sheran home, searching for the body. Six months later, Awatoyakew gave birth to their second son. The children were "taken over" by Sheran's sister Marcella, who placed them in a St Albert orphanage and paid a hundred dollars a year for the care of each. The two boys never received any direct returns from their father's holdings.

Similar legal proceedings south of the border produced similar results into the early decades of the twentieth century. Simon Pepin, a wealthy Quebec-born cattleman and founder of Havre, Montana, died in 1914. His estate was appraised at over one million dollars.[137] It included the Diamond-B Ranch of about 9,000 acres, as well as a large amount of city real estate. Around 1890 Pepin had been legally married to Rose Trottier, a Métisse from Manitoba, and they had five children (though only one daughter, Elizabeth, lived to maturity). After five years of litigation, Rose, who was by then married to a Mr Baker, succeeded in acquiring dower rights to one-third interest in the real property of the Pepin estate. She contended that her daughter had fraudulently had her confined to the Home of the Good Shepherd in Helena, taking advantage of her illiteracy and preventing her from exercising her legal rights for dower in the estate. The headline in the *Judith Basin Country Press* read "Squaw of Pepin Will Get Dower." One year later, however, this decision was overturned by the Montana Supreme Court. Rose Baker thus lost her suit for a share of the Pepin property.[138]

With reference to other colonial settings, it has been noted that in the process of stabilizing colonial rule following a crisis in authority, new limitations and restrictions were placed on the freedom and opportunity not only of indigenous women but of white women as well.[139] Far from being a land of opportunity for women, the Canadian West was patterned on a traditional patriarchal social order that dictated a dependent womanhood, and this was reinforced by federal and territorial laws which ensured that land and therefore wealth would be overwhelmingly owned and controlled by men.[140] Unlike white women in the American West, white women north of the border could be granted homesteads only in exceptional circumstances. It is perhaps no coincidence that in the Canadian West in 1886 the right of a wife to dower (a lifetime interest in one-third of her husband's property upon widowhood) was abolished by the North-West Territories *Real Property Act*. It is generally explained that common law dower created an invisible encumbrance of the title, and it was held to be inconsistent with a Torrens system of land registration.[141] The late nineteenth century was a period of intense competition for property and profit in western Canada, when lines were drawn and borders marked, and when townsites and farms were measured and parcelled out. Property had to change hands quickly, and dower stood in the way of potential profits.

There was a widely shared impression, however, that dower was abolished for other reasons as well, notably to prevent some cultural groups from gaining access to land – which meant wealth and privilege in the new economic and political order. In her autobiography *Clearing in the West*, Nellie McClung wrote about the views of a Mrs Brown of Manitou, Manitoba, whom she quoted as saying, "We have to get the vote on account of the laws. In Ontario a woman has some claim on her husband's property, but none here. That was changed because of Indian wives. The poor Indian women were cut off from any claim on a man's property. They said they had to do away with the wife's claim too, on account of the boom in 1882 when property was changing hands so fast."[142] A similar impression was given to Leo Thwaite, author of *Alberta: An Account of Its Wealth and Progress* (1912), one of a series entitled "Porter's Progress of Nations."[143] Having consulted various authorities for his chapter "Constitution, Law and Order," Thwaite had been left with a very clear idea of the matter: "In the early days of settlement many of the men married Indian squaws, and as it was considered undesirable that these should inherit their husbands' property, the Disability Act was passed, under which, to within four or five years ago, all women were squaws in the eyes of the law, and none had any inherent right to a share in her husband's estate."[144]

CHAPTER SIX

Alibis for Exclusion:
Old Frenzy, New Targets

The categories of women created in the early settlement era of 1870–1900 proved extraordinarily persistent, especially the negative images of Aboriginal women. Their morality was questioned, for example, in a number of sections of the Indian Act. If a woman was not of a "good moral character," she lost her one-third interest in her husband's estate – and a male government official was the sole and final judge of an Indian woman's moral character. As late as 1921 in the House of Commons, a Criminal Code amendment was debated that would have made it an offence for any white man to have "illicit connection" with an Indian woman.[1] Part of the rationale advanced was that "the Indian women are, perhaps, not as alive as women of other races in the country to the importance of maintaining their chastity." The amendment was not passed, however, for it was argued that the measure could make unsuspecting white men the victims of blackmail by Indian women.

White women, particularly those of Anglo-Celtic heritage, continued to be projected as the "civilizers" who had created and would continue to uphold the moral and cultural environment of the new community. C.T. Lewis's call for such women to come to the West continued throughout the late nineteenth and into the early twentieth century. Describing the Red Deer area in 1894, a *Calgary Herald* correspondent wrote, "All that is necessary to complete this veritable garden of Eden are a few Adams and Eves. The more Eves the better."[2] Of course, he meant white Eves, preferably of Anglo-Celtic origin. His comment appeared just below a paragraph in which the hope was expressed that the district would have no more

"Miss Canada: A Typical Canadian Girl" was the caption of this photograph, which was featured in the 1906 promotional pamphlet *Last Best West*, by G.L. Dodds. White women became key icons around which the West was built. (Saskatchewan Archives Board, R-A15805)

"Jewish importations from the slums of Chicago." Fears about the safety of "virtuous" women in the Canadian West were now being aimed at new targets. By 1900 there was little need to foment agitation about the presumed threat posed by the Aboriginal population, for the Indian people of the prairies were settled on reserves and segregated for the most part from the newcomers. Yet threats to the safety or virtue of white women were once again made a central issue whenever the consensus of the dominant society was needed against any group that was seen as undesirable.

An example of this took place in Alberta in 1910 and 1911 when the immigration of African Americans from Oklahoma appeared to be a distinct possibility, and some did arrive to take up homesteads. Canadian immigrations authorities, as well as many citizens of Alberta, were very concerned about this development.[3] In April 1910 the Edmonton Board of Trade passed a resolution urging the authorities to take immediate action to stop any more of this most "undesirable element" from entering the country.[4]

African Americans were the butt of jokes in western Canadian newspapers, and much attention was given to any sensational stories that could be calculated to arouse fears about them. In the spring of 1910 prominent coverage was given to the story of an African-American settler named James Chapman, who had confessed to the Mounted Police that he had helped a white woman poison her husband in Stillwater, Oklahoma, more than a year earlier. Chapman and the woman had then fled to Alberta.[5] The message conveyed was clearly that white communities had much to fear from the presence of African Americans; the sanctity of home and family was threatened. The Chapman story appeared in an Edmonton paper along with an item announcing the Edmonton Board of Trade's decision to try to stop black immigration.

In 1911 an utterly fabricated story aroused further prejudice against African Americans and the threat they might pose to white women and girls. This occurred just at the time when Henry Sneed of Oklahoma was organizing a large party of black emigrants. A first group, consisting of 194 men, women, and children, was on its way to Canada in April 1911, and a party of 200 more was preparing to follow.[6] On 5 April the headline in the Edmonton *Evening Journal* read, "Negro Thief Uses Chloroform and Binds Young Girl." It was reported that fifteen-year-old Hazel Huff had been found by a neighbour, lying unconscious on the kitchen floor with a handkerchief tied securely over her eyes, and apparently drugged by chloroform. All the rooms in the house had been rummaged, and a diamond ring and a small amount of money were missing. Hazel had been alone at the time, it was reported. The police arrested a black man named J.F. Witsue and were convinced that another black man also was involved. Hazel had told them that she had gone to the door in response to a knock and had been confronted by a black man, who had grabbed hold of her. Although she had resisted, she had been forced to give in to the overwhelming strength of her assailant. She had then been blindfolded, and a drug had been administered through a handkerchief.

This story of the assault and drugging of a little white girl spread quickly, with predictable results. A Calgary *Albertan* editorial declared, "The assault made by a colored man upon a little girl in Edmonton should open the eyes of the authorities at Ottawa as to what may be expected regularly if Canada is to open the door to all the colored people of the republic and not bar their way from open entry here."[7] Similarly, the *Calgary Herald* argued that the drugging of Hazel Huff should be seen as an indication of what would happen if more blacks were allowed to settle in Alberta.[8] The assault on the Edmonton girl was also noted in "The Black Peril," an editorial in the Lethbridge *Daily News* of 8 April, which pointed out that women were often alone on their isolated homesteads and that if more blacks were allowed to come to Canada there would be an ever-present horror. In the Saskatoon *Daily Phoenix* the headline read, "A Negro Atrocity – White Girl Flogged and Assaulted by Late Arrivals at Edmonton." Fritz Freidricks of Mewassin expressed the concern of many when he wrote to the Immigration Branch on 12 April saying, "These negroes have misused young girls and women and killed them." In rebuttal, an African-American farmer in the Lethbridge area objected to all of this, asking whether the *Daily News* knew that "black men had defended white women during the American Civil War." This argument, however, was given little attention.

Although the police had quickly arrested Witsue, they were very secretive about what charges he faced or whether he had ever appeared before the court.[9] Then, nine days after the incident, Hazel Huff admitted that she had invented the whole thing. She had lost the diamond ring and, fearing the wrath of her parents, had made up the story. She said she had decided to confess when she became frightened about the commotion the story was causing. The Edmonton chief of police had known the truth for several days but had sworn the family to secrecy, for reasons never explained. Despite Hazel's confession, however, the story continued to have an impact, and according to historian R. Bruce Shepard, it played an important role in the agitation against black immigration. The pressure to halt this immigration became intense, and a successful scheme was initiated by the federal government to stop it at its source.[10] Agents, including a black doctor from Chicago, were sent to Oklahoma to stem the "black tide." These measures proved effective, especially when combined with news of the negative reception of black settlers in Canada.

Although African-American settlers did not arrive in large numbers in western Canada, the idea that black males posed a danger to white females did not entirely dissipate. In Calgary in April 1940, a group of three hundred servicemen attacked the home of a black bandleader, and a serious riot in the city was prevented only by prompt police action. The incident apparently began at a

Saturday-night dance when a serviceman became convinced that his female companion was paying too much attention to a black musician. There was a fight, and the serviceman suffered an injured eye. The next night, the soldiers of the 49th Battalion wrecked the home of the orchestra's black leader and also attacked a white soldier who was married to the bandleader's sister. As Howard and Tamara Palmer have so rightly concluded, this event indicated that "the old myth about the danger of black males to white women" was still part of "Alberta's social landscape."[11]

The notion that the virtue and safety of white women was at risk was also pressed into service against Asian men, and it served as one of the arguments to justify the "white women's labour laws" that were enacted in the western provinces and Ontario. In 1912 the Saskatchewan Liberal government passed a law that prohibited Asian entrepeneurs – owners of restaurants, laundries, or other businesses – from hiring white women.[12] Over the next seven years, similar statutes were passed in Manitoba, Ontario, and British Columbia. This legislation was the result of an intensive lobbying effort by small businessmen and male trade unionists who were concerned about "unfair competition" from Asians who, in their view, were making inroads into their wages and profits. They were joined in this campaign by moral reformers and middle-class white women's groups. According to Constance Backhouse, these groups "decried racial intermarriage and fretted over the potential for coercive sexuality that suffused the employment relationship. White women were called into service as the 'guardians of the race,' a symbol of the most valuable property known to white society, to be protected at all costs from the encroachment of other races."[13] Although the Saskatchewan government amended this legislation slightly in 1919 to disguise the anti-Chinese focus, there was no substantive alteration in policy. Hysteria about the dangers to white women was kept alive through newspaper reports, which recounted "'sordid and revolting' stories about young white women who were introduced to Chinese men in Sunday school classes, only to come 'under the influence of the stronger personalities' of the would-be converts and find themselves tragically transformed into 'drug fiends.'"[14] Into the 1920s, organizations such as the YWCA, the Local Council of Women in Saskatoon, and the federal National Council of Women endorsed prohibitions on the hiring of white women on the grounds that they were essential for the "protection of white girls."[15] Citing Emily Murphy as his authority, a lawyer acting for the Regina Local Council of Women in 1924 in a debate before city council on the issue declared, "White girls lose caste when they are employed by Chinese."[16]

Precisely who or what constituted a "white woman," however, was becoming more difficult to define, for the Canadian West was being populated by people of increasingly diverse backgrounds. Before 1896, when the government launched its ambitious campaign to populate the prairies, there had been little problem in deciding who was "white." British-Ontarian immigration had dominated, and the only "other" women were of Aboriginal ancestry. That the matter was less clear-cut as the multicultural fabric of western Canadian society took shape is illustrated in the difficulty the authorities had in interpreting the "white women's labour law," which contained no definition of "white woman." In 1912 a Saskatoon police magistrate adjourned a trial on the subject, professing great confusion over the question of the "whiteness" of the female employees involved, who were described as Russian and German. As Constance Backhouse has argued, "In early 20th-century Saskatchewan, residents of English or Scottish origin would have been hard-pressed to identify racially with Russian or German immigrants in matters of employment or social interaction."[17] The judge in this case eventually decided that the Russian and German waitresses were indeed members of the Caucasian race. With increased immigration from central and southern Europe, groups seen as different from the dominant society for religious, cultural, or linguistic reasons were depicted in "racial" terms.

While one rationale for discouraging the immigration of certain groups was their perceived threat to women of the dominant Anglo-Celtic society, another rationale was the alleged mistreatment of women within the society of the "foreign" group. Some critics of Mormon immigration, for example, complained that Mormons threatened the safety of other white women and girls in the West and, furthermore, treated their own women in a barbarous fashion. Polygamy, a marriage system in which a man may take more than one wife, was a central religious tenet of nineteenth-century Mormonism. This was seen as an enslavement of wives and a diabolical attempt to reduce the status of women. The *Macleod Gazette* protested the Mormons' arrival in the neighbourhood and featured articles such as "In Mormondom: Domestic Barbarities of the Polygamous System."[18] This extract from an American news-paper detailed the ill-treatment of Mormon women, claiming that it led some to suicide and that even when such a woman was at death's door, her husband would heartlessly curse and revile her. A wife might leave for a time, stated the article, and on her return find that the hired girl had been installed as wife number two. The *Gazette* regularly portrayed women in Mormon communities as being held in "the bondage of ignorance and servitude" – the same type of thing that was said of Aboriginal women. In an extract from the Regina *Leader* it was argued that "no man who has regard for his peace or comfort would think of having two wives in a country in which women have become so intelligent and independent that the only sure way of living happily with one of them is to be humble and obedient."[19]

There was considerable debate in the western press about Mormon settlement, and many declared that the stories of brutal Mormon men were absurd inventions, full of errors and bigoted nonsense. But among those who were vocal in their objections, the issue of the treatment of women was paramount. Organizations such as the Woman's Christian Temperance Union (WCTU) were particularly concerned about the "perils" Mormons posed to other women in the West. As historian Howard Palmer wrote, the 1905 convention of the WCTU "pictured Mormon missionaries swarming over Saskatchewan and Manitoba persuading young, innocent girls to go to southern Alberta to live in polygamous relationships."[20] These charges were simply false.

An added threat which the Mormons posed to the status quo in the Canadian West was that Mormon women had for a long time been accustomed to vote. White women in Utah had secured the franchise in 1870. The Mormons had given women the vote to protect their social order from attack at a time when large numbers of non-Mormons were settling in Utah.[21] They also thought that the award of the franchise would demonstrate the high standing women enjoyed in their territory. Many Mormon women had been enthusiastic participants in the political process until the federal Edmunds-Tucker Act of 1887 had abolished women's suffrage in Utah. One vocal supporter of polygamy from the settlement at Cardston argued that women ought to be given the vote in the Canadian West, since polygamy was "essentially a woman's question and ought to be settled by women."[22] In the United States,

Mormon women leaders publicly defended plural marriages, arguing that their homes were morally superior to those of middle-class Protestant women.[23]

There was also great indignation expressed in the western press about the role and treatment of Doukhobor women, Russian immigrants. In 1899 the *Saskatchewan Herald* described Doukhobor marriage customs as "simpler and less ceremonious than even marriage amongst the Indians. The high contracting parties simply shake hands and kiss each other and they are man and wife."[24] Editor P.G. Laurie was harshly critical of the "ladies" who "gushingly" welcomed the Doukhobors to Canada, speaking words of comfort to "these saints in sheepskins when they had reached a land of liberty, leaving behind them all relics of serfdom and the persecutions that had all but broken their manly hearts."[25] Laurie declared that the Doukhobors made draught animals of their wives and daughters, that at three different places near Yorkton twenty-two women had been seen hitched to a breaker plough and turning over the sod, "and somewhere about seventy women at work digging with spades." To see women working in tandem in large numbers was undoubtedly a surprise to those accustomed to the homestead system, but Laurie's effort to raise anxieties about Doukhobor women ignored how hard most women worked on their farms in the Prairie West. As English journalist, Georgina Binnie-Clark, wrote after her first summer in the Qu'Appelle district, "In England I used to think that men worked whilst women gossiped. On a prairie settlement the women work and it isn't the men who gossip: I owe one debt to my life on the prairie, and that is a fair appreciation of my own sex."[26]

CONCLUSION

By 1900 it was established that there was little opportunity for Aboriginal women in the world beyond the reserves. Their categorization as a threat to the well-being of the new settlements, combined with more formal government policies, increasingly restricted them within the boundaries of the reserves. For most in the non-Aboriginal communities, contact with Aboriginal people was limited to a few local characters who were tolerated on the fringes of society and whose behaviour was the subject of various anecdotes. In many cases these were Aboriginal women, and their presence continued to feed the white community's stereotypic view of the deficiencies of Aboriginal femininity. A solitary woman known only as Liza camped on the outskirts of Virden, Manitoba, for many years until her disappearance sometime in the 1940s.[27]At that time Liza was thought to have been well over one hundred years old. She had lived winter and summer in an unheated tent by the railroad tracks, though she spent the long winter days huddled in the livery stable and also at times crept into the Nu-Art Beauty Parlour, where she sat on the floor in front of the window, warming herself in the sun. Liza smoked a corn-cob pipe as she shuffled about the streets and lanes of Virden, rummaging in garbage tins. She bathed under the overflow pipe at the water tower, sometimes clothed and sometimes not, and dried off by standing over the huge heat register in Scales and Rothnie's general store. To an extent, she was tolerated and even assisted; town employees shovelled out a path for her when she was buried under snow, and it was thought that the town fathers supplied her with food from time to time. Children were half-fascinated and half-frightened by this ancient woman. Oldtimers believed that Liza had been there well before the first settlers, that she had been one of the Sioux who escaped the pursuing American army in 1876. It was also said that she received regular cheques from the United States and that she was capable of fine handwriting – though where she had learned it no one knew.

The presence of Liza and the stories told about her served to sharpen the boundaries of community membership and to articulate what was and what was not considered acceptable and respectable.[28] Liza was the object of both fascination and repugnance in that she violated norms of conventional behaviour, dress, and cleanliness, representing the antithesis of "civilized" prairie society. Although she was a real person, what she represented was a Euro-Canadian artifact, created by the settlement. The narratives circulated about her were not those she herself would have told – of the disasters that had stripped her of family and community, or perhaps of her strategies in adopting the character role – and this folklore reflected less about Liza than about the community itself. To the white community, Liza served as an example of Aboriginal women.

In contrast to the representations made by those outside their communities, the histories told or written within the Aboriginal community about the women of these years stress the vast array of skills they possessed and their contribution to family and community. "Madame Chat-Chat," or Elise Boyer, an Ojibway woman who married a Métis farmer and lived east of Fort Ellice in Manitoba, was a midwife and traditional medicine woman.[29] She spoke many languages, including French, Cree, Saulteaux, Sioux, English, and Michif. Although she never gave birth to her own children, she raised many of her friends' and relatives' children, and was a step-mother to her husband's children. Madame Chat-Chat cut cord-wood and fenceposts, tanned hides, and made robes. It was said that she could skin any animal. She dried meat, and she made her own pemmican with dried saskatoons. While she was a great be-liever in the Roman Catholic faith, she also practised Aboriginal forms of worship, including the sweat lodge and the shaking tent ceremony. In 1967, at the age of ninety-nine, Elise Boyer was pre-sented with a Manitoba centennial corporation Order of the Crocus in grateful recognition of her contribution to the develop-ment of Canada.

Similarly, a Cree grandmother of the Duck Lake district of Saskatchewan was remembered for her ability to tan skins and make warm jackets, mittens, leggings, and moccasins.[30] She too made pemmican long after the buffalo had disappeared, using deer or moose meat when available. Her granddaughter loved to follow her and observe her at work: "Very patiently she would answer my questions, and she always made me feel that I was loved, important and truly needed."

These representations that challenge the enduring categoriza-tions of the late nineteenth century did not, until recent years, re-ceive any attention beyond the Aboriginal community. Negative stereotypes persisted, and women such as Liza served to represent Aboriginal women to the non-Aboriginal community. Meanwhile, representations of white women as the "civilizers" of the West con-tinued to receive widespread coverage, and some of the women "pioneers" of the first generation played an active role in perpetu-ating this image. In 1921 the Kiwanis Club of Calgary organized a gathering of the Pilgrim Mothers of Alberta, and this first meeting appears to have led to the formation of the Women's Southern Pioneers and Old Timers Association, which had a membership of 355 by 1925.[31] Its first function, held on Valentine's Day 1921, was open only to women who had resided in Alberta since 14 February 1891.[32] Some women of part-Aboriginal ancestry were among

those who took part in the celebration, but this was never acknowledged, for it was clearly white women who exemplified the Pilgrim
Mothers. They were women who had struck out, with their husbands, across the plains to this new and unknown region. They
were, it was declared, "from the older Canadian provinces – mostly
Scotch – practical, resourceful, enduring, thrifty, and could suit
themselves to any environment."[33] They had left spacious eastern
homes in Huron or Bruce to live in one-room shacks on the bald
alkali prairie, infested with mosquitoes in the summer and blan-
keted with snow in winter. They were the first white women in
Alberta, among whom the McDougall women loomed large: the
late Mrs George McDougall, first white woman in Saskatchewan;
Mrs John McDougall, first white woman in the foothills; and
Mrs David McDougall, second white woman in the foothills. Yet
John McDougall's first wife, Abigail Steinhauer, who was of Cree
ancestry, and their several daughters were not honoured in the
celebration.

In the *Calgary Herald*'s extensive coverage of the Valentine's Day
event, an article was included on life at the posts in fur-trade days.
This article served as a contrast to the refinements and gentility
that had arrived with the white women, thereby reinforcing
assumptions of racial superiority.[34] At Christmas in the fur-trade
era there had been a "scene of the oddest description ... Around
the stove, in various attitudes squatted the 'ladies' dressed in
bright-colored print dresses ... all chattering and giggling." It was
the custom, the author noted, for the "ladies" to kiss the factors
and staff on Christmas Day, and the article went on to describe the
ordeal of having to be kissed by "superhuman ugliness," some of
the women being "the perfect embodiment of a nightmare." Indian women were described as a "source of amusement," especially
at dances. This section of the *Herald* was followed by a tribute to the
"pioneer women" who had put an end to this rough society.

In one of the articles from the 1920s, one of Alberta's first white
women, Mrs David McDougall, spoke about the valuable assistance
of her Cree midwife, Mary Cecil.[35] Although Mrs McDougall had
been frightened of her at first, she "soon became very fond of her,
because of her kindness and faithfulness. For twenty-eight years I
had no better servant or friend, and the children loved her as well
as any white woman." Such acknowledgment was rare, however, in
the media coverage of the women pioneers.

As the celebration of the "old-time ladies" of Alberta made clear, definite meanings were attached to the category of white women of Anglo-Celtic origin in the Canadian West. These women occupied a category that was racialized as well as gendered. By the 1920s the meaning of white womanhood had shifted somewhat – the resourcefulness, ingenuity, courage, and pluck of the early white women settlers was now being emphasized, whereas in the mid-1880s it had been more useful to stress their vulnerability and their dependence on males. Throughout, however, white femininity meant virtue, domesticity, and ennobling influences, whereas Aboriginal femininity meant the opposite. As in the coverage given to the Pilgrim Mothers of Alberta, it was still useful to present the reputed deficiencies of Aboriginal women in order to highlight the reputed virtues of white women. The particular identity of white women depended for its articulation on a sense of difference from indigenous women. What it meant to be a white woman was rooted in a series of negative assumptions about the malign influence of Aboriginal women. The meanings of and different ways of being female were constantly referred to each other, with Aboriginal women always appearing deficient. The powerful ideologies of white and Aboriginal femininity functioned to inform both groups of their appropriate space and place.

Notes

1 Saskatchewan Archives Board (SAB), Regina branch, Biographical
   Clippings file, C.T. Lewis. This published poem is among the papers
   donated to the archives by his daughter Olive Lewis. It is not clear
   where it was published, but it may have been in the *Moncton Daily
   Times*, where other of his articles appeared. Beneath the poem "Girls
   Ho! For the West" is written, "P.S. Now there are too many. 1949.
   O.L." "An Ontario Girl's Lament" appeared with Lewis's poem:

   > I make complaint of a plaguey pest
   > That's known by the name of the Great North-West
   > For this wondrous land of the setting sun
   > Has taken my beaus away – every one.
   > Yes, one by one they have all cleared out,
   > Thinking it better themselves, no doubt;
   > Caring but little how far they may go
   > From the poor lone girl in Ontario.
   > First I was sweet upon Johnny J. Brown,
   > The nicest young fellow in all the whole town;
   > But he said "good-bye" and he sailed away
   > And now he's settled at Thunder Bay.
   > Next I was fishing for Farmer Lee's Dick,
   > Thought him so dull that he wouldn't cut slick,
   > But he waved his hat with a hip, hip, hurrah!
   > And said he was going to Manitoba.
   > That long lean druggist with specs on his nose,

I thought the fellow would soon propose;
He sold out his bottle shop; he was gone
Clean to the River Saskatchewan.
Fat little, plump little Johnny Grey,
I hinted he'd better get spliced and stay;
He said to me that was rather thin
And he turned his toes to Keewatin.
My Dutchman lover, Hans Ritter Von Krout,
So lame he could scarcely escort me out;
With magic ointment he greased his leg
And slid to the city of Winnipeg.
I'll sling my goods in a carpet sack,
I'll off to the West and I won't turn back;
I'll have a husband – a good one too –
If I have to follow to Cariboo.

2 C.T. Lewis, *A Revolution: The World's Return Rebate Marriage Certificate, or the Want of the West* (Qu'Appelle: The Progress, 1889).

3 Ibid., 10.

4 Ibid.

5 See, for example, *Macleod Gazette* (Fort Macleod), 4 April 1889.

6 *What Women Say of the Canadian North-West*, (Canadian Pacific Railway, 1886). The word "Aboriginal" is used throughout this study as an all-encompassing term that refers to the Métis, to those communities organized under the federal scheme of administration of "Indian Reserves" pursuant to the *Indian Act*, and to those Aboriginal people who are not statutorily defined as "Indians" (formerly known as "Non-Status Indians"). Section 35 of the *Constitution Act*, 1982, recognized and affirmed the rights derived from original occupancy, and it used the generic term "aboriginal" to refer to the Indian, Inuit, and Métis peoples. The terminology in section 35 gave impetus to the adoption of "Aboriginal" as a replacement for "Indian" as the all-encompassing term in the most generic sense. According to Paul Chartrand, "the term 'Aboriginal' is now generally used in Canada, unless the speaker's context indicates a preference for 'First Nations,' the expression that is used generally to denote the Aboriginal societies who are defined as 'Indians' by the federal *Indian Act*." The terms "Native" and "Indian" are also used at times in this study, reflecting both historical and contemporary usages, and for accuracy. In the context of the period under consideration, the term "Métis" refers to the people of mixed North American Aboriginal and Euro-

pean (mostly but not exclusively francophone) descent, who gained numerical power and influence on the western plains in the nineteenth century and who resisted westward Canadian expansion. For further elaboration on these terms and on present-day definitions, see Paul Chartrand, " 'Terms of Division': Problems of 'Outside-Naming' for Aboriginal People in Canada," *Journal of Indigenous Studies* 2, no. 2 (1991): 1–22.

7 *What Women Say of the Canadian North-West*, 7.

8 *Herald* (Calgary), 2 April 1921.

9 A similar situation has recently been described by Adele Perry, in " 'Oh I'm Just Sick of the Faces of Men': Gender Imbalance, Race, Sexuality and Sociability in Nineteenth-Century British Columbia," *BC Studies* 105–6 (Spring/Summer 1995): 27–43.

10 John Maclean, "Social Development of Southern Alberta," *Macleod Gazette*, 11 April 1889.

11 Ibid.

12 *Macleod Gazette*, 14 November 1884.

13 Maclean, "Social Development."

14 John Maclean, *Canadian Savage Folk: The Native Tribes of Canada* (Toronto: William Briggs, 1896), 344.

15 Ibid., 348.

16 Jessie M.E. Saxby, *West-Nor'West* (London: James Nisbet, 1890).

17 Ibid., 105.

18 Ibid., 107–8.

19 Ibid., 105.

20 Ibid., 102.

21 Ibid., 101–2.

22 (Mrs) George Cran, *A Woman in Canada* (London: John Milne, 1910).

23 Ibid., 109.

24 For a critique of a great deal of recent writing on "colonial discourse," see Nicholas Thomas, *Colonialism's Culture: Anthropology, Travel and Government* (Princeton: Princeton University Press, 1994).

25 Catherine Hall, *White, Male, and Middle Class: Explorations in Feminism and History* (New York: Routledge, 1992), 24.

26 Andrée Lévesque, *Making and Breaking the Rules: Women in Quebec, 1919–1939* (Toronto: McClelland and Stewart, 1994).

27 Ibid., 12.

28 Ibid.

29 Joy Parr, "Gender History and Historical Practice," *Canadian Historical Review* 76, no. 3 (1995): 363.

30 Kwame Anthony Appiah, "Race," in *Critical Terms for Literary Study*, ed. Frank Letricchia and Thomas McLaughlin (Chicago: University of Chicago Press, 1990), 277.

31 Ibid.

32 Peter Gay, *The Cultivation of Hatred: The Bourgeois Experience, Victoria to Freud* (New York: W.W. Norton, 1993), 3:77.

33 Ibid., 68.

34 Catherine Hall, *White, Male and Middle-class*; 21. The concept of "imagined community" is drawn from Benedict Anderson, *Imagined Communities: Reflections on the Origin and Spread of Nationalism* (London: Verso, 1983; revised and extended, 1991).

35 Catherine Hall, " 'From Greenland's Icy Mountains ... to Africa's Golden Sand': Ethnicity, Race and Nation in Mid-Nineteenth-Century England," *Gender and History* 5, no. 2 (1993): 216. See also Hall, "Gender Politics and Imperial Politics: Rethinking the History of Empire," in *Engendering History: Caribbean Women in Historical Perspective*, ed. Verene Shepherd et al. (New York: St Martin's Press, 1995), 48–59.

36 Vron Ware, *Beyond the Pale: White Women, Racism and History* (London: Verso, 1992). See also Phyllis Palmer, *Domesticity and Dirt: Housewives and Domestic Servants in the United States, 1920–1945* (Philadelphia: Temple Press, 1989).

37 Ibid., 18.

38 Ibid., xii.

39 Ibid., 4.

40 Ibid., 182.

41 Hazel V. Carby, *Reconstructing Womanhood: The Emergence of the Afro-American Woman Novelist* (New York: Oxford University Press, 1987).

42 Mary O'Dowd, "Women and the Colonial Experience in Sixteenth- and Seventeenth-Century Ireland," *Proceedings of the 18th International Congress of Historical Sciences* (Montreal, 1995), 73.

43 Janice Potter, "Patriarchy and Paternalism: The Case of the Eastern Ontario Loyalist Women," in *Rethinking Canada: The Promise of Women's History*, ed. Veronica Strong-Boag and Anita Clair Fellman (Toronto: Copp Clark Pitman, 1991), 59–72.

44 Ibid., 70.

45 For an examination and critique of the argument that European women introduced segregation, see Margaret Stobel, *European Women and the Second British Empire* (Bloomington: Indiana University Press, 1991); Helen Callaway, *Gender, Culture and Empire: European Women in Colonial Nigeria* (London: Macmillan, 1987); and Claudia Knapman,

White Women in Fiji, 1835–1930: The Ruin of Empire? (Sydney: Allen and Unwin, 1986). Jane Haggis raises criticisms of these woman-centred approaches to the complexities of colonialism in "Gendering Colonialism or Colonising Gender: Recent Women's Studies Approaches to White Women and the History of British Colonialism," *Women's Studies International Forum* 13, nos. 1 and 2 (1990): 105–15.

46 Ann Laura Stoler, "Rethinking Colonial Categories: European Communities and the Boundaries of Rule," *Society for Comparative Study of Society and History* (1989), 148.

47 Ibid., 147.

48 Ibid., 148.

49 Ann Laura Stoler, "Sexual Affronts and Racial Frontiers: European Identities and the Cultural Politics of Exclusion in Colonial Southeast Asia," *Society for Comparative Study of Society and History* (1992), 515.

50 Stoler, "Rethinking Colonial Categories," 154.

51 Jenny Sharpe, *Allegories of Empire: The Figure of Woman in the Colonial Text* (Minneapolis: University of Minnesota Press, 1993), 91.

52 Ibid.

53 Ibid., 4.

54 Ibid., 61.

55 Ibid., 64.

56 Ibid., 65o6.

57 Jenny Sharpe, "The Unspeakable Limits of Rape: Colonial Violence and Counter-Insurgency," *Genders* 10 (Spring 1991): 36.

58 Sharpe, *Allegories*, 92.

59 Catherine Hall, "Competing Masculinities: Thomas Carlyle, John Stuart Mill and the Case of Governor Eyre," in Hall, *White, Male and Middle Class*, 255.

60 Ibid., 285.

61 Norman Etherington, "Natal's Black Rape Scare of the 1870s," *Journal of Southern African Studies* 15, no. 1 (1988). See also Amirah Inglis, *"Not a White Woman Safe": Sexual Anxiety and Politics in Port Moresby 1920–1934* (Canberra: Australian National University Press, 1974). I am grateful to Lucy Denton, University of Calgary graduate student in history, for these references.

62 Sharpe, *Allegories*, 89.

63 Ibid.

64 Jennifer S.H. Brown, *Strangers in Blood: Fur Trade Company Families in Indian Country* (Vancouver: University of British Columbia Press, 1980), 212–13.

65 See Sylvia Van Kirk, "The Impact of White Women on Fur Trade Society," in *Sweet Promises: A Reader in Indian-White Relations in Canada*, ed. J.R. Miller (Toronto: University of Toronto Press, 1991), 180–204.

66 Sylvia Van Kirk, "'The Reputation of a Lady': Sarah Ballenden and the Foss-Pelly Scandal," *Manitoba History* 11 (Spring 1986): 4–11.

67 Ibid., 10.

68 Erica Smith, "'Gentlemen, This Is No Ordinary Trial': Sexual Narratives in the Trial of the Reverend Corbett, Red River, 1863," in *Reading beyond Words: Contexts for Native History*, ed. Jennifer S.H. Brown and Elizabeth Vibert (Peterborough: Broadview Press, 1996), 364–80.

69 Ibid., 370.

70 Ibid., 367.

71 Many of these themes are elaborated in Sarah Carter, *Lost Harvests: Prairie Indian Reserve Farmers and Government Policy* (Montreal: McGill-Queen's University Press, 1990).

72 Lewis G. Thomas, *The Prairie West to 1905: A Canadian Sourcebook* (Toronto: Oxford University Press, 1975), 2.

73 Ibid., 15.

74 John L. Tobias, "Canada's Subjugation of the Plains Cree, 1879–1885," *Canadian Historical Review* 64, no. 4 (1983).

75 Walter Hildebrandt, "P.G. Laurie: The Aspirations of a Western Enthusiast" (MA thesis, University of Saskatchewan, 1978); John N. Jennings, "The North West Mounted Police and Indian Policy, 1873-1896" (PHD dissertation, University of Toronto, 1979).

76 P.B. Waite, *Canada, 1874–1896: Arduous Destiny* (Toronto: McClelland and Stewart, 1971), 149.

77 This poem also appeared in G. Mercer Adam, *From Savagery to Civilization: The Canadian North-West: Its History and Its Troubles* (Toronto: Rose Publishing, 1885), 388.

78 Gay, *The Cultivation of Hatred*, 68.

79 *Saskatchewan Herald*, 18 May 1885.

80 Bob Beal and Rod Macleod, *Prairie Fire: The 1885 North-West Rebellion* (Edmonton: Hurtig Publishers, 1984), 277.

81 James Levernier and Hennig Cohen, *The Indians and Their Captives* (Westport: Greenwood Press, 1977), xxi–xxii.

82 Ibid., xiii.

83 Colin Calloway, ed., *North Country Captives: Selected Narratives of Indian Captivity from Vermont and New Hampshire* (Hanover, NH: University Press of New England, 1992).

84 See John Demos, *The Unredeemed Captive: A Family Story from Early America* (New York: Alfred A. Knopf, 1994).

85 Patricia N. Limerick, *The Legacy of Conquest: The Unbroken Past of the American West* (New York: W.W. Norton, 1988), 46.

86 Annette Kolodny, *The Land before Her: Fantasy and Experience of the American Frontiers, 1630–1860* (Chapel Hill: University of North Carolina Press, 1984), 21–6.

87 June Namias, *White Captives: Gender and Ethnicity on the American Frontier* (Chapel Hill: University of North Carolina Press, 1993). See also Christopher Castiglia, *Bound and Determined: Captivity, Culture-Crossing, and White Womanhood from Mary Rowlandson to Patty Hearst* (Chicago: University of Chicago Press, 1996). Other recent studies include Kathryn Z. Derounian, "The Publication, Promotion and Distribution of Mary Rowlandson's Indian Captivity Narrative in the Seventeenth Century," *Early American Literature* 23 (1988): 239–61; Julie Ellison, "Race and Sensibility in the Early Republic: Ann Eliza Bleecker and Sarah Wentworth Morton," *American Literature* 65, no. 3 (1993): 445–74; Tara Fitzpatrick, "The Figure of Captivity: The Cultural Work of the Puritan Captivity Narrative," *American Literary History* 3 (1991): 1–26; Carroll Smith-Rosenberg, "Subject Female: Authorizing American Identity," *American Literary History* 5, no. 3 (1993): 481–511; Teresa A. Toulouse, "'My Own Credit': Strategies of (E) Valuation in Mary Rowlandson's Captivity Narrative," *American Literature* 64, no. 4 (1992): 655–76; and Susan Walsh, "'With Them Was My Home': Native American Autobiography and *A Narrative of the Life of Mrs. Mary Jemison*," *American Literature* 64 no. 1 (1992): 49–70.

88 Carroll Smith-Rosenberg, "Captured Subjects/Savage Others: Violently Engendering the New American," *Gender and History* 5, no. 2 (1993): 177–95.

89 Ibid., 179.

90 Ibid.

91 David Murray, *Forked Tongues: Speech, Writing and Representation in North American Indian Texts* (Bloomington: Indiana University Press, 1991), 95n8.

92 See Julie Cruikshank, *The Stolen Women: Female Journeys in Tagish and Tutchone*, Canadian Ethnology Service, paper no. 87 (Ottawa: National Museum of Man Mercury Series, 1983).

93 I am drawing on the version given by Julian Ralph, *On Canada's Frontier: Sketches of History, Sport, and Adventure, and of Indians, Missionaries and Fur Traders of Western Canada* (New York: Harper, 1892) 24–5.

94 Hugh Dempsey, "Natos-api," *Dictionary of Canadian Biography* (Toronto: University of Toronto Press, 1990), 12:779.

95 Priscilla K. Buffalohead, "Farmers, Warriors, Traders: A Fresh Look at Ojibway Women," *Minnesota History* 48, no. 6 (Summer 1983): 243.

96 Namias, "White Captives," 3–4.

97 Quoted in ibid., 10.

98 Kay Schaffer, "Eliza Fraser's Trial by Media," *Antipodes* 5, no. 2 (1991): 116.

99 Kay Schaffer, "Colonizing Gender in Colonial Australia: The Eliza Fraser Story," in *Writing Women and Space: Colonial and Postcolonial Geographics,* ed. Alison Blunt and Gillian Rose (New York: Guilford Press, 1944), 101–20. See also Schaffer, "Australian Mythologies: The Eliza Fraser Story and Constructions of the Feminine in Patrick White's *A Fringe of Leaves* and Sidney Nolan's 'Eliza Fraser' Paintings," *Kunapipi* 11, no. 2 (1989): 1–15, and Shaffer, "Eliza Fraser's Trial by Media," 114–19.

100 Schaffer, "Colonizing Gender," 107.

101 See C. Alice Baker, *True Stories of New England Captives Carried to Canada during the Old French and Indian Wars* (Greenfield, Mass.: E.A. Hall, 1897; rpt., Pointer Ridge: Heritage Books, 1990); J.M. Bumsted, "Carried to Canada: Perceptions of the French in British Colonial Captivity Narratives, 1690–1760," *American Review of Canadian Studies* 13, no. 1 (1983); James Axtell, "The White Indians of North America," in *The European and the Indian: Essays in the Ethnohistory of Colonial North America* (New York: Oxford University Press, 1981); Colleen Gray, "Captives in Canada, 1744–1763" (MA thesis, McGill University, 1993); Barbara E. Austen, "Captured … Never Came Back: Social Networks among New England Captives in Canada, 1689–1763," and Alice N. Nash, "Two Stories of New England Captives: Grizel and Christine Otis of Dover, New Hampshire," both in *New England/New France,* ed. P. Benes, Dublin Seminar for New England Folklife, annual proceedings 1989 (Boston: Boston University Press, 1992).

102 Levernier and Cohen, *The Indians and their Captives,* xiii.

103 See Gray, "Captives in Canada," 89. Drawing on the captivity narrative of the Reverend Mr John Norton, Gray argues that the apparent "kindness" extended by the French was "an integral element of a military interrogation system which was instituted the moment an individual became a captive and followed him/her into the walls of the Quebec prison."

104 Baker, *True Stories*, 35–68.

105 Ibid., 57n3.

106 Ibid., 321–9.

107 Demos, *The Unredeemed Captive*.

108 Ibid., 142.

109 Ibid., 146.

110 Ibid., 165.

111 Ibid., 142.

112 Ibid., 169.

113 Clifton Johnson, *An Unredeemed Captive* (Holyoke, Griffith, Axtell and Cody, 1897).

114 Ibid., 54.

115 Demos, *The Unredeemed Captive*, 143.

116 Ibid., 166.

117 Leland Donald, "Captives or Slaves? A Comparison of Northeastern and Northwestern North America by Means of Captivity Narratives," *Culture* 5, no. 2 (1985): 18–19. See also *The Adventures and Sufferings of John R. Jewitt Captive of the Maquinna*, ed. H. Stewart (Vancouver: Douglas & McIntyre, 1987).

118 John Tanner, *The Falcon: A Narrative of the Captivity and Adventures of John Tanner*, introd. Louise Erdrich (1830; rpt., New York: Penguin Books, 1994), xi.

119 M. L'Abbé G. Dugast, "The First Canadian Woman in the Northwest," *Transactions of the Historical and Scientific Society of Manitoba* 62 (Winnipeg: Manitoba Free Press, 1902).

120 Ibid., 15.

121 Richard White, "Frederick Jackson Turner and Buffalo Bill," in *The Frontier in American Culture: Essays by Richard White and Patricia Nelson Limerick*, ed. James R. Grossman (Berkeley: University of California Press, 1994), 29.

122 Reproduced in Robert M. Utley, *Indian, Soldier, and Settler: Experiences in the Struggle for the American West* (St Louis: Jefferson National Expansion Historical Association, 1979), 55.

123 Provincial Archives of Manitoba (PAM), card index to the Anglican parish registers, Red River Settlement.

124 PAM, George Gunn Papers, box 5, file 21, "Sketch of Tully Tragedy."

125 *Nor'Wester* (Red River Settlement), 15 October 1860.

126 Ibid., 8 November 1865.

127 Ibid., 22 September 1866.

128 *Thorold Post,* 19 June 1885.

129 Fanny Kelly, *Narrative of My Captivity among the Sioux Indians* (Toronto: Maclear, 1872). Although I have also located a fourth Canadian edition of this book (Toronto: Maclear, 1878), I have not been able to find any copies of the second and third editions.

130 There is controversy about Fanny Kelly's date of birth. Although she herself wrote 1845, it may have been 1842. See the introduction by Clark and Mary Lee Spence, eds., to Kelly's *Narrative of My Captivity among the Sioux Indians* (Chicago: R.R. Donnelley, 1990), xxxv and 3n1. Her tombstone in Glenwood Cemetery, Washington, DC, gives her date of birth as 15 November 1842.

131 Orillia Public Library, William Sword Frost Scrapbook, "Assessment Roll of Orillia Village and Township for Year 1844." Thanks to Donald Smith, Department of History, University of Calgary, for his correspondence with Frances E. Richardson of the Orillia Public Library.

132 Kelly, *Narrative* (1872 edn.), 15.

133 Kelly, *Narrative,* ed. Spence (1990 edn.), xxxv–xxxvi.

134 Ibid., xxxvii.

135 Ibid., 127.

136 Ibid., 229.

137 Ibid., 323.

138 Alan W. Farley, "An Indian Captivity and Its Legal Aftermath," *Kansas Historical Quarterly* (1955), 7.

139 Kelly, *Narrative* (1872 edn.), 269–70.

140 Kelly, *Narrative,* ed. Spence (1990 edn.), lvii.

141 Farley, "An Indian Captivity," 1.

142 Sarah L. Larimer, *The Capture and Escape; Or, Life among the Sioux* (Philadelphia: Claxton, Remsen and Haffelfinger, 1870).

143 Farley, "An Indian Captivity," 9.

144 Kelly, *Narrative,* ed. Spence (1990 edn.), 327.

145 Farley, "An Indian Captivity," 9.

146 Ibid., 10.

147 Kelly, *Narrative,* ed. Spence (1990 edn.), 331.

148 Ibid., 328.

149 Fanny Kelly, *Narrative of My Captivity among the Sioux Indians,* 3rd edn. (Chicago: R.R. Donnelley, 1891), vi.

150 *Ottawa Daily Citizen,* 27 September 1877.

151 Kelly, *Narrative,* ed. Spence (1990 edn.), 331.

152 Kelly, *Narrative* (1872 edn.).

153 Ibid., viii.

154 Ibid., 23.

155 Fanny Kelly, *Narrative of My Captivity among the Sioux*, 4th Canadian edn. (Toronto: Maclear, 1878), viii.

156 Ibid.

157 Ibid., vii.

158 Walter Hildebrandt and Brian Hubner, *The Cypress Hills: The Land and Its People* (Saskatoon: Purich Publishing, 1994), and Robert M. Utley, *The Lance and the Shield: The Life and Times of Sitting Bull* (New York: Henry Holt, 1993), chs. 15–18.

159 Utley, *The Lance and the Shield*, 344.

160 Kelly, *Narrative*, ed. Spence (1990 edn.), lvi.

161 Howard H. Peckham, *Captured by Indians: True Tales of Pioneer Survivors* (New Brunswick, NJ: Rutgers University Press, 1954), 230.

162 Utley, *The Lance and the Shield*, 60–3.

163 Kelly, *Narrative*, ed. Spence (1990 edn.), 336.

CHAPTER TWO

1 Canada, House of Commons, *Debates*, 8 June 1885, 2357.

2 *Globe*, 13 July 1885.

3 Theresa Gowanlock and Theresa Delaney, *Two Months in the Camp of Big Bear: The Life and Adventures of Theresa Gowanlock and Theresa Delaney* (Parkdale: Times Office, 1885), 83–91. See also Anson A. Gard, *Pioneers of the Upper Ottawa and the Humours of the Valley*, South Hull and Aylmer edn. (Ottawa: Emerson Press, 1906), 23. Thanks are due to Diane Aldred, Aylmer, for her research in locating the tombstone of Theresa Fulford in St Paul's Roman Catholic Cemetery on the Aylmer Road.

4 Ibid., 9. See also S.A. Martin, "Johnson, Theresa Mary (Gowanlock)," *Dictionary of Canadian Biography* (Toronto: University of Toronto Press, 1990), 12:478.

5 St Catharines Public Library, burial records, St Ann's 11 United Churchyard: "Theresa M. Johnson, wife of John Gowanlock, who on April 1 1885 was taken prisoner by Big Bear during the massacre of Frog Lake, NWT and after 2 months captivity was rescued by Col. Strange, d. Sept. 12, 1899, age 36 yr, 11 m. 15 d." Thanks are due to Roy A.C. Johnson of Ridgeville, Ont., family genealogist and historian, for sharing his research and providing copies of the *Johnson Reporter.*

6 Gowanlock and Delaney, *Two Months*, advertisement on the final page of the book, n.p.

7   Carlotta Hacker, *The Indomitable Lady Doctors* (Toronto: Clarke, Irwin, 1974), 39, 42.

8   *Land of Red and White* (Heinsburg: Frog Lake Community Club, 1977), 25.

9   C.D. Denney, "In Memory of Mary Rose (Pritchard) Sayers: The Last Witness," *Saskatchewan History* 24, no. 2 (Spring 1971): 63, 67, and Douglas W. Light, *Footprints in the Dust* (North battleford: Turner-Warwick Publications, 1987), 125n2.

10   "The Wanderings of John Pritchard, 1805," Outfit 273, *Beaver*, June 1942.

11   Light, *Footprints in the Dust*, 208. See also Guillaume Charette, *Vanishing Spaces: Memoirs of a Prairie Métis* (Winnipeg: Editions Bois-Brulés, 1976), 126.

12   Joe Dion, *My Tribe the Crees* (Calgary: Glenbow-Alberta Institute, 1979), 91–2.

13   Canada, House of Commons, *Sessional Papers* 18, no. 3 (1885): 148–9.

14   Hugh A. Dempsey, *Big Bear: The End of Freedom* (Vancouver: Douglas & McIntyre, 1984), 145.

15   Ibid., 145.

16   Ibid., 145–6.

17   Many different accounts, including those of William Bleasdell Cameron, George Stanley (Musunekwepan), Theresa Delaney, Theresa Gowanlock, and W.J. McLean, are included in Stuart Hughes, ed., *The Frog Lake "Massacre": Personal Perspectives on Ethnic Conflict*, Carleton Library no. 97 (Ottawa: McClelland and Stewart, 1976). A detailed account of the events and background to Frog Lake is contained in Norma Sluman and Jean Goodwill, *John Tootoosis: A Biography of a Cree Leader* (Ottawa: Golden Dog Press, 1982). See also Dion, *My Tribe the Crees*; Charette, *Vanishing Spaces*; "My Own Story: Isabelle Little Bear, One of the Last Remaining Links with the Riel Rebellion," in *Reflections: A History of Elk Point and District*, ed. Mary Bennett (Winnipeg: Inter-Collegiate Press, 1977), 197–202; and the accounts contained in *Land of Red and White* (Heinsburg: Frog Lake Community Club, 1977) and *Fort Pitt History Unfolding, 1829–1985* (Frenchman Butte: Fort Pitt Historical Society, 1985).

18   G.M. Adam, *From Savagery to Civilization: The Canadian North-West, Its History and its Troubles* (Toronto: Rose Publishing, 1885), 305.

19   Sluman and Goodwill, *John Tootoosis*, 57.

20   Ibid., 59, and Isabelle Little Bear, "My Own Story," 199.

21   Charette, *Vanishing Spaces*, 158–9.

22   Canada, House of Commons, *Sessional Papers* 15, no. 5 (1881): xv.

23 Allen Ronaghan, "Who Was This 'Fine Young Man'? The Frog Lake 'Massacre' Revisited," *Saskatchewan History* 47, no. 2 (1995): 13–19.
24 Dempsey, *Big Bear*, 214–15.
25 Bob Beal and Rod Macleod, *Prairie Fire: The 1885 North-West Rebellion* (Edmonton: Hurtig Publishers, 1984), 203.
26 George Stanley (Musunekwepan), "An Account of the Frog Lake Massacre," in *The Frog Lake "Massacre,"* ed. Stuart Hughes (Ottawa: McClelland and Stewart, 1976), 164–5.
27 Ibid., 165.
28 See Dion, *My Tribe the Crees*, and Jimmy Chief's recollections in *Fort Pitt History Unfolding*, 101.
29 Edward J. McCullough et al., *The Camps of Big Bear and Oo-nee-pow-o-hay-oos* (Calgary: Fedirchuk, McCullough and Associates, 1991), ii.
30 *Fort Pitt History Unfolding*, 101.
31 *Free Press* (Ottawa), 8 June 1885. William Bleasdell Cameron, *Blood Red the Sun* (1926; revd. edn., Vancouver: Wrigley Printing Co., 1950).
32 Gowanlock and Delaney, *Two Months*, 19, 28, 33.
33 Desmond Morton, *The Last War Drum: The North-West Campaign of 1885* (Toronto: Hakkert, 1972), 127–44.
34 Kenneth L. Holmes, "Murray, Alexander Hunter," *Dictionary of Canadian Biography* (Toronto: University of Toronto Press, 1972), 10:540–1.
35 Robert Watson, "Chief Trader Alexander Hunter Murray and Fort Youcon," *Beaver*, June 1929, 213.
36 *Globe*, 25 June 1885.
37 Ibid. Seekaskootch was also known as Cut Arm.
38 Glenbow-Alberta Institute, G.G. Mann Papers, "Episodes of the Riel Rebellion."
39 Elizabeth McLean, "The Siege of Fort Pitt," Outfit 277, *Beaver*, December 1946, 22.
40 Duncan McLean with Eric Wells, published as "The Last Hostage" in Harold Fryer, ed., *Frog Lake Massacre* (Surrey, BC: Frontier Books, 1984), 81-2.
41 Elizabeth McLean, "The Siege of Fort Pitt," 22.
42 Saskatchewan Archives Board (SAB), Campbell Innes Collection, box 2, file B9, William Cameron, "History of the Saskatchewan Uprising," 45.
43 Elizabeth McLean, "Prisoners of the Indians," Outfit 278, *Beaver*, June 1947, 15.
44 *Toronto Daily Mail*, 23 April 1885.
45 Ibid., 14 April 1885.
46 *Daily Patriot* (Charlottetown), 14 April 1885.

47 Ibid., 25 April 1885.
48 *Toronto Daily Mail*, 23 April 1885.
49 *Manitoba Daily Free Press*, 8 June 1885.
50 Battleford National Historic Park, Campbell Innes Collection, Diary of Lieut. R.S. Cassels, North-West Field Force, 1885, typescript copy, 26.
51 *Toronto Daily Mail*, 24 April 1885.
52 John G. Donkin, *Trooper in the Far North-West* (1889; rpt., Saskatoon: Western Producer Prairie Books, 1987), 158.
53 Glenbow-Alberta Institute, "Telegrams Relating to the Riel Rebellion," 116, J.S. McDonald to *Sun*, Winnipeg, 12 April 1885.
54 *Manitoba Daily Free Press*, 27 June 1885.
55 *Daily Patriot*, 13 July 1885.
56 Adam, *From Savagery to Civilization*, 365.
57 Nathalie Kermoal, "Les femmes métisses lors des événements de 1870 au Manitoba et de 1885 en Saskatchewan" (paper presented to the Canadian Historical Association, Carleton University, Ottawa, June 1993).
58 Battleford National Historic Park, Campbell Innes Collection, Cassels diary, 22.
59 Kitty (McLean) Yuill, "The Crossing of the Big Muskeg of Loon Lake, Sask., 1885" (address given at the Fiftieth Anniversary of the Riel Rebellion, the North-West Field Force Association, Toronto, 15 April 1935), typescript copy in collection of Edgar Mapletoft, Frenchman Butte, Saskatchewan.
60 See, for example, *Free Press* (Ottawa), 20 May 1885.
61 *Free Press* (Ottawa), 2 June 1885.
62 Gary Abrams, *Prince Albert: The First Century, 1866–1966* (Saskatoon: Modern Press, 1966), 79.
63 *Missionary Outlook*, June/July 1885, 101–2.
64 Jenny Sharpe, "The Unspeakable Limits of Rape; Colonial Violence and Counter-Insurgency," *Genders* 10 (Spring 1991): 35.
65 Catherine Hall, "Competing Masculinities: Thomas Carlyle, John Stuart Mill and the Case of Governor Eyre," in Hall, *White, Male and Middle Class* (New York: Routledge, 1992), 285.
66 Quoted in John Hawkes, *The Story of Saskatchewan and its People* (Regina: S.J. Clarke, 1924), 1: 226.
67 *Montreal Daily Star*, 16 May 1885.
68 *Toronto Daily Mail*, 25 April 1885.
69 *Daily Patriot*, 16 May 1885.
70 Walter Hildebrandt, *The Battle of Batoche: British Small Warfare and the Entrenched Métis* (Ottawa: Parks Canada, 1985).

71 *Toronto Morning News,* 25 May 1885.

72 *Macleod Gazette,* 6 June 1885.

73 Donkin, *Trooper in the Far North-West,* 144.

74 *London Advertiser,* 13 May 1885; Sharpe, "Unspeakable Limits," 33.

75 *London Advertiser,* 21 May 1885.

76 *Free Press* (Ottawa), 29 May 1885.

77 *London Advertiser,* 21 May 1885.

78 Morton, *The Last War Drum,* 133.

79 Rudy Wiebe and Bob Beal, eds., *War in the West: Voices of the 1885 Rebellion* (Toronto: McClelland and Stewart, 1985), 138, excerpt from Joseph Hicks of Major Halton's Scouts, May 1885.

80 Charles R. Daoust, *Cent-vingt jours de service actif: Récit historique très complet de la campagne du 65ème au Nord-Ouest* (1886; English translation by Roberta Cummings, Wetaskiwin: City of Wetaskiwin, 1982), 58.

81 Excerpts from John P. Pennefather, *Thirteen Years on the Prairies* (1892), in Harold Fryer, *Frog Lake Massacre* (Surrey: Frontier Books, 1984), 61, 71.

82 *Macleod Gazette,* 6 June 1885.

83 Quoted in Ibid.

84 *Macleod Gazette,* 6 June 1885.

85 Nellie L. McClung, *Clearning in the West: My Own Story* (Toronto: Thomas Allen and Son, 1976), 183.

86 Ibid., 183–4.

87 Richard H. Bartlett, "Citizens Minus: Indians and the Right to Vote," *Saskatchewan Law Review* 44 (1979–80): 163–94.

88 D.N. Sprague, *Canada and the Métis, 1869–1885* (Waterloo: Wilfrid Laurier Press, 1988), 176.

89 Quoted in Bartlett, *Citizens Minus,* 173.

90 Ibid., 179.

91 *London Advertiser,* 5 May 1885.

92 As reprinted in the *Daily Patriot,* 27 May 1885.

93 *Pree Press* (Ottawa), 22 May 1885.

94 Bartlett, *Citizens Minus,* 180–1.

95 *Free Press* (Ottawa), 28 May 1885.

96 A list of those in the "procession" of escaped captives who arrived at Fort Pitt on 5 June was included in the *Minneapolis Pioneer Press,* 25 June 1885: "Mrs. Gowanlock, Mrs. Delaney (white); Joseph Glader, wife and child, Frog Lake; Gregoire Donaire, Frog Lake; John Movan, wife and four children, Fort Pitt; Alfred Smith, Hudson's Bay Company employee [*SIC*], wife and four children, Fort Pitt; John Pritchard, Indian interpreter, wife and eight children, Frog Lake; Joseph

Dupree's wife and child, Frog Lake; Abraham Montour, wife and six children, Cold Lake; Pieter Bondrean, wife and two children, Onion Lake; André Dreneau, Frog Lake – two whites, forty-three half-breeds."

97 *Minneapolis Pioneer Press*, 25 June 1885.

98 Ibid.

99 See ibid.; also *Toronto Evening News*, 9 June 1885, *Globe*, 23 June 1885, and *Montreal Daily Star*, 23 June 1885.

100 *Globe*, 23 June 1885.

101 *Toronto Evening News*, 9 June 1885.

102 *Globe*, 25 June 1885.

103 *Globe*, 17 July 1885.

104 *Daily Patriot*, 27 June 1885.

105 Ibid.

106 Ibid.

107 Ibid.

108 *Montreal Daily Star*, 23 June 1885.

109 *Minneapolis Pioneer Press*, 25 June 1885.

110 *Globe*, 23 June 1885.

111 *Toronto Daily Mail*, May 19 1885.

112 Light, *Footprints in the Dust*, 512.

113 *Globe*, 7 July 1885.

CHAPTER THREE

1 G.M. Adam, *From Savagery to Civilization: The Canadian North-West, Its History and Troubles* (Toronto: Rose Publishing, 1885), 301.

2 *Globe*, 24 June 1885.

3 *Macleod Gazette*, 21 July 1885.

4 *Week* (Toronto), 18 June 1885.

5 *Macleod Gazette*, 21 July 1885.

6 C.D. Denney, "In Memory of Mary Rose (Pritchard) Sayers: The Last Witness," *Saskatchewan History* 24, no. 2 (Spring 1971): 66–7.

7 Saskatchewan Archives Board (SAB), Campbell Innes Papers, box 8, file 42, clippings from the Saskatoon *Star-Phoenix*, 1925.

8 Violet Loscombe, *Pursuit of Peace: Historic Tales of Battleford* (North Battleford: Battleford North West Historical Society, 1986), 117.

9 SAB, Effie Storer Papers, box 4, file 9, "A Story of Frog Lake," 15.

10 Ibid., 16.

11 *Thorold Post*, 17 July 1885.

12 *Manitoba Free Press*, 20 April 1910.

13 *Canadian Statesman*, 31 July 1885.

14 Loscombe, *Pursuit of Peace*, 146.

15 *Macleod Gazette*, 9 March 1886. According to Doug Light, Mrs Burke was a Métisse.

16 *Saskatchewan Herald*, 3 December 1887.

17 *Saskatchewan Herald*, 6 July 1885.

18 *Toronto Evening News*, 9 June 1885.

19 See, for example, Thomas B. Strange, *Gunner Jingo's Jubilee* (London: J. MacQueen, 1893).

20 *Daily Free Press* (Ottawa), 2 June 1885, excerpted from the *Chicago Daily News*, n.d.

21 Adam, *From Savagery to Civilization*, 303.

22 Ibid., 302.

23 Ibid., 306.

24 *Canadian Statesman*, 29 May 1885.

25 Glenbow-Alberta Institute (GAI), Jessie DeGear Papers, file 26, scrapbook no. 6, 74–5, clippings from an unidentified Winnipeg newspaper.

26 SAB, Effie Storer Papers, box 4, file 9, "A Story of Frog Lake," 19.

27 *Canadian Statesman*, 17 July 1885 (from *Daily Manitoban*, 7 July 1885).

28 Gowanlock and Delaney, *Two Months*, 56.

29 *Huron Expositor*, 17 July 1885.

30 *Daily Free Press* (Ottawa), 25 July 1885.

31 Ibid.

32 *Canadian Statesman*, 31 July 1885.

33 Mary Jane Edwards et al., eds., *The Evolution of Canadian Literature in English, 1867–1914* (Toronto: Holt, Rinehart and Winston, 1973), 42.

34 Quoted in Gowanlock and Delaney, *Two Months*, 63.

35 *Globe*, 13 July 1885.

36 *Thorold Post*, 15 January 1886.

37 Stuart Hughes, ed., *The Frog Lake "Massacre,": Personal Perspectives on Ethnic Conflict*, Carleton Library no. 97 (Ottawa: McClelland and Stewart, 1976), 1.

38 *Thorold Post*, 15 January 1886.

39 Ibid., 6.

40 Kay Schaffer, "Colonizing Gender in Colonial Australia: The Eliza Fraser Story," in *Writing Women and Space: Colonial and Postcolonial Geographies*, ed. Alison Blunt and Gillian Rose (New York: Guilford Press, 1994), 107.

41 Page numbers in parentheses are from Theresa Gowanlock and Theresa Delaney, *Two Months in the Camp of Big Bear: The Life and*

Adventures of Theresa Gowanlock and Theresa Delaney (Parkdale: Times Office, 1885).

42 Kay Sheaffer, "Eliza Fraser's Trial by Media," *Antipodes* 5, no. 2 (1991): 107.

43 Richard Van Der Beets, *The Indian Captivity Narrative: An American Genre* (Lanham: University Press of America, 1984), 29.

44 *Globe*, 23 June 1885.

45 In the accounts of many (including Isabelle Little Bear's "My Own Story") the camp was located about one mile from the settlement at Frog Lake. On the way, a "little knoll" allowed a last glimpse of the site of Frog Lake. Recent archaeological research undertaken by Fedirchuk McCullough and Associates located the camps of Big Bear and Oo-nee-pow-ohay-oos on a large flat terrace overlooking Frog Creek, with the site of the town of Frog Lake not within seeing distance. See Edward J. McCullough et al., *The Camps of Big Bear and Oo-nee-pow-o-nay-oos (FI0.4)* (Calgary: Fedirchuk, McCullough & Associates, 1991).

46 *Minneapolis Pioneer Press*, 25 June 1885.

47 National Archives of Canada (NA), RG10, vol. 3719, file 22649.

48 Van Der Beets, *The Indian Captivity Narrative*, 26–7.

49 Quoted in ibid., 27.

50 Charles Pelham Mulvaney, *The History of the North-West Rebellion of 1885* (Toronto: A.H. Hovey, 1885).

51 George H. Ham, *Reminiscences of a Raconteur* (Toronto: Museum Book Co., 1921), 88–9.

52 Ibid., 88.

53 Gowanlock and Delaney, *Two Months*, 55.

54 Michel Foucault, *The Archaeology of Knowledge*, trans. A.M. Sheridan-Smith (New York: Pantheon, 1972).

55 Sara Mills, *Discourses of Difference: An Analysis of Women's Travel Writing and Colonialism* (London: Routledge, 1991), 68.

56 Ibid., 78.

57 Mary Louise Pratt, "Conventions of Representation: Where Discourse and Ideology Meet," *Georgetown University Round Table on Language and Linguistics* (Washington, DC: Georgetown University Press, 1982), 145.

58 *Montreal Herald and Daily Commercial Gazette*, 19 November 1885.

59 Ibid.

60 *Thorold Post*, 2 October 1885.

61 Elizabeth M. McLean, "The Siege of Fort Pitt," Outfit 277, *Beaver*, December 1946, 22–5; "Prisoners of the Indians," Outfit 278, *Beaver*, June 1947, 14–17; "Our Captivity Ended," Outfit 278, *Beaver*, September 1947, 38–42.

62 Elizabeth McLean, "The Siege," 22.

63 Elizabeth McLean, "Prisoners," 17.

64 Elizabeth McLean, "Captivity Ended," 39.

65 Elizabeth McLean, "Prisoners," 15.

66 Elizabeth McLean, "Captivity Ended," 39.

67 Ibid., 40.

68 Kitty McLean (Mrs K.M. Yuill), "The Crossing of the Big Muskeg of Loon Lake, Sask. 1885." Typescript copy in the collection of Edgar Mapletoft, Frenchman Butte, Saskatchewan.

69 S.B. Steele, *Forty Years in Canada* (Winnipeg: Russell, Land and Co. 1915), 228.

70 Kitty McLean, "The Crossing," 2.

71 Kitty (Katherine) McLean, "Adventures of Kitty," "His Twin from the Great Beyond," "The Mounties Arrived in Splendour," "My First Formal: The Gift Dance," "I Smoke the Peace Pipe," "How We Read the News," "A Gentle Man and His Gift," "Honest Thief," and "The Tool of God," all in *Nor'Wester* 100, no. 1 (July 1970).

72 Kitty McLean, "My First Formal," 40.

73 Amelia M. Paget, *The People of the Plains* (Toronto: Ryerson Press, 1909).

74 *Daily Herald* (Calgary), 23 October 1906.

75 See NA, RG10, vol. 4018, file 276916.

76 Ibid., E.S. Caswell to D.C. Scott, 3 March 1909.

77 Paget, *People of the Plains*, 98–9.

78 Ibid., 13–15.

79 Ibid., 15.

80 John Maclean, *McDougall of Alberta: A Life of Rev. John McDougall*, D.D. *Pathfinder of Empire and Prophet of the Plains* (Toronto: Ryerson Press, 1927), 150.

81 NA, RG10, vol. 3719, file 22–649, L. Vankoughnet to Sir John A. Macdonald, 24 July 1885, and order-in-council, 14 November 1885.

82 Hughes, *The Frog Lake "Massacre,"* 1.

83 Robert Fulford, "Big Bear, Frog Lake, and My Aunt Theresa," *Saturday Night*, June 1976, 9–10. See also Robert Fulford, "How the West Was Lost," *Saturday Night*, July 1985, 5–8.

84 Anson A. Gard, *Pioneers of the Upper Ottawa and the Humours of the Valley*, South Hull and Aylmer edn. (Ottawa: Emerson Press, 1906), 23.

85 NA, RG10, vol. 3719, file 22649, Mrs M.L. Walsh et al. to minister of the interior, 14 April 1915.

86 Hughes, *The Frog Lake "Massacre,"* 1.

87 NA, RG10, vol. 3719, file 22649, N.O. Coté, controller, to W.W. Cory, deputy minister of the interior, 5 May 1915.

88 *Saskatchewan Herald*, 29 September 1899.

89 NA, RG10, vol. 3831, file 63891, assistant deputy and secretary to W.J. Hyde, 7 October 1912.

90 Ibid., E. Forster Brown to Department of Indian Affairs, 20 January 1913.

91 Walter Hildebrandt, "Official Images of 1885," *Prairie Fire* 6, no. 4 (1985): 31–8.

92 *Free Press* (Ottawa), 2 June 1885.

93 *Toronto Daily Mail*, 30 November 1885.

94 Theresa Johnson Gowanlock, "Memories of Frog Lake," *Family Herald and Weekly Star*, 20 October 1955, 26–7. An article by Sylvia Bough (now Sylvia Lee) entitled "Theresa Gowanlock's Ordeal," *Western People*, 21 March 1985, alerted me to this 1955 article. Lee is doubtful that the article was written by Mrs Gowanlock. I am grateful to Sharon Gerein of Regina for sending me Sylvia Lee's article. The quotations that follow are all from the 1955 publication.

95 University of Saskatchewan Archives, Special Collections Department, Shortt Collection, A.S. Morton Papers, C555/1/1.29, "Theresa" by Mrs Storer, Moose Jaw. The quotations that follow are from this manuscript.

96 Gowanlock, "Memories of Frog Lake," 26.

97 SAB, Effie Storer papers, 4: 9, "A Story of Frog Lake, part of unpublished manuscript. According to the information contained in the finding aid to the Storer Papers at the SAB, Effie Laurie Storer was born in Windsor, Ontario, in 1867. She moved with her family to Red River in 1869 and then to Battleford in 1882. She married J.H. Storer, a corporal in the NWMP who was later killed in France during the Great War. Effie Storer was a newspaperwoman and journalist, working first in her father's *Saskatchewan Herald* office and later on the Regina *Leader-Post* and Moose Jaw *Times-Herald*. She died in Saskatoon on 18 May 1951 at the age of eighty-four.

98 SAB, Dr W. Menzies Whitelaw Papers, finding aid, 1.

99 Ibid., file 5, Effie Storer Correspondence, Storer to Whitelaw, 4 July
    1949.

100 Ibid., Storer to Whitelaw, 28 December 1949.

101 Edmund Collins, *Annette, the Metis Spy: A Heroine of the N.W. Rebellion*
     (Toronto: Rose Publishing, 1886), 65–6, and, by the same author,
     The Story of Louis Riel: The Rebel Chief (Toronto: J.S. Robertson and
     Brothers, 1885), 147–8.

102 John Mackie, *The Rising of the Red Man: A Romance of the Riel Rebellion*,
     2nd edn. (London: Jarrold and Sons, 1914).

103 Ibid., 29.

104 Ibid., 61.

105 Rudy Wiebe, *The Temptations of Big Bear* (Toronto: McClelland and
     Stewart, 1973); Mel Dagg, *The Women on the Bridge* (Saskatoon: This-
     tledown Press, 1992).

106 Sherrill E. Grace, "Western Myth and Northern History: The Plains
     Indians of Berger and Wiebe," *Great Plains Quarterly* 3, no. 3 (Sum-
     mer 1983): 148.

107 Fulford, "Big Bear, Frog Lake and My Aunt Theresa," 9–11.

108 William B. Cameron, *Blood Red the Sun* (1926; revd. edn., Calgary:
     Kenway Publishing Co., 1950), 223.

109 Diane Parenteau, "Historic Study Uncovers Big Bear's Camp," *Wind-
     speaker*, June 1991.

110 See McCullough et al., *The Camps of Big Bear and Oo-nee-pow-o-hay-oos*.

CHAPTER FOUR

1   *World* (New York), 2 February 1890.

2   Ibid., 11 February 1890.

3   Ibid., 2 February 1890.

4   Ibid., 7 February 1890.

5   Ibid.

6   *River Press* (Fort Benton), 12 February 1890.

7   *Macleod Gazette* (Fort Macleod), 6 February 1890.

8   *World*, 2 February 1890.

9   All of this detail is contained in the *World*, 11 February 1890.

10 National Archives of Canada (NA), RG10, vol. 3803, file 50704,
    W. McGirr to E. Dewdney, 15 August 1888.

11 NA, RG18, vol. 40, file 217–1890, Supt. J. McIllree to commissioner,
    19 February 1890.

12 *World*, 2 February 1890.

13 James Sanderson, "Tales of the Canadian Prairies," in *The Best from Alberta History*, ed. Hugh Dempsey (Saskatoon: Western Producer Prairie Books, 1981), 10–11.

14 Saskatchewan Archives Board (SAB), Campbell Innes Papers, A113, 8, Clippings 46, "Wood Mountain Tales: The Belle of the Qu'Appelle."

15 See *Fort Macleod – Our Colourful Past: A History of the Town of Fort Macleod from 1874 to 1924* (Fort Macleod: Fort Macleod History Committee, 1977), 268–9; personal interview with Kirsten Grier, great-grand daughter of D.J. Grier, Calgary, 19 May 1993.

16 Beverley A. Stacey, "D.W. Davis: Whiskey Trader to Politician," *Alberta History* 38, no. 3 (Summer 1990).

17 Hugh A. Dempsey, *Red Crow: Warrior Chief* (Saskatoon: Western Producer Prairie Books, 1980), 76–7.

18 *Macleod Gazette*, 1 May 1890.

19 *Manitoba Daily Free Press*, 24 February 1890.

20 Provincial Archives of Alberta, Diary of Rev. L. Doucet, typescript copy, translated, Nakoda Institute.

21 *Macleod Gazette*, 17 May 1887.

22 *Calgary Herald*, 1 April 1887.

23 Ibid.

24 *Macleod Gazette*, 17 May 1887.

25 *Calgary Herald*, 1 April 1887.

26 *Macleod Gazette*, 3 May 1887.

27 Ibid.

28 *Calgary Herald*, 22 January 1890.

29 Sarah Carter, *Lost Harvests: Prairie Indian Reserve Farmers and Government Policy* (Montreal: McGill-Queen's University Press, 1990), 150–5.

30 *Lethbridge News*, 13 April 1887.

31 NA, RG18, vol. 45, file 953–90.

32 *Macleod Gazette*, 26 July 1895.

33 Provincial Archives of Alberta, Diary of Rev. L. Doucet.

34 *Manitoba Daily Free Press*, 25 February 1890.

35 *Fort Macleod – Our Colourful Past*, 363.

36 *Minnedosa Valley Views* (Winnipeg: Intercollegiate Press, 1982), 177.

37 Rev. Alfred Garrioch, "Female Moses of the Peace," *Alberta Folklore Quarterly* 1, no. 4 (1945).

38 NA, RG10, vol. 3560, file 75, pt 2, Allan Macdonald to J.A. Markle, 22 October 1895.

39 *Manitoba Free Press*, 4 January 1898.

40 Ibid., 11 January 1898.

41 Ibid.

42 *Journal* (New York), 18 January 1898.

43 *Manitoba Free Press*, 3 February 1898.

44 Ibid., 4 March 1898. See also *Memories Are Forever* (Manor and District Historical Society, 1982): 381–2.

45 NA, RG10, vol 3909, file 107422, A. Turton to Department of Indian Affairs, 29 October 1893.

46 Ibid., Agent T.J. Campbell to deputy superintendent of Indian affairs, 10 November 1893. See also *Manitoba Free Press*, 2 July 1895.

47 *Manitoba Free Press*, 7 March 1898.

48 Ibid., 4 March 1898.

49 Ibid., 7 March 1898.

50 Ibid.

51 NA, RG10, vol. 3909, file 107422, T.W. Aspdin to David Laird, 18 April 1898.

52 Ibid.

53 Ibid.

54 Ibid.

55 *Leader* (Regina), 5 May 1898.

56 NA, RG10, vol. 3909, file 107422, James W. Kyle to David Laird, 13 May 1898.

57 Ibid., W.A. Jones to James G. Reid, 19 July 1898.

58 *Memories Are Forever*, 382.

59 Ibid.

CHAPTER FIVE

1 Mary E. Inderwick "A Lady and Her Ranch," in *The Best from Alberta History*, ed. Hugh Dempsey (Saskatoon: Western Producer Prairie Books, 1981), 65–77. In 1882 the North-West Territories were divided into four provisional districts named Assiniboia, Saskatchewan, Alberta, and Athabasca. Many thanks are due to Hugh Dempsey for sharing his research with me and for his valuable suggestions as to other sources.

2 For an examination and critique of this argument, see Margaret Strobel, *European Women and the Second British Empire* (Bloomington: Indiana University Press, 1991). See also essays by Ann Laura Stoler, "Carnal Knowledge and Imperial Power: Gender, Race and Morality in Colonial Asia," in *Gender at the Crossroads of Knowledge: Feminist Anthropology in the Postmodern Era*, ed. Micaela di Leonardo (Berkeley: University of California Press, 1991), 51–101, and "Rethinking

Colonial Categories: European Communities and the Boundaries of Rule," in *Colonialism and Culture*, ed. Nicholas B. Dirks (Ann Arbor: University of Michigan Press, 1992), 319–52.

3 Vron Ware, *Beyond the Pale: White Women, Racism and History* (London: Verso, 1992), 17.

4 See Sarah Carter, *Lost Harvests: Prairie Indian Reserve Farmers and Government Policy* (Montreal: McGill-Queen's University Press, 1990).

5 Rayna Green, "The Pocahontas Perplex: The Image of Indian Women in American Culture," in *Unequal Sisters: A Multicultural Reader in U.S. Women's History*, ed. Ellen Carol DuBois and Vicki L. Ruiz (New York: Routledge, 1990), 15–21.

6 John McDougall, "A Criticism of 'Indian Wigwams and Northern Camp-Fires,'" (1895), 12–13.

7 See, for example, Canada, House of Commons (CHC), *Sessional Papers 14* 34, no. 11 (1900): xxviii, l66; *Toronto Daily Mail*, 2 March 1889; and Pamela Margaret White, "Restructuring the Domestic Sphere – Prairie Indian Women on Reserves: Image, Ideology and State Policy, 1880–1930," PHD diss, McGill University, 1987).

8 CHC, *Sessional Papers 14* 33, no 12 (1899): xix.

9 Ibid., 34, no. 11 (1900): xxiii.

10 W.H. Withrow, *Native Races of North American* (Toronto: Methodist Mission Rooms, 1895), 114.

11 CHC, *Sessional Papers 27* 43, no. 15 (1909): 110.

12 National Archives of Canada (NA), RG10, vol. 3860, file 82319–6, Inspector Alex McGibbon's report on Onion Lake, October 1891.

13 Egerton Ryerson Young, *Stories from Indian Wigwams and Northern Campfires* (Toronto: William Briggs, 1893), 148.

14 Egerton Ryerson Young, *By Canoe and Dog Train among the Cree and Saulteaux Indians* (Toronto: Willliam Briggs, 1890), 63.

15 "Along the Line. The Indian Work. Saskatchewan District" (letter from Rev. J. McDougall, Morley, November 1892), *Missionary Outlook*, April 1893, 53.

16 *Toronto Daily Mail*, 23 January 1886.

17 Saskatchewan Archives Board, (SAB), Effie Storer Papers, box 2, file 5, "Indian Life," 2.

18 Jane Fishburne Collier, *Marriage and Inequality in Classless Societies* (Stanford: Stanford University Press, 1988).

19 Ibid., 82.

20 Ibid., 82, 119.

21 Robert H. Lowie, "Marriage and Family Life among the Plains Indians," *Scientific Monthly* 34 (1932): 463.

22 See, for example, Alan Klein, "The Political-Economy of Gender: A Nineteenth-Century Plains Indian Case Study," in *The Hidden Half: Studies of Plains Indian Women*, ed. P. Albers and B. Medicine (Lanham, Md.: University Press of America, 1983).

23 See, for example, Patricia Albers, "Sioux Women in Transition: A Study of Their Changing Status in Domestic and Capitalistic Sectors of Production," in *The Hidden Half*, ed. Albers and Medicine; and Carolyn Garrett Pool, "Reservation Policy and the Economic Position of Wichita Women," *Great Plains Quarterly* 8 (Summer 1988).

24 Kathleen Jamieson, "Sex Discrimination and the Indian Act," in *Arduous Journey: Canadian Indians and Decolonization*, ed. J. Rick Ponting (Toronto: McClelland and Stewart).

25 See Constance Backhouse, *Petticoats and Prejudice: Woman and Law in Nineteenth-Century Canada* (Toronto: Women's Press, for Osgoode Society, 1991).

26 Catherine Cavanaugh, "The Limitations of the Pioneering Partership: The Alberta Campaign for Homestead Dower, 1909–25," *Canadian Historical Review* 74, no. 2 (June 1993).

27 Quoted in Peggy Pascoe, *Relations of Rescue: The Search for Female Moral Authority in the American West, 1874–1939* (New York: Oxford University Press, 1990), 59. See also "Nez Percé Women's Industrial Society, 1890," *Gender and History* 7, no. 1 (April 1995): 1–4.

28 *Globe*, 1 February 1886.

29 *Toronto Daily Mail*, 23 January 1886.

30 *Macleod Gazette*, 23 June 1886.

31 *Globe*, 1 February 1886.

32 Mariana Valverde, *The Age of Light, Soap and Water: Moral Reform in English Canada, 1885–1925* (Toronto: McClelland and Stewart, 1991), 90–1.

33 David J. Carter, *Samuel Trivett: Missionary with the Blood Indians* (Calgary: Kyle Printing and Stationery, 1974), 37–40.

34 CHC, *Debates* 1 (1886): 720–1.

35 E.C. Morgan, "The North-West Mounted Police: Internal Problems and Public Criticism, 1874–1883," *Saskatchewan History* 26, no. 2 (Spring 1973): 56–9.

36 Quoted in ibid., 56.

37 Quoted in John Hawkes, *The Story of Saskatchewan and Its People* (Regina: S.J. Clarke, 1924), 1:534.

38 CHC, *Debates*, 21 April 1880, 1638.

39 *Toronto Daily Mail*, 2 February 1886.

40 John Maclean, "The Half-breed and Indian Insurrection," *Canadian Methodist Magazine* 22, no. 1 (July 1885): 173–4.

41 NA, RG10, vol. 3753, file 30613, Edgar Dewdney to Bishop of Saskatchewan, 31 May 1886.

42 Glenbow-Alberta Institute (GAI), J.F. Macleod Family Fonds, file 14, 1878101A, J.F. Macleod to Mary Macleod, 29 July 1878.

43 Jean D'Artigue, *Six Years in the Canadian Northwest* (Toronto: Hunter Rose, 1882), 70.

44 F.J.E. Fitzpatrick, *Sergeant 331: Personal Recollections of a Member of the Canadian North-West Mounted Police from 1879–1885* (New York: F.J. Fitzpatrick, 1921), 75.

45 R.B. Nevitt, *A Winter at Fort Macleod*, ed. Hugh A. Dempsey (Calgary: Glenbow-Alberta Institute, 1974), 49.

46 Ibid., 54.

47 GAI, Simon John Clarke Papers, "Anglo Canadian News Service," Series A, no. 218, "Simon John Clarke."

48 Ibid., entry for 20 October 1879.

49 GAI, Diary of William H. Metzler, typescript copy, entry for 30 June 1882.

50 *Fort Benton Record*, 15 December 1876.

51 GAI, "Diary of Regimental no. 247, Trumpeter Fred A. Bagley, North-West Mounted Police. 1874 to 1880. '81 & '84. Transcribed at Banff, Alberta, 1938," entry for 13 February 1880.

52 SAB, Campbell Innes Papers, vol. 2(b), 7, "Diary of a Mountie. W.H. Cox, 1880–85."

53 SAB, R834, file 17(b), 15, John O'Kute-sica correspondence.

54 Ruth M. Daw, "Sgt.-Major H.H.G. Bray, the Forgotten Horseman," in *Men in Scarlet*, ed. Hugh Dempsey (Calgary: McClelland and Stewart West, 1975), 49.

55 Fort Walsh National Historic Park, London M. Modien, "The McKay Family: People of the Little Bearskin," unpublished manuscript, 1986, 56–7.

56 Hugh Dempsey, private collection, taken from Blood Indian correspondence for the agents' letterbooks, vol. 2, 1881–89, William Pocklington's report for 9 October 1885. See also Hawkes, *The Story of Saskatchewan and Its People*, 1:109 ff.

57 Roderick C. Macleod, "Walsh, James Morrow," *Dictionary of Canadian Biography* (Toronto: University of Toronto Press, 1994), 13:1072.

58 *Blackfoot Heritage: 1907–08*, (Browning: Blackfeet Heritage Program, n.d.), 171.

59 A.B. McCullough, "Papers Relating to the North West Mounted Police and Fort Walsh," Manuscript Report Series 213 (Ottawa: Parks Canada, Department of Indian and Northern Affairs, 1977), 132–3.

60 GAI, S.J. Clarke diary, typescript, entries for 21 December 1880 and 11 January 1881.

61 *Blackfoot Heritage: 1907–08*, 171.

62 NA, RG18, vol. 35, file 499–1889, L. Herchmer to comptroller, 23 May 1889.

63 NA, MG29-F52, R.N. Wilson diary, entry for 14 January 1883.

64 T. Morris Longstreth, *The Silent Force: Scenes from the Life of the Mounted Police of Canada* (New York: Century Co., 1927).

65 Ibid., 116. Perhaps the most candid NWMP diary is that of James T. Stanford, written in 1876–77 at Fort Macleod, where Stanford was in charge of stores and rations. It contains numerous entries such as "Had a go at a squaw on my bed," Had a go at a squaw in the root house," and "Had a go at a Cree squaw got her in to mud my shack" (University of Missoula Archives, K. Ross Toole Collection, Mike and Maureen Mansfield Library, Conrad Family Collection, James T. Stanford diary, 1876–77). See entries for 7 November 1876 and 1, 7, 11, and 13 December 1876.

66 *River Press* (Fort Benton), 29 December 1880.

67 University of Missoula Archives, K. Ross Toole Collection, Mike and Maureen Mansfield Library, Conrad Family Collection, box 5, file 31, James Stanford to Mrs C.E. Stanford, 3 October 1875.

68 C. Frank Turner, "Custer and the Canadian Connections," *Beaver*, Outfit 307, Summer 1976, 10.

69 For information on W. D. Jarvis, I am grateful to Dr William Beahen, Royal Canadian Mounted Police, and his correspondence with Dr Donald Smith, 15 October 1993.

70 Sandra Gwyn, *The Private Capital: Ambition and Love in the Age of Macdonald and Laurier* (Toronto: McClellanad and Stewart, 1984), 77.

71 Ibid.

72 John McDougall, *On Western Trails in the Early Seventies: Frontier Pioneer Life in the Canadian Northwest* (Toronto: William Briggs, 1911), 222.

73 SAB, R834, file 17(b), John O'Kute-sica correspondence, 3.

74 Ibid., 4.

75 See, for example, NA, RG18, vol. 2182, file RCMP 1895, pt 2, S.B. Steele to commissioner, Fort Macleod, 20 July 1895; and Glenbow Archives, Edward Sanders Family Papers, Gilbert E. Sanders diaries, M1093, file 38, 20 October 1885.

76 Robert Jefferson, *Fifty Years on the Saskatchewan* (Battleford: Canadian North-West Historical Society, 1929).

77 F. Laurie Barron, "Indian Agents and the North-West Rebellion," in *1885 and After: Native Society in Transition*, ed. F. Laurie Barron and James B. Waldram (Regina: Canadian Plains Research Centre, 1986), 36.

78 Norma Sluman and Jean Goodwill, *John Tootoosis: A Biography of a Cree Leader* (Ottawa: Golden Dog Press, 1982), 37.

79 NA, RG10 William Henry Cotton Collection, undated newspaper clipping, "Through the Saskatchewan."

80 NA, RG10, Hayter Reed Papers, Chief Thunderchild to Hayter Reed, 15 July 1893. See also vol. 16, inquiry into allegations against agent P.L. Clink.

81 Ramon A. Gutierrez, *When Jesus Came, the Corn Mothers Went Away: Marriage, Sexuality and Power in New Mexico, 1500–1846* (Stanford: Stanford University Press, 1991), 51.

82 *Globe*, 4 June 1880.

83 *Macleod Gazette*, 16 March 1886.

84 Ibid., 23 March 1886.

85 *Toronto Daily Mail*, 2 February 1886.

86 *Macleod Gazette*, 16 March 1886.

87 CHC, *Debates* 1 (1886): 730.

88 NA, RG10, vol. 3772, file 34983, William Donovan to L. Vankoughnet, 31 October 1886.

89 Provincial Archives of Alberta, Diary of Rev. L. Doucet, typescript copy, translated, Nakoda Institute.

90 *Globe*, 4 June 1886.

91 *The Facts Respecting Indian Administration in the North-West* (Ottawa, 1886), 9.

92 Ibid., 12.

93 CHC, *Sessional Papers 19 24*, no. 15 (1891): 62.

94 *Moosomin Courier*, 13 March 1890.

95 Joe Dion, *My Tribe the Crees* (Calgary: Glenbow-Alberta Institute, 1979), 114.

96 SAB, R176, vol. 1, 22 "Women's Canadian Club Convention 1924: Essays on Pioneer Days." (Author's name has been deleted from the essay.)

97 Ibid., vol. 2, 15, "The Neighborhood of Battleford," by Mrs. J.A. Reid, "An Old Time Resident."

98 Elizabeth M. McLean, "Prisoners of the Indians," *Beaver*, Outfit 278, June 1947, 15–16.

99 David Hamer, *New Towns in the New World: Images and Perceptions of the Nineteenth Century Urban Frontier* (New York: Columbia University Press, 1990), 17, 213.

100 Elizabeth Keith Morris, *An Englishwoman in the Canadian West* (London, 1913), 57. Thanks to Pernille Jakobsen for bringing this quotation to my attention in her MA thesis, "Touring Strange Lands: Women Travel Writers in Western Canada, 1876–1914" (MA thesis, University of Calgary, 1996).

101 *What Canadian Women Say of the Canadian North-West* (Montreal: Montreal Herald, 1886), 42–5.

102 Ibid., 44.

103 NA, RG10, vol. 1009, file 628, 596–635, L. Vankoughnet to John A. Macdonald, 15 November 1883.

104 S.W. Horrall, "The (Royal) North-West Mounted Police and Prostitution on the Canadian Prairies," *Prairie Forum* 10, no. 1 (Spring 1985).

105 NA, RG10, vol. 3673, file 10986, clipping from the Edmonton *Bulletin*, 7 January 1883.

106 CHC, *Sessional Papers II* 27, no. 14 (1906): 82.

107 Constance B. Backhouse, "Nineteenth-Century Prostitution Law: Reflection of a Discriminatory Society, *Histoire sociale/Social History* 18, no. 36 (November 1985), 420–2.

108 Ibid., 422.

109 CHC, *Sessional Papers.* Annual Report of the Commissioner of the North-West Mounted Police Force for the year 1889, reprinted in *The New West* (Toronto: Coles, 1973), 101.

110 *Saskatchewan Herald,* 15 March 1886.

111 Ibid., 13 March 1888.

112 *Calgary Herald,* 5 March 1885.

113 See, for example, Carolina Antoinetta J.A. Van de Vorst, "A History of Farm Women's Work in Manitoba" (MA thesis, Deparament of Anthropology, University of Manitoba, 1988).

114 Lyn Hancock with Marion Dowler, *Tell Me Grandmother* (Toronto: McClelland and Steward, 1985), 139.

115 Ibid.

116 *Macleod Gazette,* 18 July 1888.

117 Ibid.

118 John D. Higginbotham, *When the West Was Young: Historical Reminiscences of the Early Canadian West* (Toronto: Ryerson Press, 1933), 260–1.

119 R.C. Macleod, *The North-West Mounted Police and Law Enforcement, 1873–1905,* (Toronto: University of Toronto Press, 1976), 145. See also NA, RG18, vol. 24, file 667–1888.

120 Donald Smith, "Bloody Murder Almost Became Miscarriage of Justice," *Herald Sunday Magazine*, 23 July 1989, 13. Thanks to Donald Smith, Department of History, University of Calgary, for allowing me to draw upon his sources on this case.

121 James Gray, *Talk to My Lawyer: Great Stories of Southern Alberta's Bar and Bench* (Edmonton: Hurtig Publishers, 1987), 7.

122 See Major Charles Boulton, *Reminiscences of the North-West Rebellions* (Toronto: Grip Printing and Publishing, 1886), 512.

123 *Calgary Weekly Herald*, 17 July 1889.

124 Quoted in Smith, "Bloody Murder," 15.

125 *Calgary Herald*, 24 July 1889.

126 Ibid., 11 September 1889.

127 Ibid., 6 March 1889.

128 Ibid.

129 See Christine Bolt, *Victorian Attitudes to Race* (Toronto: University of Toronto Press, 1971); Philip D. Curtin, *The Image of Africa: British Ideas and Action, 1780–1850* (Madison: University of Wisconsin Press, 1964); V.G. Kiernan, *The Lords of Human Kind: European Attitudes toward the Outside World in the Imperial Age* (Harmondsworth: Penguin Books, 1972); Douglas A. Lorimer, *Colour, Class and the Victorians* (Leicester University Press, Holmes and Meier Publishers, 1978); and Philip Mason, *Patterns of Dominance* (London: Oxford University Press, 1971).

130 This is suggested by Backhouse, "Nineteenth-Century Canadian Prostitution Law," 422.

131 Mariana Valverde, *The Age of Light, Soap, and Water: Moral Reform in English Canada, 1885–1925* (Toronto: McClelland and Stewart, 1991).

132 NA, RG18, vol. 1039, file 87–1886, pt. 1.

133 Sylvia Van Kirk, *"Many Tender Ties": Women in Fur Trade Society, 1670–1870* (Winnipeg: Watson and Dwyer, 1980), 241; Constance Backhouse, *Petticoats and Prejudice: Women and the Law in Nineteenth-Century Canada* (Toronto: Osgoode Society, 1991), ch. 1.

134 Quoted in Van Kirk, *Mary Tender Ties*, 241.

135 Brian Slattery and Linda Charlton, eds., *Canadian Native Law Cases*, vol. 3, *1891–1910* (Saskatoon: Native Law Centre, 1985), 636–44.

136 Georgia Green Fooks, *Fort Whoop-Up: Alberta's First and Most Notorious Whisky Fort* (Lethbridge: Whoop-Up Country Chapter Historical Society of Alberta, 1983), 43.

137 *Judith Basin Country Press*, 11 October 1926.

138 *Havre Daily News*, 29 December 1927.

139 Jenny Sharpe, *Allegories of Empire: The Figure of Woman in the Colonial Text* (Minneapolis: University of Minnesota Press, 1993).
140 Catherine Cavanaugh, "The Limitations of the Pioneering Partnership: The Alberta Campaign for Homestead Dower, 1909–1925," in Catherine Cavanaugh and Jeremy Mouat, *Making Western Canada: Essays on European Colonization and Settlement* (Toronto: Garamond Press, 1996), 191.
141 Ibid.
142 Nellie McClung, *Clearing in the West: An Autobiography* (Toronto: Thomas Allen and Sons, 1965), 306.
143 Leo Thwaite, *Alberta: An Account of Its Wealth and Progress*, Porter's Progress of Nations Series (Chicago: Rand McNally, 1912).
144 Ibid., 38.

CHAPTER SIX

1 Canada, House of Commons, *Debates*, 26 May 1921, 3908.
2 *Calgary Herald*, 23 March 1894.
3 R. Bruce Shepard, "Plain Racism: The Reaction against Oklahoma Black Immigration to the Canadian Plains," *Prairie Forum* 10, no. 2 (1985): 365–82, "Diplomatic Racism: Canadian Government and Black Migration from Oklahoma, 1905–1912," *Great Plains Quarterly* 3, no. 1 (1983): 5–16.
4 Shepard, "Plain Racism," 369.
5 Ibid., 368.
6 Ibid., 367–8.
7 Quoted in ibid., 371.
8 I am indebted to the research of R. Bruce Shepard for this entire section on the Huff scandal and its impact on Oklahoma black immigration to the West.
9 *Evening Journal* (Edmonton), 6 April 1911.
10 Shepard, "Plain Racism," 379.
11 Howard and Tamara Palmer, eds., *Peoples of Alberta: Portraits of Cultural Diversity* (Saskatoon: Western Producer Prairie Books, 1985), 387–8.
12 Constance Backhouse, "White Female Help and Chinese-Canadian Employers: Race, Class, Gender and Law in the Case of Yee Clun, 1924," in *Canadian Women: A Reader*, ed. Wendy Mitchinson et al. (Toronto: Harcourt Brace Canada, 1996).
13 Ibid., 282.
14 Ibid., 287.

15 Ibid., 288.

16 Ibid., 291.

17 Ibid., 264.

18 *Macleod Gazette*, 15 November 1887.

19 Ibid., 14 March 1888.

20 Howard Palmer, "Polygamy and Progress: The Reaction to Mormons in Canada, 1887–1923," in *The Mormon Presence in Canada*, ed. Brigham Y. Card et al. (Edmonton: University of Alberta Press, 1990), 122.

21 Richard White, *"It's Your Misfortune and None of My Own": A History of the American West* (Normon: University of Oklahoma Press, 1991), 356–7.

22 *Macleod Gazette*, 15 July 1889.

23 Peggy Pascoe, *Relations of Rescue: The Search for Female Moral Authority in the American West, 1874–1939* (New York: Oxford University Press, 1990), 22.

24 *Saskatchewan Herald*, 3 February 1899.

25 Ibid., 2 June 1899.

26 Georgina Binnie-Clark, *A Summer on the Canadian Prairie* (London: Edward Arnold, 1910), 278.

27 "Talk about Stories," *Anecdotes and Updates: Virden Centennial, 1982* (Virden: Empire Publishing, 1982), 57–9.

28 Diane Tye, "Local Character Anedotes: A Nova Scotia Case Study," *Western Folklore* 48 (July 1989): 196.

29 *Fort Ellice History* (Altona: D.W. Friesen, 1985), 161–2.

30 Marguerite Perillat, "This and That Over the Years," in *Their Dreams ... Our Memories: A History of Duck Lake and District* (Altona: D.W. Friesen and Sons, 1988), 746.

31 *Morning Albertan* (Calgary), 22 January 1925.

32 *Calgary Herald*, 12 February 1921.

33 *Calgary Herald*, 2 April 1921.

34 Ibid.

35 Elizabeth Bailey Price, "Pioneers of the Foothills," *Maclean's*, 1 July 1927, 85.

Index